PHYSICAL THEORY

OF

ANOTHER LIFE.

BY

ISAAC TAYLOR.

"I think that I shall be able to prove to you by these reasons that the soul is something immortal......"

TRANSLATION OF THE GREEK MOTTO.

"In truth, if the human family is to live anew, the future stage of its existence offers itself to our curiosity as a proper branch of the physiology of the species; and it only remains to be asked whether we are in possession of any sufficient materials for prosecuting the subject."

AUTHOR.

NEW YORK:
WILLIAM GOWANS.

1853.

PREFACE

TO THE FIRST EDITION.

During the years that have elapsed since the Author projected his literary course, a great change has taken place in the relative position and the reciprocal feelings of the religious parties that divide the country. Eight or ten years ago, and even later, many auspicious indications of peace and union met the eye; and an enterprise might seem hopeful which had for its object the removal of obsolete causes of disagreement. It then seemed as if, at last, ancient misconceptions might safely and successfully be dealt with.

But an unlooked-for course of events has dissipated, for the present, these happy presages, and has given a vehement excitement to sentiments which the lovers of peace had fondly believed were fast disappearing; so that it would now be idle to hope for a dispassionate hearing upon subjects that touch the differences between party and party.

In its bearing upon his own literary projects and engagements, the Author has felt, every day with fresh force, that the revolution of public feeling to which he has alluded, must render the prosecution of the plan he had devised, and which he has announced, and in part executed, peculiarly difficult, if not impracticable; as well as hopeless of a beneficial issue. The subjects included in his plan have become the very themes of eager contention; nor could he believe that, while satisfying his own convictions of truth, he should be able to avoid the taking a side, and the ranging—or the being ranged, with one body of Christians against others. In fact, he has found himself nearing the abyss of strife; and he steps back in haste.

The present state of ecclesiastical excitement will however, no doubt, in a few years subside, and a calmer season once again smile upon the Christian commonwealth. Should he live to see the happy days of tranquillity and good-will, the Author would gladly resume the difficult, and, as he believes, important subjects, which at present he lays down. He now returns to the favourite and peaceful themes of his earlier meditations and studies; and is most happy to find himself in a region not exposed to storms.

There are two perfectly distinct modes in which the influence of the highest truths may be increased: the one is to remove, so far as it may be done, the prejudices and perversions that have been amassed around them. The other method is, forgetting any incidental causes of obstruction, to hold forth, in its native brightness, the substance of those truths. The Author, in his desire,—he believes a sincere desire,—to promote, to the utmost of his power, these inestimable principles, at first attempted to accomplish his object in the former method; he now attempts it in the second.

PREFACE

TO THE PRESENT EDITION.

The Author hopes that no reader will so far misunderstand his intention, in the present instance, as to suppose that a train of thought professedly *theoretic*, or hypothetical, and on a subject connected with which we have no direct information beyond what the Scriptures incidentally convey, is to be allowed to interfere with, or to supersede, any article of our religious belief. An attempt *so* to theorize would be in an equal degree reprehensible and absurd. The Author hopes, and believes, that the following pages do not contain a single sentence which, fairly interpreted, can lay him open to blame on this ground. At any rate, the very distinct profession which he is now making of his reverent regard to the Inspired Testimony, may be admitted to carry him clear of all just exceptions.

As to the actual tendency of the conjectures, and the analogical reasoning, which this volume comprises, the Author has now some good reason to believe that it is altogether favourable to piety, with modest, meditative, and serious minds. It is impossible to provide against the incidental harm that may accrue to those who are wanting in right dispositions.

So far as the speculations and conjectures propounded in this volume touch upon the philosophy of human nature, whether in its physiological or intellectual branches, the Author continues to believe that the hints he has suggested, if pursued, would lead to consequences of some importance, and especially that they would open such views of the WORLD OF MIND as must decisively exclude certain modern doctrines, of injurious tendency. Should he find leisure to do so, the Author would be glad to develop, a little further, his opinions on these subjects, and to confirm them by an appeal to facts. How gladly would he walk awhile in the peaceful and uncontested paths of philosophy—especially when philosophy offers, or seems to offer, her aid in deepening our convictions of the highest truths!

STANFORD RIVERS,
July 1, 1839.

CONTENTS.

CHAPTER | PAGE

I. Preliminary Cautions, and Statement of the Subject . . . 9

II. The Conditions of Corporeity, whether animal or spiritual . 25

III. The probable Prerogatives of Spiritual Corporeity, as compared with Animal Organization:—the first of those Prerogatives 42

IV. The second and third supposed Prerogatives of the Spiritual Economy 52

V. The fourth of these Advantages 61

VI. The fifth and sixth hypothetical Prerogatives of the Spiritual Body 70

VII. The seventh probable Advantage of the Future Life . . . 81

VIII. The eighth Prerogative, according to our Hypothesis, of Spiritual Corporeity 88

IX. The ninth Point of Advantage belonging to the contrast between Animal Organization and Spiritual Life 99

X. The balanced probability of Happiness or Misery involved in the Physical Theory of another Life 106

XI. Probable point of contrast between the Animal and Spiritual Body, in the principle of their construction, respectively . 122

XII. The Transition of Human Nature from Animal to Spiritual Corporeity, a part of the established order of things . . . 129

XIII. The Survivance of Individual Character, and of the Moral Consciousness 143

CHAPTER PAGE

XIV. Correspondence between the Present and the Future Employment of the Active Principles of Human Nature . . 152

XV. Introductory to some Conjectures concerning the Relation of the Material to the Spiritual Universe 162

XVI. The first Conjecture concerning the Material Universe, viewed as the theatre of an Intellectual System 175

XVII. The second Conjecture 186

XVIII. The third Conjecture 222

XIX. The general ground of Conjectural Reasoning concerning what is unseen or future 235

XX. On the Advancement of Pneumatology 253

PHYSICAL THEORY

OF

ANOTHER LIFE.

CHAPTER I.

PRELIMINARY CAUTIONS, AND STATEMENT OF THE SUBJECT.

WE may easily imagine the knowledge of a future life to have been conveyed to us through some other channel than that of the Christian writings. In that case we should have felt to have been in no danger of culpable presumption while seeking further information, concerning the destiny of the human family, in any mode which might have come within our reach; and if the means of our obtaining this further knowledge had been natural and ordinary, we should, without scruple, have prosecuted our inquiries in the very spirit, and with all the freedom, that belong to other physical researches.

But if, indeed, the human family is to live anew, it cannot be denied that the future stage of its existence may excite our curiosity as a proper branch of the physiology of the species; and it then only remains to be asked, whether we are actually in possession of any sufficient materials for prosecuting such an inquiry: if we be, the circumstance that our expectation of immortality forms a part of our belief as Christians, and that it is sustained by the sanction of divine authority, need not be held to bar our researches, or to prevent our doing what otherwise we should certainly attempt, if there were ground to suppose that a careful analysis of human nature might enable us to form an idea of the functions and prerogatives of our approaching mode of existence.

What is to be guarded against, as well in respect to the sanctity of religion, as in deference to the principles of good sense and sound philosophy, is, in the first place, the mere indulgence of the imagination; for it is assuredly not from that quarter we can expect substantial aid; and, in the second place, we should reject the supposition, that any hypothesis, formed on a subject of this kind, how plausible soever it may seem, is, or can be, more than a rational conjecture; or that it can rightfully have any force in disturbing our religious convictions. On the path we are about to pursue, no practical evil can arise so long as we carefully abstain from the error of confounding the deductions of reason with the testimony of the inspired writers; nor ever allow any part of the authority, or of the serious and sacred import that attach to the latter, to be extended to the former. To intrude into "things not seen," under the influence of a "fleshly mind," is a grave fault, and especially so if, on the strength of even the most reasonable theory, we are led to bring into question a particle of that which the text of Scripture, duly interpreted, requires us to believe.

Yet there is a path, as I humbly think, which runs clear of both the errors above mentioned,-and in following it awhile, as I propose to do, I shall endeavour to discard the gay dreams of the fancy fraught with the images of earth; and shall hold every thing light which countervails, or which will not readily consist with, the sure words of Christ and his apostles. Our conjectures are conjectures merely; or even if in any instance they might challenge a somewhat higher value, they are to be considered as matters of science, not of piety; nor is our faith in any way implicated in them; nor can our Christianity be compromised in the remotest manner by the establishment, or by the refutation of any such speculations. Whether they be confirmed, or whether they be confuted, still, as expectants of that "life and immortality" which is brought to light by the gospel, we look on with no solicitude while reason attempts the arduous path that is opened to her efforts.

It is very true that Christianity has suffered damage by vain and presumptuous intrusions into its mysteries; but it may also be injured, and perhaps in a more fatal, although a more silent manner, by the cold withdrawment of all attention and of all curiosity from the high themes of meditation which it involves. In fact this is the very danger to which our religion is now exposed; and a too eager regard to things unseen is certainly not the fault of the times we live in. There may then be a seasonableness in the endeavor to engage attention upon the tranquil but vivifying anticipation of another life; and it must always be true that a distinct and familiar conception of it is likely to aid us, as well in resisting the seductions of the present life, as in sustaining its pains and sorrows; nor does all the help we can obtain of this kind prove enough to insure a due repose of mind amid those agitating alternations of hope and fear that attend our path.

If it be true that human nature, in its present form, is only the rudiment of a more extended and desirable mode of existence, we can hardly do otherwise than assume that the future being must lie so involved in our present constitution as to be discernible therein; and that a careful examination of this structure, both bodily and mental, with a view to the supposed reconstruction of the whole, will furnish some means of conjecturing what that future life will be, at least as to its principal elements. It remains then to be seen whether something of this sort may not actually be effected; and in attempting it we are not left totally at large, or without hints of the path we should attempt; for if the inspired writings be always listened to where they give any distinct testimony, and are narrowly scrutinized also in every instance of a casual allusion to facts not explicitly revealed, they furnish a guidance such as may save endless wanderings in a false direction. Nevertheless in using this guidance, the conditions that belong to it should be borne in mind, lest we should be led astray by taking it for what it is not. These conditions must then be briefly adverted to before we advance further.

Nothing, it is manifest, remains to be desired in philosophy beyond the attainment of absolute truth; and therefore, as the inspired writings, within their province, convey truth, and truth only, it might seem that, on every subject to which their evidence extends, we have but to admit it, and there to rest. Yet it must not be forgotten that truth, in the Scriptures, is always presented under some special aspect, or as if seen from a particular position, or as bearing upon some definite human affection or immediate duty: it is not truth in the abstract: it is indeed a pure element; but it is a particle only of that element; and therefore it will not arrest the inquiries of minds of philosophic cast, which, by instinct, ascend from what is partial to what is general, and are impelled to pursue the universal wherever they touch particulars. Such minds may indeed (and if sound they often will) see good reason for stopping short where they find the means of acquiring further knowledge to be totally wanting; nor will they be slow to confess their ignorance in all such instances. Nevertheless they cannot but resist the interdiction of those who would require them to profess that such detached particles are actually the whole truth, and all that could possibly be known.

There is to be observed a manifest distinction between what immediately concerns us in relation to the divine government, and which it is indispensable we should well understand; and what relates to the constitution of the invisible world, to other orders of being, or to the future physical condition of the human race. It is to subjects of the former sort, chiefly, that the inspired writers direct our attention; while they only glance, incidentally and very hastily, at subjects of the latter class. Not only do they abstain from conveying truth in universal and abstract terms, but they very rarely touch at all any theme that can be considered as a proper object of scientific curiosity. This is now well understood, and therefore the attempt is no longer made to discover latent systems of physical science in the language of the Bible; and it is agreed on all hands that although Moses and the prophets contradict nothing which our modern science has demonstrated, it formed no part of their commission to imbed a scheme of the universe in the Hebrew text. And if physics and astronomy are not to be sought there, neither are metaphysics, nor psychology, nor pneumatology to be inquired for from the inspired writers, notwithstanding that these subjects are much more nearly related to the principles of religion than are the former. What we may fairly rely upon is this, that, in their incidental allusions to the constitution or the destinies of the great intellectual system, and while they are passing over ground where we have no other direct means of information, the inspired writers never lead us astray; or, when fairly interpreted, give rise to suppositions that are altogether unfounded, and contrary to fact. And more than this we may well believe that, so far as they go, they furnish us with an incidental guidance, of which we may safely avail ourselves while pursuing inquiries of a scientific kind. In relation to the unseen world, Scripture is to be listened to much as we might listen to an ambassador from a distant country, who, while earnestly discharging the special duties of his mission, and while urging at large the political and commercial interests of his sovereign, might make many allusions and employ many phrases, which, when collected and attentively considered, would serve to convey some general notion of the climate, usages, and wealth of his native land.

It is thus then that we propose to keep an ear open to the apostolic voice, while endeavoring, by another process than that of biblical interpretation, to unfold the rudiments of the future life;—always respecting the sacred canon, and ever and again reverting to it as an infallible means of keeping ourselves near to the true path of inquiry. And with the very hope of making an auspicious commencement, and with the view of starting from solid ground, so that our first steps at least may be sure, we shall devote a page to an apostolic affirmation, which indeed might serve as the text of our dissertation—"There is," says St. Paul, "a natural body, and there is a SPIRITUAL BODY:"—the natural, or animal first, and then the spiritual; and these, while agreeing in certain general conditions, are contrasted in some important respects; yet both serve as the vehicle and instrument of the higher principle of our nature.

The animated argument carried on through the fifteenth

chapter of the first epistle to the Corinthians, stands alone, or nearly so, in the body of Scripture, as well as to its subject, as its style; for we meet with nothing elsewhere within the inspired pages so much resembling a physiological disquisition, or any thing that goes so far in setting before us, at one view, the natural history of man, considered as destined to immortality. And yet this argument does not depart so widely from the customary style of Scripture, as to be otherwise than topical in its terms, and popular, rather than scientific, in its mode of reasoning and in its illustrations. While, therefore, it may suggest the course we should pursue, and prevent our setting out in a wrong direction, it cannot be held to supersede the sort of inquiry which we have now before us.

The leading affirmation of St. Paul's argument we may consider to be the one just quoted, and the import of which we may properly inquire into, as a preliminary to the statement of our theory of another life.

"THERE IS A SPIRITUAL BODY." It is then BODY, and not spirit, to which the reasoning of the apostle, in this instance, relates. He is treating of the transition which human nature is destined to pass through, from one condition of corporeal existence to another; and he speaks of the laying down a body that is gross, or at least infirm, perishable, and ignoble, and the taking up a body that shall be potent, illustrious, and permanent. For aught we know, there may be, in the universe, pure immateriality, or a state of absolute separation from matter; and moreover, such a state of sheer incorporeity may perhaps await the human race in some stage of its progress towards its ultimate condition; but, clearly no abstraction of this kind is either affirmed or implied in the passage before us; nor does it enter into St.

Paul's argument, even by so much as a passing allusion, or a solitary phrase, thrown in to save a collateral truth. We should indeed be far from thence inferring that an immaterial state, in the fullest sense of the term, is not in itself possible, or may not actually have to be passed through by mankind; for arguments drawn from negative evidence are at all times extremely fallacious. Nevertheless, so far as this passage goes, the doctrine of an absolute incorporeity,* as possible to human nature, may be true, or it may not. The distinctive, or foremost principle of Christianity—namely, the resurrection of the dead, demands no such doctrine, nor does the apostle (who was personally well qualified to judge of the hidden, yet real connection of principles) deem it necessary to his conclusion, or at all pertinent to his subject to affirm it. If questioned on the point, whether the human soul is ever actually and entirely separated from matter, it is not improbable that he would have dismissed the inquiry as altogether irrelevant to religion, and as a theme proper to be discussed among the professors of abstruse science, with which he, as a teacher of Christianity, had nothing to do.

That which Christianity requires us to believe is the actual survivance of our personal consciousness *embodied*, and the perpetuity of our sense of good and evil, and our continued sensibility to pain and pleasure, and the unbroken recollection, in another life, of the events and affections of the present state. What Christianity decisively affirms is to this effect, that the Life—moral, intellectual, and active, or corporeal, is not commensurate with, or dependent upon, the present animal organization; but that it may, and that it will, spring up anew from the ruins of its earthly habitation. "Destroy *this* body," and the man still lives; but

* See Cudworth.

whether he might live immaterially, is a mere question of philosophy, which the inspired writers do not care to decide. In almost all instances it is with facts, rather than with abstruse principles, that they have to do; and in relation to our present subject, after having peremptorily affirmed that human nature is to survive in another state, and that it is to rise embodied from the ashes of its present animal organization, St. Paul leaves speculations at large, neither denying nor affirming any hypothesis that may consist with the facts which alone are important to our religious belief.

Let it then be distinctly kept in view, that although the essential independence of mind and matter, or the abstract possibility of the former existing apart from corporeal life may well be considered as tacitly implied in the Christian scheme, yet that an *actual* incorporeal state of the human soul, at any period of its course, is not necessarily involved in the principles of our faith, any more than it is explicitly asserted. This doctrine, concerning what is called the immateriality of the soul, should ever be treated simply as a philosophical speculation, and as unimportant to our Christian profession. The question then, concerning pure immateriality, we regard as having been passed, untouched, by St. Paul; nor do we consider it as in any specific manner important to the inquiries upon which we are about to enter. Nevertheless, there may be an advantage in concisely stating what seems to be the present relative position of the two parties in the old controversy concerning matter and mind:—a controversy now very likely to die away for ever.

The antagonist principles then are thus balanced.—Two classes of facts, readily distinguishable, present themselves to our consciousness:—those of the one class we involuntarily attribute to an external world, and think of as the consequences of our connection with matter, or as the effects which its properties produce upon our minds. But those of the other class we as invariably regard as belonging more immediately to the mind, and as arising from itself; and they are, many of them at least, of a sort which we may easily imagine to have place, if there were no external world, or if the mind had no sentient knowledge of its existence. Theory and speculation apart, the entire mass of our consciousness resolves itself, naturally and easily, into these two elements; and it is only by the temporary force of some arbitrary system of philosophy, that we can be brought to regard the two elements as essentially one and the same; and, by the very constitution of our minds, we reluctate every moment at the violence done them by any such means.

But notwithstanding the remonstrances of common sense, the attempt has in every age been renewed, on the one side by the materialist, and on the other by the spiritualist (if we may so use the term), to melt down these two elements into a mass, or to annul the distinction between them;—the one, by affirming that mind is mere organization, or a product of matter; and the other, by alleging that those varied sensations or states of the mind which, by "a natural prejudice," we attribute to an external material world, are in fact nothing more than peculiar conditions of the mind itself; and that there neither is an external world, nor could be; or that, even if there were, no substantial proof of its existence could possibly reach us.

Now the two parties, if indeed two such parties may still be said to be extant, have nearly come to an agreement on one point, namely, that our belief of the reality of matter and of mind can never be made to stand together as collateral truths, equal in authority, and resting upon the same sort of evidence, and ascertained by the same process of reasoning. If at last they are to consist one with the other the one must be assumed as intuitively certain, and as incapable of proof by reasoning; while the other must thence be derived in the way of inference, and must, however well proved, yet take a secondary place in the order of things known. Which of the two then shall we assume as needing no proof, and employ as a fulcrum of argument in proving the other, or in disproving it?

The materialist—and in this argument the materialist must take the atheist as his companion, the materialist says —"It is impossible for me to doubt the existence of matter; for it is under my touch, it is before my eyes, and its properties are the subject of the only sciences that are absolute in their methods of reasoning, and infallible in their results. But as to mind, otherwise than as it is merely a function of animal organization, or a product of cerebral secretions, I know nothing, and can know nothing of it, and the inquiry concerning it ever has been, and must always remain obscure and unsatisfactory."

But the spiritualist contemns this summary treatment of the argument by his antagonist, as crude, and as altogether illogical, and such as can satisfy none who are competent strictly to analyze their own consciousness. He affirms that this statement of the case by his opponent takes for granted the very facts that are to be proved; and in reply to the materialist, he says—"All that I contend for, and which I affirm to be intuitively certain, and to be known without proof, you first tacitly assume, and then formally deny. What, I ask, are all these sensations of touch and sight, and what are these demonstrations of mathematical science, of which you speak, but so many *states of the mind* —so many mental phenomena, as I may term them, which, while they necessarily imply the existence of mind, do but render the existence of matter, probable; or at best demonstrate its reality by a circuit of reasoning. I will grant you that an external world may exist, and I believe that it does exist: but this very belief, let it rise as high as it may, together with the argument that sustains it, are still only so many elements of my mental consciousness, and can never nullify or annihilate that of which they are parts." This scepticism concerning the reality of matter, and an external world, which is of a far more subtile and sweeping kind than that of the materialist concerning mind, he finds it impossible to supplant; and he feels himself undermined in his assault upon spiritualism, his foot sinking whichever way he endeavours to advance. His opponent therefore leaves him with this defiance—"Prove the existence of an external world, if you please, or if you can;—and I too believe it to exist; but I believe it by inference; and therefore hold it as a truth, if not inferior in certainty, yet assuredly as subordinate to that primary truth—the existence of mind."

Now even if it were granted that a due regard to the constitution of the human mind—its physiology, obliges us to receive its instinctive and involuntary conviction of the reality of an external world as a proper evidence of its existence, and as superseding all reasoning on the subject, so that the two truths should be considered as alike intuitively known, still the spiritualist will retain the advantage he has gained over his opponent; for it is manifest that, if there be room at all for any hesitation or skepticism in relation to either truth, it is matter, not mind, that is in jeopardy. The very ground of the assumption that the existence of an external world ought to be admitted as certain, without reasoning, is nothing else but a consideration of the laws or constitution of the mind. Mind therefore, and its elementary principles, stands first in logical order; and the existence of matter follows, if not as an inference, yet as a truth not to be affirmed until after another has been granted.

The bearing of this controversy upon Christianity may thus be stated.—The doctrine of the materialist, if it were followed out to its extreme consequences, and consistently held, is plainly atheistic, and is therefore incompatible with any and with every form of religious belief. It is so because, in affirming that mind is nothing more than the product of animal organization, it excludes the belief of a pure and uncreated mind—the cause of all things; for if there be a supreme mind, absolutely independent of matter, then, unquestionably, there may be created minds, also independent of matter. But if the materialist is ready to admit, as he usually does, the divine existence, and the pure spirituality of the divine nature, and if he professes to mean nothing more than that created minds are in fact always embodied, and that, apart from some material structure or animal organization, there is no consciousness or activity, then, and in this sense understood, materialism becomes a doctrine of little or no importance to our faith as Christians, for it may consist well enough with what is affirmed in the Scriptures concerning the immortality of man, the resurrection, the intermediate state, and the existence and agency of invisible orders. On the other hand, although the great principles of theology are saved and respected by the spiritualist, yet, if he goes so far as to call in question the reality of the external world, and the material universe, it will not be without having recourse to very subtile modes of reasoning, and to abstruse distinctions, that he can reconcile this sort of skepticism with the plain sense and explicit affirmations of the inspired volume. Moreover, as Christianity, by its characteristic temper, distastes philosophic refinements of all sorts, it will reject a theory which tends to introduce a species of mysticism, scarcely less atheistic than the bolder doctrine of the materialist. To bring into doubt, in any way, (and it is of little moment in what way, or on what pretext,) that which the common sense of mankind has always assumed to be certain, is—if not to shake the evidence of all truth, yet to paralyze the faculty by which evidence of any kind is seized and held. Whether you rob a man of his treasure, or disable the hand that grasps it, you do him an equal injury; or perhaps we should say that the latter is the worse wrong of the two.

Our present passing reference to this controversy may be dismissed with affirming the probability that it will ere long become totally extinct; for as the atheistic materialist finds himself dislodged from his too hastily assumed position, by a skepticism more profound and refined than his own, he is not likely again to provoke discussion on the subject; while, on the other hand, the spiritualist, who would never have entertained or advanced his skepticism, concerning the external world, if he had not been incited to do so, as a summary means of dealing with the atheist, will no longer have any urgent motive for reviving the argument, after it has been generally confessed that philosophic atheism is indefensible. Thus, as we may fairly hope, the two worlds of matter and mind will henceforward be permitted quietly to coexist, as good neighbours and allies.

But be this as it may, the doctrine of the Scriptures concerning the destiny of man stands untouched:—or, to revert to the argument of St. Paul on the subject of the resurrection, it is altogether independent of any such abstruse questions, inasmuch as it is Body, and not spirit, about which he is reasoning. His interrogatories and his replies may be reduced to these—Have the dead ceased to exist? Have those who are fallen asleep perished? No;—for there is a spiritual body, and another vehicle of human nature, as well as a natural body; and therefore the dissolution of this animal structure leaves the LIFE untouched. The animal body is not itself the life, nor is it the cause of life; nor again is the spiritual body the life, nor the cause of it; but the one as well as the other are the instruments of the mind, and the necessary medium of every productive exercise of its faculties.

What the Christian Scriptures then, and St. Paul, specifically, affirm, is not any abstruse metaphysical doctrine, concerning mind and matter; but the simple physiological fact, of two species of corporeity, destined for man: the first, that of our present animal and dissoluble organization, which we share, in all its conditions, with the irrational sentient tribes around us; and the second—a future spiritual structure, imperishable, and endowed with higher powers, and many desirable prerogatives.

Now having the sanction of this inspired affirmation of these two kinds of corporeity, and intending to inquire concerning the probable prerogatives of the future human body, it is natural that we should first state what appear to be the essential conditions of corporeal existence, whether animal or spiritual, so that before we come to ask wherein the spiritual body shall excel the animal body, we may understand what it is in which the two must be supposed to agree.

We assume then the reality, and the independence of mind and matter; and yet suppose that, although intrinsically unlike, and capable of existing, the one without the other, nevertheless that, as they coexist, so are they intimately blended, and reciprocally affect each other within the circle of sentient and active life. Body, whether animal or spiritual, is a third essence—a middle nature, and the medium of the reciprocity of the two unlike substances. Body is the tangential point of the two worlds of mind and matter; or it is the amalgam of two substances wherein the properties of both are so blended as to constitute a mean, essentially unlike what could have resulted from any possible construction of the one, by itself. The body is to the mind the means of a mode of existence, and the organ of an exertion of powers which, in its corporeal state, it could never have known and exercised. If, metaphorically speaking, matter is refined and ennobled by its union to mind, it is the mind that is really the advantaged party in the connection; for it is absolutely indifferent to matter whether it be left in a grosser state, or be wrought into a more elaborate form. On the contrary, by compounding itself with matter, mind takes possession of a world foreign to itself; and, in a sense, doubles its powers of action, and extends its sphere of existence.

CHAPTER II

THE CONDITIONS OF CORPOREITY, WHETHER ANIMAL OR SPIRITUAL.

The blending of mind and matter in the bodily structure of the sentient and rational orders, we may be assured, is a method of procedure which, if it be not absolutely indispensable to the final purposes of the creation, subserves the most important ends, and carries with it consequences such as will make it the general, if not the universal law of all finite natures, in all worlds. A little attention to what is involved in the idea of corporeal existence will incline us to believe that it is the basis of intellectual activity—of moral agency, and of communion or sociality among intelligent orders.

In stating these common prerogatives, or consequences of corporeity, we of course leave out of view whatever seems proper to animal organization merely; and we then ascend by abstraction, as high as we can go, toward the few essential conditions of the combination of mind and matter.

And first, without question, we must affirm that Body is the necessary means of bringing Mind into relationship with space and extension, and so, of giving it—Place. Very plainly, a disembodied spirit, or we ought rather to say, an unembodied spirit, or sheer mind, is nowhere. Place is a relation of extension; and extension is a property of matter: but that which is wholly abstracted from matter, and in speaking of which we deny that it has any property in common therewith, can in itself be subject to none of its conditions; and we might as well say of a pure spirit that it is hard, heavy, or red, or that it is a cubic foot in dimensions, as say that it is *here* or *there*, or that it has come, and is gone. It is only in a popular and improper sense that any such affirmation is made concerning the Infinite Spirit, or that we speak of God as *everywhere* present. God is in every place in a sense altogether incomprehensible by finite minds, inasmuch as his relation to space and extension is peculiar to infinitude. Using the terms as we use them of ourselves, God is not here or there, any more than he exists now and then. Although therefore the idea may not readily be seized by every one, we must nevertheless grant it to be true that, when we talk of absolute immateriality, and wish to withdraw mind altogether from matter, we must no longer allow ourselves to imagine that it is, or that it can be, in any place, or that it has any kind of relationship to the visible and extended universe. But in combining itself with matter, by the means of a corporeal lodgment, mind brings itself into alliance with the various properties of the external world, and takes a share in the conditions of solidity, and extension. Thenceforward mind occupies one place, at one time, moves from place to place, and may follow other minds, and be followed by others;—it may find and be found; it may be detained, or be set at large; it may go to and fro within a narrow circle, or it may traverse a wide circle; and while, by this same means, the material universe is opened to its acquaintance, it is also itself restricted in its opportunities of acquiring knowledge by its subjection to the laws of gravitation and motion: we may then with some degree of confidence, on these grounds, regard a corporeal state as indispensable to the exercise of active faculties, and to a scheme of government, and to a social economy.

That which is finite—a finite mind, for example, must, as we are inclined to think, become subject to some actual limitations, and must undergo some specific relations, before its faculties can come into play, or be productive of effects. There is reason to conjecture (perhaps stronger terms might be used) that none but the Infinite Spirit can be more than a latent essence, or inert power, until compacted by some sort of restraint. The union with matter, or the coming into a corporeal state, may be in fact, not a degradation to mind, but the very means of its quickening—its birth into the world of knowledge and action. The first consequence of this birth is, as we have said, the acquirement of locality in the extended universe.

But in the second place, a relationship not at all less important than the preceding, is undoubtedly dependent upon the union of the mind with matter, or upon its corporeity, —namely, its relationship to time.

Consequences the most momentous, and which perhaps we do not often think of, connected as well with our intellectual and active, as with our moral life, attach to our connection with that equable motion by which duration is at once measured and made sensible to us. Nor is it easy so much as to conceive of a social economy and system of government, in a world where all were not held to one and the same rate of intellectual movement, through their contemporary periods. Familiar as we are, and have always been, with the equal periods that are marked for us by the celestial and telluric revolutions, we think it only natural, and a matter of course, that our individual consciousness of duration should flow on equably, and that this consciousness of time in one mind, should pretty nearly keep pace with the same feeling in other minds. But a little attention to some familiar facts, as well as to the reason of the thing, will convince us that, for this equable consciousness, or perception of the steady flow of time, we are wholly indebted to external and artificial means, deprived of which, our notion of duration, and our recollection of the successive parts of it, would be the most variable and illusory of all the conditions of our existence; nay, utterly irregular and unfixed, so that, according to the ever-varying velocity of our mental states, a minute might seem a century, or a century a minute. We must indeed still, as finite beings, know ourselves to be flowing along a line, or as existing instant by instant; but we should have no means, either of deter mining the rate, or of rendering it equable.

Let the reader, by a little effort, imagine himself to be totally cut off from all connection with the clock-work of the material universe;—uninformed of the alternations of day and night, and of summer and winter—remote from the swing of the pendulum, and unconscious also of the beating of the pulse, of the heaving of the chest, of the sensations of hunger and satiety, of sleep and wakefulness;—in such a state of absolute seclusion from all the mechanical and animal indices of equable motions—that is to say, knowing nothing of time, he must very soon, or as soon as the previously acquired habit of the mind had become indistinct, cease to be conscious of any other difference between a long period and a short one, than that which might be derived from the actual equableness of his thoughts and emotions; and if these at some seasons, as in fact they do, followed one the other with incalculable rapidity, while at another season a single idea or emotion remained fixed in the mind, there would be no possible means of his ascertaining whether, since a certain mental state or epoch, he had existed an hour, a day, a year, a century, or a thousand years. Thus insulated from equable motion, we should not be able to correct our individual consciousness of duration by comparing it with that of others under like circumstances; for while one, by the peculiar constitution of his mind, would tell us an eternity had elapsed since we last conferred with him; another, either more inert, or more addicted to dwell upon abstractions, would say—it was only yesterday when we compared eras. To MERE MIND, a long period means nothing else but a period in which it has passed through many and various states with a vivid consciousness and distinct recollection of each; and a short period is one during which few ideas or emotions have sluggishly followed each other, or have intently engaged it; or, whether few or many, have clean passed from the memory. Yet the former may in fact have been only a tenth, or a hundredth part of the latter. Every one's experience in dreaming, or in sickness, may furnish him with facts illustrative of the unfixedness and illusory quality of our consciousness of duration, when entirely deprived of the external means of collating our mental history with the regular motions of the material world.

It is motion that measures duration, and Time is duration, measured into equal parts by the equable motion of bodies through space. But as motion belongs to matter, of which it is a condition, and is that wherein duration and extension combine to form a common product, so mind must become related to extension, in order to its having any knowledge of motion, or to its being able to avail itself of the measurement of duration; in other words, it is only in connection with matter that it can know any thing of time.

Minds embodied, not only learn to measure out their own existence equally, and to correct the illusions of which otherwise they would be the sport, but also, by an insensible habit, they come to exist at a more even velocity, if we may so speak, than could else be possible, and learn unconsciously to put a curb upon the excessive and dangerous rapidity of thought; while in other cases a spur is supplied for the sluggishness of the mind, or a remedy found for its undue fixedness; and thus all minds are brought to move together, at nearly the same rate, or at least as nearly so as is essential for securing the order and harmony of the social system. We should not indeed be warranted in affirming that mere minds, or unembodied spirits, could not, by any means, purely immaterial, become conscious of the equable lapse of duration; but we see in fact that it is exclusively through the corporeal alliance of mind with the external world, that this important rectification of its consciousness is effected; nor would it be difficult to specify some very momentous consequences attaching to the government of the moral system, that may perhaps be found to result from the suspension, or from the restoration of this means of knowing the lapse of time. In truth, a speculation of this kind, if pursued in all its bearings, might lead to our taking a new view, not merely of the economy of the human system, but of that world of animal life and enjoyment by which we are surrounded. We are accustomed to take it for granted that all creatures are living at one and the same rate, or that they are *going by our clock;* whereas in fact, if we duly consider the analogies of the system of nature, we shall see reason to conjecture that, while perhaps some species of animals are living much slower than ourselves, others may be living inconceivably faster. It is by no means unphilosophical to imagine that the ephemera of a summer's noon, which we are apt to pity as short lived, may, in the compass of their few sunny hours, be running through a century of joyous sensations; and if the microscope, which exposes to our view the vivacious tenants of a drop of water, had the power also of laying open the whirl of the sentient faculty of these tribes, it might appear, to our amazement, that the busy history of a thousand years is condensed into their life of a day, or an hour, so that the diminutiveness of their visible organs would be even less astonishing than the compression of their consciousness. These speculations are, however, foreign to our immediate purpose.

Nevertheless we must yet follow them so far further, as to point out a not improbable consequence of the principle upon which the visible universe is constructed:—we mean that of the subdivision of the mass into spheres, revolving in precise times; and each world, as it seems, being furnished with a double or treble measurement of time, by its annual and diurnal rotations, by its cycle of seasons, and by the revolution of its satellites. In looking abroad upon the thickly peopled fields of space, wherein all worlds are seen to be made subject to the law of equable motion, who can resist the belief that this stupendous machinery (whatever other purposes its revolution may subserve) is a vast horology—a register of duration, to all rational tribes, and a means, indispensable to the purposes of universal government, of holding all minds to the due symphony of time. As all minds, by the means of corporeity, are connected with extension, and are limited to place, so are all, by the same means, and by the revolution of the worlds they inhabit, bound down to time. There may be intelligent orders, so fiery in temperament, that, but for this physical check—this necessity of keeping place with the slow march of the planetary bodies, they would outrun their term, and leave their ranks in the steady movement of the great social system. Or are there, on the other hand, any minds secluded from the sight of the visible heavens, and shut out from every means of reckoning years and centuries? Such may be passing through a state and process during the continuance of which the perception of time would be no boon.

In the third place, as the corporeal alliance of the mind with matter is seen to be in fact the means of exposing it passively to be acted upon by the properties of the material world, and thus of making it liable to pleasures and pains not proper to itself, and to some of the most intense kind; so may this connection be universally necessary for the same end. In truth, the pleasures and the pains to which the mind is laid open by its amalgamation with matter in the body, are so intense, as to take the lead, for the most part, in determining its active and moral destiny. If indeed the mind were not inherently susceptible of impressions from the properties of matter, it is not any animal organization that could have rendered it so. Nevertheless it is probable that sensation is the result of corporeity, or an effect not taking place apart from that intimate blending of the two alien substances of which the body is the medium; or it may be only as embodied that the perceptions of the mind become definite and distinct. In illustration of this alleged consequence of coporeity, as the necessary means of rendering the mind conscious of the properties of matter, we might refer to the instances, so frequent in chemical science, in which two substances remain in juxtaposition, without in any manner affecting each other, or combining, until the presence of a third substance puts their affinities into action. It is thus that the presence of heat, or of electricity, or of oxygen, or of water, is the means of forming innumerable compounds, or of dissolving them. And so, as there is room to conjecture the unknown principle of life may be the *third power*, or element, the agency of which brings mind into conscious connection with matter, rendering it sensible of light and colours, of heat, solidity, sound, tastes, smells, motions, and all their variations of intensity. Embodied, the mind, by a process of natural and involuntary education, becomes familiar with a certain set or circle of the properties of the material world; and though still unconscious, probably, of many other of its properties, yet gains an acquaintance with it in all the points that are important to its present welfare; and thus, as in a foreign school, brings its otherwise latent faculties into exercise. Moreöver it is as embodied that the mind comes under the potent discipline of organic pleasures and pains—and how large a portion of its history hinges upon this susceptibility! There is no reason (at least we have no reason) to believe that, apart from body, or in a purely incorporeal state, the mind could either enjoy or suffer in any other manner than intellectually. Probably the whole of that peremptory and efficacious impulse which is necessary for putting the intellectual and moral faculties in activity, and for maintaining their activity, springs from this exposure of the mind to the stimulating properties of matter;—that is to say, from its corporeal constitution.

But then, and in the fourth place, this same intimate connection between mind and matter, while it exposes the mind, passively, to the influence of the inferior element, becomes, in return, the means of its exerting a power, and how extensive and mysterious a power is it, over the solid masses around it. Mind, embodied, by a simple act or volition, originates motion. That is to say, its will or desire, through the instrumentality of muscular contractions, as applied to the body itself, or to other bodies, puts it or them in movement. This power of the mind in overcoming the *vis inertiæ* of matter, and the force of gravitation, is the only active influence, in relation to the material world, which we have a certain knowledge of its possessing; for, as is obvious, the various combinations of substances that are brought about by the skill of man, are all indirectly effected through the instrumentality of the muscular system; nor can it be ascertained whether the chemical changes and assimilations that are carried on in the secreting glands, and the viscera, are effected by an unconscious involuntary mental operation. This organic influence excepted, supposing it to exist, the mechanical power of the mind is the only one it enjoys; but this it enjoys, as we shall again have occasion to observe, in no mean degree. It may, without much hazard, be assumed that motion, in all instances, originates in an immediate volition, either of the supreme, or of some created mind, and that this power is exerted by the latter through the means of a corporeal structure. In what way this same power may in future be extended or enhanced, we shall soon have to inquire.

Hitherto we have considered those consequences or prerogatives of corporeity which have an immediate relation to the material world, and in which consists the mind's direct alliance with matter. But there are other consequences of this same alliance that fall in upon the mind itself, and which, if they do not originate some of its operations, or modes of feeling, yet modify them to a great extent.

Thus, and in the fifth place, it is to its corporeal connection with the external world that must be attributed the mind's liability to various mixed emotions, as well pleasurable as painful, of the class called imaginative. These emotions, often of the most powerful kind, and which are neither merely animal or organic, nor purely intellectual or moral, mingle with all other elements of our nature, and modify, abate, or stimulate every function of the active and moral life. The sense of fitness, of beauty, of sublimity, of terror, of harmony and music, and their opposites, give rise, in their various complex forms, to sentiments and to modes of action such as are scarcely more foreign to what belongs to brute life, than they are to what might belong to mind in a state of absolute abstraction from matter. Each of these sensibilities and tastes, with its endless combinations, is, in a sense, a product of the material universe, and is directly consequent upon a corporeal mode of existence.

The imaginative sentiments might perhaps, at a first view, be regarded as adapted to a temporary purpose only, inasmuch as they constitute a reconciling medium between the animal and the intellectual principles. But, in considering them further, it appears that they go beyond this lower office, and in fact mingle themselves with the very highest and purest of our moral feelings. We ought then to reckon them among the noble and permanent elements of our nature, and so must assume that they will belong to the spiritual, as they have belonged to the animal body. If man were animal only, he would neither need, nor indeed could he possess, an imaginative faculty; or, on the other hand, if he were rational only, or moral only, the class of sentiments that arise from this faculty he would spurn (could he even conceive of them) as degrading, or as illusory;—inasmuch as they present something which is either more, or which is less than absolute truth, reason, and rectitude. Or if man, being at once animal, moral, and rational, were yet wholly destitute of imagination and of its sensibilities, he would painfully want harmony and combination; and he would be compelled, every hour, to pass, with a shocking abruptness, from one mode of existence, and from one principle of life to another, without the aid of any transition-feelings. But as we are actually constituted, we find within the circle of our mental economy nothing so purely rational (not even mathematical truth) and nothing so simply moral, as not, through the medium of imaginative tastes, to be brought into alliance, remotely at least, with our animal sensations; nor, on the other hand, is there any thing so merely sensual as not to be, in some measure, relieved, ennobled, or graced, by an intermixture of ideas of beauty and order. Now the body, with its sensibilities, is manifestly the means of effecting this harmony of the various elements of our mental constitution, and so of generating complex sentiments of a sort which we should most reluctantly lay aside, even although the primary purpose they were intended to subserve, in relation to the present life, were superseded.

Our speculation must not hastily be condemned as a mere subtilty, when we assume it to be probable that the correspondence of finite minds with the Infinite Mind needs to be attempered by an admixture of those imaginative sentiments which take their rise from the corporeal constitution. Those organic and quelling impressions of beauty, sublimity, majesty, and those feelings of awe, and of ecstasy, and that adoration in which a latent dread or terror imparts intensity to the happier feeling of affection—all these mixed emotions shall perhaps be found necessary, as well for keeping finite minds in the place that becomes them, as for enabling them to sustain the immediate presence of the bright and absolute perfection. The imaginative sentiments may thus serve at once to facilitate a nearer approach to the ineffable glory than would otherwise have been possible, and to fence off the mount of vision, if we may so speak, against dangerous intrusions. If this conjecture be well founded, we may be inclined to suppose that all rational orders are made to commence their course under the condition of animal organization, wherein they may become thoroughly imbued with these imaginative sentiments, which, in a refined form, they are to carry on with them throughout their immortality. Does this conjecture receive support from the apostolic doctrine—"There are bodies celestial, and bodies terrestrial—there is a natural body—and a spiritual body—Howbeit *that is not first* which is spiritual, but that which is *natural;* and *afterward* that which is spiritual." This order, or regular process, this transition, is it the universal law of the intelligent creation?

Not to multiply distinctions, and lest we should seem to refine too much, we may class under this same head, those various modifications of the moral sentiments, both in the way of abatement and of enhancement, which arise from our corporeal sympathies and animal desires. Neither love nor anger, nor the sense of jnstice, nor the emotion of pity, neither shame, remorse, hatred, amity, ambition, humility, hope or fear, is what it would have been if there had been no concomitant organic sensations. These emotions of the moral nature, and especially when they come to form habits or dispositions, and constitute individual character, are unquestionably modified, to a very great extent, by the peculiarities of the physical temperament; and hence arise various modes of feeling, of a complex kind, which must be traced to the body, as their source. Now even if these physical modifications of the moral nature might be dropped with the dissolution of the animal frame, so that the moral sentiments should return to an elementary state, it is not certain that we should be gainers by the change; on the contrary, it is easy to imagine that a new power and intensity, a vividness and a spring shall be imparted to the moral principles from their sympathy with the organic energies of the spiritual body. At present we are conscious of the fact that activity and force are infused into the moral sentiments, even the most exalted of them, by their alliance with animal sensations; it is so with the domestic affections, and with general benevolence, and pity, courage, and ambition: the rule of analogy therefore leads us to suppose that similar effects will follow from a similar combination, in the future construction of human nature.

Once more, and in the sixth place, the corporeal alliance of mind and matter is, in the present state, and as we may strongly conjecture it will be, the means of so defining our individuality in relation to others, as is necessary for bringing minds under the condition of a social economy. The purposes of such a system demand, in the first place, what may be called the seclusion, or the insulation of each spirit; or its impenetrability by other spirits. Communication and exchange of thought must, under any plan of free agency, be voluntary; there must rest with each member of the community a power of reserve; and then, the means of communication being arbitrary, must be absolutely under the command of the individual. Now the body is not the open bower or tent of the soul into which any one may walk at pleasure; but it is its castle, from which all other minds may, at pleasure, be excluded. Perhaps unembodied spirits (if such there be) may lie open to inspection, or may be liable to invasion, like an unfenced field, or a plot of common land. But although such a state of exposure might involve no harm to beings either absolutely good, or absolutely evil, we cannot imagine it to consist with the safety or dignity of beings like man; or, indeed, to be proper to a mixed economy.

But further; a social system demands the means of immediate recognition individually; and this, in the present state, is provided for by the endless, yet distinct peculiarities of bodily conformation, and by that law of the animal organization which gives to each peculiarity of the mind, and temper, and temperament, a characteristic exterior expression. It must not be positively affirmed that these purposes could not, in the nature of things, be secured without the aid of a corporeal structure; yet there is some reason to question whether sheer spirits could (except by immediate acts of the divine power) be individually dealt with, and governed, or could be known and employed, or could be followed and detained, or could form lasting associations, and be moulded into hierarchies and polities, or could sustain office, and yield obedience, in any certain manner, if at all. At least is it true that all these functions and social ends are now in fact dependent upon corporeity; and it is only fair to assume that they demand a bodily structure in every case where minds are to live and act in concert with others.

The supposition has already been advanced that the definite or productive agency of finite natures demands that mind be compacted, or bound down to those conditions of limitation which attach to matter, and which mind undergoes in becoming allied to matter. Now the same principle, if it be good, must imply, and even more clearly, this same limitation of minds, as the condition of their being definitely related one to another, and of their acting one upon another, and one with another. We imagine then, that by the medium of corporeity, the mind is *defined*, and that its powers are rendered applicable to definite purposes.

In thus naming what appear to be the common conditions or prerogatives of corporeal existence, whether natural or spiritual, we of course do not include any of those adjuncts of the present life which make part of our animal organization merely, and which may readily be conceived of as dropped, along with the perishable body. After setting off all such temporary faculties of the body, and which are subservient only to the well being of the animal structure itself—to its preservation, or to its reproduction, we reach those properties or consequences of the corporeal constitution which are directly subservient to the mind, and which may therefore, on good grounds, be regarded as belonging to corporeity abstractedly, and which are likely to attach to the future spiritual body. Such, manifestly, are—the occupation of place, or a relationship to space and extension—the consciousness of equable motion, or a knowledge of time,—the consciousness of the properties of matter, or sensation—an active power over matter, to originate motion—the susceptibility to imaginative emotions, and to mixed moral sentiments—and a defined, recognizable individuality.

Besides these properties or consequences of the corporeal union of mind and matter, as above described, others of a more abstruse kind might be named which affect the processes of reasoning; but it may be better to confine ourselves, at present, to what is the most simple and indisputable, and especially because fit opportunities will arise, in pursuing our inquiry, for adverting to some of these more intricate subjects. In truth a strict analysis of our mental operations would hardly leave one free from a reasonable supposition of being extensively modified by the interaction of mind and body, or of being what it is in consequence of the dependence of the mind upon the organization and functions of the brain. Plainly it is so with the memory, with the association of ideas, with the power of attention, with the processes of comparison, calculation, and reasoning, and with the inventive faculty, and the perception of analogies.

Having thus inquired what it is which ought to be attributed in common to the animal and to the spiritual body, and which must belong as well to the future as to the present lodgment of the human mind, we are next to ask (on the ground of physical probability) what it is wherein the difference between the one and the other will consist; or, in other words, what are likely to be the prerogatives of the latter, as compared with the former; or in what manner the actual powers of the present structure of human nature may be conceived of as expanded or advantaged, consistently with those great principles of analogy which we find to attach to the divine operations in all their departments.

CHAPTER III.

THE PROBABLE PREROGATIVES OF SPIRITUAL CORPOREITY, AS COMPARED WITH ANIMAL ORGANIZATION :—THE FIRST OF THOSE PREROGATIVES.

In now approaching the hypothetical part of our subject, I must again remind the reader of the important distinction between the mere creations of the imagination and the legitimate results of analysis and abstraction. Plainly it is not the imagination that can render us aid in conceiving of a new and different mode of existence; since this faculty is but the mirror of the world around it, and must draw all its materials from things actually known. It may exalt, refine, ennoble, enrich what it finds; and it may shed over all the splendour of an effulgence such as earth never actually sees; yet it must end where it began, in compounding elements and in recombining forms, furnished to its hand; and if ever it goes, or seems to go, beyond these limits, the product is grotesque or absurd, not beautiful: there is no grace or charm in that which trenches upon the actual forms of nature. But the faculty of analysis may boldly, and safely, outstep the imagination; and it may, by a careful examination of the constituents of human nature, considered in their abstract value, be able, in accordance with sound principles of analogy, to point out other modes of construction, such as, while they employ only small actual changes of form, involve high prerogatives. In some of these instances it may not be difficult to assign a reason why such prerogatives should not have been granted to man, in his present condition; and yet it may be equally easy to show that they are abstractedly possible, and that they are compatible one with another, and that they comport with the probable purposes of a higher range of intellectual and moral life.

And be it always remembered that, although hypothesis is not truth—or we should rather say, is not truth ascertained, yet, when legitimately used, it is the most ready and effective of all the means in our power for acquiring truth. It is by hypothesis, framed with at once a bold and a cautious sagacity, that the boundaries of science are extended; and it is in the use of this method that facts and principles which once seemed to be placed far beyond the reach of human intelligence, have at length been brought to form a part of our well-established modern philosophy. At the least, or where nothing can be done beyond the mere statement of a rational and consistent theory, this, while carefully kept apart from matters of certainty and faith, may serve the important purposes, first, of superseding a multitude of difficulties, themselves drawn from hypothetical sources; and secondly, of affording a provisional aid to meditative minds, in loosening from things sensual and temporary, and in bringing vividly home to their convictions the bright expectation of a future and undecaying felicity.

Nothing can be more absurd than the supposition that any efforts of the mind, how strenuous soever, can enable it to conceive, even in the faintest manner, of a mode of existence essentially and totally unlike our actual mode of life; for this were to imagine ourselves to be endowed with a real creative faculty. But the task we now undertake, although arduous, is altogether of another sort; inasmuch as it is proposed to specify the conditions of a mode of existence, differing from the present *as little as may be*, and yet in a manner that shall secure the highest advantages. On a line of conjecture like this, sobriety may be mistress of our course, nor need we set a single step, without a sufficient reason for the direction we take. That the principle of analogy will hold good, in connecting the present with the future constitution of human nature, is a persuasion which, while the material universe is before us, it is scarcely possible to resist; and that such an analogy will actually run on from the present to the future, the language of Scripture plainly implies. But if so, then it cannot be thought a hopeless task to trace the rudiments at least of the future, amid the elements of the present life. Our part then is to examine, in succession, the several constituents of our corporeal existence, and to consider of what extensions each faculty may be susceptible, or how it might be set at large from the limitations that actually confine it.

We take perhaps the most accessible path on this field of hypothesis by considering, in the first place, the least intellectual of the faculties of the mind—namely, its power to originate motion—a power shared by all classes of beings that give evidence of consciousness or sensation. Wherever there is feeling, there is also muscular power and will. Now this power, mysterious as it is, may be conceived of as applied in a very different manner, and so as to involve a great and desirable extension of our range of corporeal activity and enjoyment. It was an ancient opinion, to which modern philosophy also inclines—that motion, in every case, is the product of mind, and that though transmitted and continued through various means, it never commences except in a volition, either of the Supreme Mind, or of created minds. This doctrine may well have been suggested by our consciousness, with which it exactly comports. The mere volition is followed by muscular action, and the process is absolutely simple and instantaneous; nor does any thought of the physical apparatus—the muscular contractions, the tendinous attachments, or the bony fulcra, enter into the mental operation. In fact the power of the mind over matter involves no *process* at all; there is no circuit of acts or preparations; motion follows will, just as perception follows the impact of vibrations—without an interval; will and motion are immediately conjoined, and the organic and mechanical structure by which it is effected are modes only through which the power of the mind is defined, and is directed in a particular line of movement.

The *vis inertiæ* of matter, the tendency of gravitation, and the resistance of the atmosphere, or of more dense fluids, are all instantaneously overcome by a direct mechanical force—a force which is not that of bones, tendons, and muscular fibres, but the force of mind. Bones, tendons, nerves, and muscles, do, in fact, come between mind and the extraneous mass; but it is as instruments only, and as a staff or a cord intervenes between the hand and the body that is moved by it. The expansive force of heat, as applied in the vaporization of water, is not a more direct mechanical force than is the impulsive power of the mind in man and other locomotive animals. We are accustomed, indeed, to say that the mind acts mechanically, only by exciting muscular irritability and the tension of fibres. But is not this assumption gratuitous? Our consciousness does not suggest any such belief:—in rapidly and forcibly moving the hand—in striking a blow, we know nothing of contractile fibres, or of muscles, or of a circuitous despatching of orders from the mind to the brain, and from the brain along the nervous chords,.to such and such muscles, as the case may demand. The mind is in the hand, or the arm, and there it originates the motion; it is not, or not if our consciousness speak true, in the anatomical or physiological mechanism. This complex apparatus performs its part, at the moment when called upon, with as little of our control or interference as the heart, and the intestines, and the liver perform their constant offices.

Nor is the mechanical power of the mind of a slender or evanescent sort, like certain barely perceptible magnetic influences, which, although they may just be detected in a nicely conducted and elaborate experiment, elude common observation, and are incapable of being so far enhanced as to propel the smallest solid mass. The mind impels matter with the celerity of lightning, and with a force that is bounded, as it seems, only by the adhesive strength of the engine it employs; that is to say, by the solidity of the bones, the tenacity of the ligatures and tendons, and by the degree in which the irritability of the fleshy substance may be wrought upon. That the inherent power of the mind is in fact limited by the strength of the materials it employs (just as the expansive force of steam is limited only by the strength of copper and iron) becomes evident in those instances in which, from want of due caution, it actually breaks up or rends its own animal machinery. Acting through the medium of a lever of that sort in which velocity is gained at the cost of power, it yet puts in motion masses greater in bulk and heavier than the animal frame; and were the whole muscular energy of a robust man to be applied in one direction, and through the means of a lever of the first order, it would be sufficient to crush or to burst far stronger materials than those which compose the animal body. An habitual and unconscious discretion is, in truth, acquired early in life, which checks our muscular efforts, and leads us to refrain from the full exertion of the power we might exert, lest injury should be done to the vascular system, or to the tendons, or to the ligatures and fascia.

A man in full health is capable of far greater efforts than he ordinarily permits himself to make; and when this habitual restraint is thrown aside, as in cases of sudden peril, or of delirium and madness, the inherent mechanical force of mind is displayed, and it is seen that one lunatic or one desperate man exerts a power with which five or six in their ordinary senses can hardly cope. This same force, otherwise applied, would be enough, and much more than enough, to overcome the *vis inertiæ* and the gravitation of the body, and to impart to it a velocity greater than that of the swiftest of birds.

Furthermore, in the animal structure the force of the mind is limited, not only in its *amount* by the strength of the organic material, but in its *direction* also by the system of articulation, and by the specific arrangement of the muscles. A door, however impelled, can only revolve on its hinges; the piston can play perpendicularly only; and the limbs have their appointed movement—prone or supine, lateral or rotatory, and always in conformity with a definite mechanism. One part of this mechanism consists of the nervous communication between the limb and the brain. Sever or tie the nervous chord, and the muscles no longer receive from the cerebral mass or spinal process that pabulum of irritability which they require; the mind, in that case, does not take effect upon the limb—the limb wanting its galvanic excitement. It may be said, indeed, that the nervous chord is the channel, not of muscular excitement, but of *volition*, which, taking place in the brain, is supposed to run along the thread, conveying itself duly to this, that, and the other muscles, to flectors, pronators, supinators,

&c., as may be needed for the performance of the intended movement. But how is any such gratuitous supposition proved, or even made to appear probable? All we are conscious of is—the volition; and all we learn from physiology is, that muscular contraction requires a certain galvanic influence, of which the brain appears to be the secreting viscus, and the nerves the channel. The hand cannot follow the mind unless it be constantly supplied with blood by the heart, and with galvanic excitement by the brain; nor can the stomach digest food unless, in the same manner, it be supplied with both, from the heart and from the brain: but it is not the heart that digests the food, nor is it the brain that digests it; but the living assimilative power, with its solvents, in the coats of the stomach; and thus, as we suppose, it is not the brain that moves the hand, in any other sense than that in which it may be said that the heart does so; although the functions of both are indispensable to motion; but it is the mind, present in the hand and arm, that is really the moving power.

But the inference we have in view, in connection with our immediate subject, is not dependent upon any hypothesis we may adopt concerning the occult process of muscular movement; for whether we suppose, as I am inclined to do, that the mind impels the limb immediately, and that the influence derived from the brain, through the nervous chord, is subsidiary only; or whether we think that volition, affecting the brain immediately, is thence conveyed to the muscles, it will still be true that mind puts matter in movement; only under the last-named supposition the influence must be considered as chemical; whereas, on the former supposition, it is simply mechanical. In the one case, as well as the other, inert matter is put into vehement action, and it is quite as easy to conceive of the one species of movement, as of the other, as originated by the mind.

We are then free to adopt the hypothesis, which seems the simpler of the two, namely, that animal motion springs immediately from the inherent mechanical power of the mind over matter, which it impels at will, hither and thither, with a velocity like that of light, and with a force that, so far as we know, is limited only by the tenacity of the tendinous chords, and by the strength of the coats of the vessels.

But in like manner as sensation is confined, in the animal organization, to particular points, or to surfaces of nervous excitability; so is the mechanical force of the mind restricted to those flexions and rotations which the joints will admit of, and which the muscles may perform. Nothing more therefore can be done by a machinery such as this, but change the relative position of the limbs, and so, by throwing the centre of gravity forward or backward, on this side or on that, to effect locomotion. The flight of birds, the swimming of fishes, and the walking, running, and leaping of land animals are mere adaptations of an altered relative position of the limbs, taking effect suddenly and forcibly upon resisting bodies.

Let it however be supposed that muscular action takes place in the mode of chemical excitement, which we have stated; and in this case it is easy to conceive of the very same power (nor need it be greater) acting upon, or through the medium of, a corporeal structure absolutely infrangible and indestructible; and it would then suffice for effecting locomotion by impulsion upon a resisting medium in a manner analogous to the flight of birds, but greatly surpassing it in velocity. This supposition, though easily admitted, I should not entertain; but should prefer the hypothesis that, in the future spiritual body, whether or not the mechanical apparatus is to be altogether superseded, the entire corporeal mass shall be liable to a plenary mental influence equably diffused, and although still subject to the *vis inertiæ* and gravitation that are proper to matter, that both shall be overcome, at will, by the embodied mind, so that the locomotion of the whole shall follow volition, as now the relative motion of the limbs follows it. This implies nothing more than the setting the inherent mechanical power of the mind at large, and the breaking up its restriction to the muscular structure, and the osseous articulations. A body thus informed throughout, by the energy of mind, might be either subtile and ethereal, like the magnetic fluid; or it might be as dense and ponderous as gold, or as adamant; for the most elastic gas is not in itself at all more self-motive than a block of granite; and it is a mere illusion to imagine that the one might more readily be affected by the volitions of mind than the other. The seraph who steers his course at pleasure from sun to sun, and who overtakes the swiftest of the planets in its orbit, may corporeally possess an invisible and imponderable ether, or (which is equally credible) he may command a gigantic body, solid as porphyry. The two suppositions stand on the same ground of abstract probability; for matter, in relation to mind, is one and the same, and is always inert and passive.

The first article then of our hypothesis concerning the future spiritual body, involves nothing more than an extension of a power now actually exerted by the mind, and which is easily conceived of as set free from its muscular restrictions, in such a manner as should allow of locomotion by simple volition, as well as of the power to put external masses in movement. Nevertheless, inasmuch as a corporeal structure must involve the limitations that attach necessarily to matter, it may well be supposed that this locomotive faculty, how wide soever its range, will yet be—a force related to other forces, and counterpoised by a definite resistance;—it will have its calculable velocity and its limit, which it will not pass.

A fit occasion will present itself in the following pages, for adverting to the probable uses and consequences of this enlarged power of locomotion; but that it actually awaits human nature might be plausibly inferred on the ground that the muscular force is now felt to be—a power restrained; that is to say, a faculty equal to much more than is as yet permitted to it; and perhaps, with not a few individuals, the conscious muscular energy is strictly analogous to that of a strong man fettered and handcuffed, who meditates what he will do when set at large. Is there not a latent, or a half latent instinct in the mind which speaks of a future liberty of ranging at will through space? There are some, perhaps, who will admit that they have indistinct anticipations of this sort, quite as strong as are those moral and intellectual aspirations after immortality which have been considered good presumptive proofs of the reality of a future life. The author would be very slow to seek support to an argument, such as the one now in hand, from scriptural expressions which, probably, ought to be interpreted in a spiritual sense only; he will therefore merely name the often-quoted passage, (Isaiah xl. 31,) as *possibly* having a secondary reference to the future corporeal powers of the sons of God: "They shall renew their strength—they shall mount up with wings as eagles; they shall run, and not be weary; they shall walk, and not faint."

CHAPTER IV.

THE SECOND AND THIRD SUPPOSED PREROGATIVES OF THE SPIRITUAL ECONOMY.

Thus far our hypothesis trenches very little upon the ground of mere conjecture, and it would be easy to go on in the same direction, imagining the mind, in its new corporeal lodgment, to gain a power over some other of the properties of matter, besides the *vis inertiæ* and gravitation; and that it may be able to put in activity certain chemical affinities. Of this supposed influence we find what is very nearly an actual instance, or at the least, an indication, in the chemical assimilations, and the secreting functions, which belong to animal life, and which, if not immediately effected by an unconscious mental agency, are unquestionably to a great extent under the influence of the mind, acting upon them in the way, sometimes of acceleration, and sometimes of abatement. Animal life, in its various functions, or that mysterious energy which we name, but can never define, and never expose to view, may perhaps consist in the power of mind over such of the properties of matter as may be made available for the purposes of animal organization. Mind, allied to matter, unconsciously indeed, but as directed by the creative energy, combines or dissolves, takes up or rejects, the elements with which it comes in contact, and thus lives, if we might so speak, by its own discretive act. Now this same power over the chemical affinities of matter, may, like the power of the mind over masses of matter, be enlarged in another state. But we leave this conjecture and pass on.

Nothing however can be more natural than the supposition that the passive power of the mind, or its consciousness of some of the properties of matter through the senses, shall, in the future corporeal frame, be made to include other of those properties. The mind, as we have already observed, is no doubt inherently percipient of light, heat, sound, solidity, as well as of the several properties that affect the olfactory and gustatory organs; for if it were not so, there is no reason to believe that any organic apparatus—any expansion of nervous filaments, could endue it with this faculty. On the same ground we assume the mind to possess an inherent or essential mechanical force; yet a force that can be exerted only through the instrumentality of a corporeal structure. But as the several species of perception are rendered distinct, and are adapted to the various purposes of animal and rational life by being separately attached, each to its organ, these contrivances, admirable as they are, must be regarded as so many limitations of the general percipient faculty of the mind, and as restricting it, as well in regard to the extent and the delicacy of its perceptions, as to the variety or kinds of them. The organs of sense are particular adjustments of nervous sensibility, intended to concentrate the mind, at different times, upon single properties of the external world, with a view to the better securing of definite purposes. The senses are *adits* of knowledge; and because adits, therefore exclusive and restrictive means of information. It is upon the retina, and there only, that the mind converses with light and colours: it is within the tympanum, and there only, that the mind converses with the modulated vibrations of the air; it is upon the tongue that it discriminates certain chemical differences of the substances to be taken into the stomach. But we cannot suppose that, abstractedly, these several properties might not affect the mind in any other mode, or at any other points; doubtless it might bring its percipient faculty into contact with these properties of matter more at large and under fewer limitations; and it might also gain acquaintance with other properties than those to which the five organs of sensation extend. We may easily suppose the medullary substance to be laid open to sensation otherwise than it actually is, and also to be endued with a more exquisite or refined sensibility. The discrimination of colours, through the touch, by the blind, and the many instances that have occurred in which the want of one or more of the senses has been compensated by an enhanced sensibility of the remaining organs, afford proof enough, or as we should perhaps say, give indication of what may be called the versatility of the percipient faculty, and they establish the fact that this power is inherently much greater than, under ordinary circumstances, it seems to be.

The animal organization, with its medullary mass and its nervous expansions, may be regarded, not merely as a means of sensation, but as a means of abatement, or if it were as a sheath, defending the percipient faculty of the mind, except at certain points, from the too forcible impressions which would otherwise be made upon it by the external world. The body, as we suppose, is to the mind an envelope, or a rough coating, which serves to prevent its being either overborne, or unduly stimulated by the otherwise continuous influx of various and powerful excitements. The mind perhaps, in this its present initial stage of existence, might scarcely be able to assert its rational supremacy, or to exercise its proper, intellectual, and moral functions, if it were exposed to as much sensation as it is inherently capable of receiving. But in its next stage of life, and when its active and higher principles have become mature, it may be well able to sustain, and advantageously to use, a much more ample correspondence with the material world, than would now be good, or even possible.

The boldest supposition we can entertain, on this subject, ought not to be regarded as unphilosophical or extravagant, while we have so many proofs before us of those vast extensions of our means of knowledge that have accrued from the improvement of the merely mechanical aids of the senses. Let the well-known facts be simply stated and duly considered.—The nearest of the fixed stars is at a greater distance from our system than 19,200,000,000,000 miles, and the most remote of those that are *distinctly visible* by the telescope, are probably twice that distance, or much more. Nevertheless the transmission of light through that incalculable space is exact and precise; and when, by the means of the refracting power of some few lenses, the remote object is made to subtend a larger angle than it does to the naked eye, then the eye with ease converses with that object, and perceives that what seemed one, is actually two stars, and that these two revolve around a common centre of gravity; and moreover, that the curve they move in is not a circle, but an ellipse. Thus this infinitely small difference between one kind of orbit and another, has actually become perceptible to the human eye. It is manifest therefore that, as well the materials of knowledge as the faculty of knowing, are immensely more extensive than, to the unassisted senses, they appear. Now it cannot be deemed extravagant to suppose that, instead of the aid furnished to the eye by the telescope, the percipient faculty itself might be so exposed to the emanations or vibrations of light, as to be able to distinguish at once, what now it does distinguish by the aid of refraction. And if it might do this, who shall say it might not do still more? Is it philosophical to place any limit to the range of perception? we think not; and on the contrary, regard it as altogether a probable supposition, that the same mind, which now discerns spheres, and distinguishes their motions at a distance incalculably remote, may hereafter be so advantaged, in its organic structure, as to discern bodies, and their movements, on the surfaces of the planets of our system, near as they are to us comparatively. If this be a wild hypothesis, it is an hypothesis like that which assumes that the infant who now crosses the nursery, may in time, and by the use of the very same locomotive powers, perambulate the globe. The actual discoveries of modern science are such as to render every thing credible which can be proved to come within the compass of analogy.

Whatever is true, or may be made to appear probable, in relation to vision, may be assumed, *mutatis mutandis*, in relation to the other senses; and it is not needful here to insist upon the particulars. Our principle is—That perception is, at present, a circumscribed faculty; and we rationally anticipate an era when it shall throw off its confinements, and converse at large with the material universe, and find itself familiarly at home in the height and breadth of the heavens.

The five senses, we have said, may be regarded as limiting the percipient faculty, not merely as to the amount or extent of the impressions we receive, but in regard also to the kinds of sensation which the mind may be inherently capable of admitting. By the means of these senses we become acquainted with some few of the properties of matter; but at the most it is only a few, and the intimate researches of our modern physical science leave no room to doubt that there are many agencies in activity about us, which, although they make themselves known in their ultimate consequences, are not directly cognizable either by the eye, the ear, the touch, the taste, or the smell. The external world, as at present perceptible to man, in five species, may, to other sentient natures, be perceptible in twenty or in fifty kinds. If the mind may know the differences of hot and cold, hard and soft, loud or harsh and melodious, red and yellow, sweet and bitter, it may discriminate other differences, or qualities that belong to matter, or every other such quality. In truth it is more easy to conceive of the mind as conversant with all properties of the external world, than as conversant with some, while it is insensible of others. Mind, as we have said, must be natively conscious of the vibratory, emanative, and pungent powers of the external world; but if so, then we may assume that it only needs to be freed from the husk of animal organization, to know, on all sides and perfectly, that which now it knows at points only, and in an abated degree. The ancient philosophy supposed there to be four elements, or perhaps a fifth; but we now reckon fifty; and in like manner, as now we think of five species of perception, hereafter we may become familiar with a hundred, or a thousand.

Yet this is not all that may fairly be assumed as probable, and as strictly analogous to our present powers—mere conjecture not admitted. The senses, such as they are under the present animal organization, in no instance go further than to give us information concerning the last product of certain combined qualities or conditions of matter. Thus, for example, we perceive colours, but we know nothing (by the sense of sight) of that state of the surfaces of bodies, the effect of which is that they imbibe some of the elements of light, and throw off others: the petals of the poppy imbibe and assimilate the yellow and the blue, and with a most decisive antipathy reject the fierce red of the sun's rays; while, again, the gentle violet cherishes the more powerful element of light, and refuses the pale and feeble. So do the chemical qualities of substances affect the tongue and palate, and the membranes of the nose, with a certain product of their combination; but this combination itself and its ingredients, and the reason of its affinity, remain occult. But it is conceivable that this INNER FORM of matter, as it has been termed, may, as well as the external species, be perceptible, so that the specific cause of solidity, fluidity, crystallization, decomposition, colour, taste, smell, musical relation, and other states, movements, and transitions of matter, may be as immediately perceptible as are now the ulterior products of those states. Thus, besides knowing effects, we should also know causes; or, to speak more correctly, we should be able to trace forms and affinities, a stage or two higher than now we can. Instead of looking only at the dial-plate of nature, and of noting the hands and the figures, we should be admitted to inspect the wheel-work and the springs; and this inner perception of real forms might well consist with the simultaneous perception of external species; just as our dissection of an animal does not prevent or supersede our discernment of its form.

The material universe (and the same, with still more meaning, may be said of the intellectual universe) is a vast profound, upon the surface of which we float, and of which, by direct consciousness, we know nothing beyond the surface. Science, with its methods of inference, carries us a little way beneath the forms and semblances of things, and only a little. Meantime we cannot suppose the interior to be, from any abstract necessity, incognizable by the human mind. Our knowledge of nature is like our acquaintance with the globe we inhabit, superficial only; and the operations of the miner, like those of the natural philosopher, expose to our view a few fathoms of the depth, but yet leave the abyss unexplored. Nevertheless it is assuredly possible, abstractedly, that the very bowels of our planet should be inspected by the human eye. And so we may assume, concerning the inmost recesses of the mechanism of the material world, that they might be known by man.

Nor need any jealousy be entertained, as if this exposure of the secrets of nature should tend to abate our reverence toward the Creator, or breed in the human mind a presumptuous familiarity with the divine operations. It may indeed be well, and even necessary, while in the present world, where the Creator himself is veiled from our sight, that an impenetrable veil of mystery should be thrown over the procedures of his power and wisdom; and that so a check should be given to the audacity of reason, and an awe and modesty imposed upon minds ready enough to build a tower of pride that shall reach to heaven. In the path of any such intellectual arrogance, we meet an impassable obstacle, resulting from the secrecy that attaches to the processes and the construction of the material world, —a secrecy such as no means of analysis, how exact and assiduous soever, can break through. Our ambition and self-esteem receive here an effectual rebuff. But it may, and probably will be otherwise, when we reach a more advanced stage of our existence, and come where the far more stupendous mysteries of the divine nature, and of the spiritual universe, shall begin to unfold themselves to our view. Then it will be found that the lower, and comparatively unimportant wonders of the material world, may be looked at with a familiar intuition; and this first page of our schooling, which now concentrates all our faculties, being fully understood, shall leave us at leisure to learn a higher lesson.

We ought assuredly to believe that He who has endowed his rational family with powers fitting them to comprehend the reason of his works, and with a disposition to admire what they understand, will not, in the end, hide from them any thing which they might know with safety and advantage; and that gradually, as one temporary motive of concealment after another is superseded, the veil will be drawn aside, so that what once was inscrutable shall be openly displayed. These progressive revelations, instead of inflating intellectual vanity, must tend rather to inspire an ever-growing awe of the inexhaustible wealth of the Infinite Intelligence, inasmuch as every such new discovery shall be attended with a new and glimmering perception of things heretofore not imagined to exist, or so much as whispered of among even the best informed of the elders of immortality.

CHAPTER V.

THE FOURTH OF THESE ADVANTAGES.

The above-named probable extensions of the physical powers, in the future spiritual body, have relation to the correspondence of the mind with the external world; and some other like advantages, less clearly supported by analogy, might be added; but passing any such conjectures, we go on to consider those new adjustments of the corporeal structure, the effect of which would be to confer advantage upon the mind itself, in relation to the exercise of its intellectual and moral faculties.

It can hardly be necessary, as a preliminary to this portion of our hypothesis, to prove that all the faculties of the mind, even the loftiest of them, as well as the very purest of the emotions, are, in their present corporeal lodgment, subject to much modification, and much abatement, in consequence of the dependence of the mind upon the animal organization. In every mental process, and in every movement of the affections, there is an attendant organic action—a subsidiary operation of the brain, and of the arterial system, not to say of other vital organs; and inasmuch as this accompaniment is necessarily clogged with the conditions that attach to inert matter, the mind is so far bound down to those conditions, and is restrained from moving at any other rate than that which the body can safely follow, and duly perform its part. Reason (in man) is not absolute reason, but a reasoning faculty dependent, to a great extent, upon, and characterized by, the particular cerebral conformation, and by the constitution or temperament of the individual. The same manifestly is true of the moral sentiments.

Among these intellectual powers, intimately affected by the original structure, and by the pathology of the body in each individual, the memory stands foremost. The memory is, in a peculiar sense, a function of the brain; and as in the admission of images of the external world, every thing depends upon the sensorium, so likewise in the retention and the reproduction of these ideas, the physical structure, and the actual condition, or healthy action of the cerebral organ, determine its power and its activity. The memory grows with the growth of the body; strengthens with adolescence, is the contemporary of animal energy; and is the first of the mental powers to betray the incipient decay of the vital force: the gray head, the impaired sight, the trembling limb, and the faithless memory tell of the advance of years, even while reason, and perhaps imagination, scarcely seem to decline. Again, it is the memory that is the most directly affected by external injuries of the head, or by those diseases that spend their violence upon the brain. It is the memory, moreover, that asks for, and admits those artificial aids which bespeak its intimate alliance with corporeal impressions. Thus it is that any very peculiar physical sensation, recurring after a long interval, brings to our recollection the incidental circumstances and the mental state, at the time of its first occurrence. Instances of this sort are various, and have often been adduced, nor can it be necessary here to relate them.

It is therefore obvious, that this organic mental faculty, as at present possessed even by the most highly favoured individuals, is susceptible of much enhancement and extension, merely by an improvement of the corporeal constitution. In this there is nothing conjectural. But it may be well to consider what is probably implied in such an augmentation of the memory.

Let it then be kept in view that, as sensation, in its several kinds, or the consciousness we have of the external world, is a specific adaptation of the inherent power of the mind to perceive the properties of matter, so is the memory a particular adaptation of that original and essential faculty of the mind by which it retains a consciousness of its past states, and knows them to be past, and to have been real, and clearly distinguishes them from simple cogitations. Sensation has respect to the particular uses and purposes of the present animal and intellectual life; and so likewise the faculty of memory, as now enjoyed, has respect to the special purposes of our present condition: so much of it is granted to us as we actually need, but not more; or at least by no means all that is abstractedly possible. As sensation is a limited consciousness of the external world, so is memory a limited and incidental recollection of our past states of feeling; it is a partial exercise of a larger power, which, in adapting itself to the occasions of active life, forfeits, or holds in abeyance, its plenary prerogatives. Considered as a function of the brain, the memory retains what it retains, and reproduces what it reproduces, according to the law of an arbitrary, and often accidental connection of ideas. The power which, in its original capacity, might have filled a broad field, does in fact only beat a narrow path, and gropes its way backward over the ground it has traversed, in search of what it has dropped. Or, to change our comparison, the memory is a book, the blank leaves of which are constantly filling, but of which the written portion never lies outspread before us; and, moreover, the paper being of frail texture, and the ink evanescent, and the entries often made in haste, or carelessly, they soon become totally illegible. The memory furnishes a partial and fortuitous sample of facts; but it by no means (not even in the most eminent instances) exhibits a complete collection of whatever it has received.

Yet with all its incompleteness and its frailties the memory serves sufficiently the ordinary purposes of life, active, intellectual, and moral; nor is it very difficult to imagine the reasons which may make even these disparagements a necessary part of our condition in the present state. Perhaps if our impressions of the past were not in some such manner liable to be abated, and borne down, or obscured and obliterated, there would, in most minds, be certain vivid recollections which would continue to usurp the entire consciousness, and so exclude the present, with its fainter sensations, its interests and its duties; and we might thus be liable to long seasons of abstraction, during which we should stand like statues amid the urgent affairs of the passing moment. Such, in fact, is the misfortune of a class of morbid minds. But this necessity for abating the vividness of the memory is temporary only; and it is easy to imagine such an enhancement of the active force of the mind, in relation to the passing moment, as should fully counterpoise the influence of even the most distinct and vivid recollection of scenes gone by. Let but the voluntary principle be proportionately invigorated, and then the mind might enjoy a permanent and bright consciousness of all that it has ever known, felt, and performed:—it might thus repossess itself of its entire past existence, and might continue to enjoy (or to endure) an ever-growing and entire recollection of its various successive states; it might every moment live its whole life over simultaneously, and with infallible accuracy might be conscious of all the circumstances and shades of every portion of its being. However much such a full consciousness of the past might seem to exceed, in kind, as well as in amount, our present partial and fallacious recollections, it would nevertheless be only the same power of mind, set free from physical obstructions and infirmities.

The memory, even in its present state, and affected as it is by the conditions of animal life, might be brought near to the perfection we have supposed (and in a few recorded instances it has been) if it were only exempted from accidental obstructions arising from a turgid state of the cerebral vessels—a flaccid state of the cerebral substance—a slight compression—a confusion connected with some derangement of the digestive organs, and the like. The spiritual body then, in itself indestructible and exempt from the liability to animal decay, may allow the mental faculty to spread itself out to the full;—as if an inscription, which heretofore had been committed to a leaf, or papyrian scroll, was now transferred to a fair and ample surface of Parian marble.

Memory, we say, is a corporeal-mental power, and it is so, not only as physiologically dependent upon the state of the cerebral mass, but also in a higher and more intellectual sense, which should not be lost sight of in relation to our present argument. Mind, absolutely unembodied, and cut off from all connection with the material universe, would not (as we have conjectured) retain the power of noting the epochs of its existence, or be conscious of the equal periods of duration. In such an insulated condition, it is probable, that the entire consciousness, comprising as well the acts of the mind, as its passive states, and its emotions, instead of constituting a continuous history, or a series of changes, the one coming on as the other recedes, would assume the appearance of a various aggregate of ideas, as if simultaneously existing, and would be associated with no notion of the past and the present, nor be attended with an anticipation of the future. Whether such a condition of being could consist at all with the exercise of active faculties is not clear; but it is hard to think that it would comport with that progressive development of principles and of character which belongs to the moral life. The moral life is, in a peculiar sense—A HISTORY: it is a process, involving successive stages, through the course of which the unalterable laws of the spiritual economy are in turn brought to bear upon the dispositions and conduct of those who are subject thereto. Take away memory, and we go near to annul government, and to destroy accountability.

Now it is as *embodied*, and as thereby conversant with material objects, that the mind learns to arrange its consciousness in a series, or in other words, exercises memory. For this faculty, although not exclusively conversant with material objects, yet rarely, if ever, entertains any notions, as constituting part of our past history, unless connected with things seen, heard, and felt. Pure abstract conceptions may indeed keep their place in the mind; but whenever the having entertained such conceptions is *remembered*, it is only as they may have been accidentally conjoined with circumstances of place, or company, or with physical sensations. The memory leans upon the material world.

On both these accounts then, that is to say, first, because it is peculiarly dependent upon the bodily organization, and secondly, because it is mainly conversant with images of the external world, the faculty of memory is one which, with the highest probability, we may expect to be greatly extended and improved in a new and a more refined corporeal structure. The important consequences of such an extension of memory it can hardly be necessary to specify. A rational agent, whatever were his other powers, who should be totally destitute of memory (if indeed we can at all form such a conception) must occupy a very low place in the scale of being; nor could either the vividness of his momentary impressions, or the energy or grasp of his reasoning faculties, in any degree compensate for the want of an intelligent recollection of his past existence. On the other hand, a being of inferior original endowments, but yet gifted with a perfect consciousness of the whole of his past course, could hardly fail rapidly to accumulate intellectual wealth, and to outstrip those of his competitors who were not gifted in the like manner. After a time, such a being would possess an *amount of consciousness*, if we may so speak, which in itself would be opulence and power. Man, in the present life, occupies a middle position, between these two supposed cases; for his memory, with all its imperfections, and although it retains at command a small portion only of what is committed to its keeping, yet retains enough to secure to itself the fruits of experience and study; and in what it actually embraces and performs, it gives a promise of far greater things, when it shall be lodged in a corporeal structure, liable to no decay or disturbance.

A little steady reflection will open to any one who pursues the idea, many momentous consequences involved in the supposition of an entire continuous recollection of our past existence; or of what might be termed, a PLENARY MEMory. In relation to the maturing of the moral life, it is this vivid consciousness of the whole series of our actions and emotions that is needed for penetrating the mind with a sense of its own condition, and for rendering it its own equitable censor. It is manifest that those egregiously false estimates, which we so often entertain of our own merits, gain entrance by favour of an oblivion of the most considerable and characteristic portions of our moral life. It is from a full and incessant recollection of the past, that are to arise, if at all, and in a due and necessary intensity, those strivings of the spirit with itself, and those compunctious agonies of the heart, whence improvement may result. The trite motto on a sun-dial, *non sine lumine*, might aptly be transferred to the human conscience, in relation to memory; and we may believe that when its full light, unabated and perpetual, shall be brought to bear upon the soul's sense of good and evil, then shall be developed, in its dread power, the force of the moral principle, as implanted by God in our bosoms.

The abstract possibility of an entire restoration of memory, or of the recovery of the whole that it has ever contained, need not be questioned; or if it were, an appeal might be made to every one's personal experience; for we suppose there are none to whom it has not happened to have a sudden recollection,—a flashing of some minute and unimportant incident of early life or childhood; and perhaps after an interval of forty or sixty years. With some persons, these unconnected and uncalled-for reminiscences are frequent and very vivid; and they seem to imply that although the mind may have lost its command over the stores of memory, and may no longer be able to recall at will the remote passages of its history, yet that the memory itself has not really parted with any of its deposits, but holds them faithfully (if not obediently) in reserve, against a season when the whole will be demanded of it. Might not the human memory be compared to a field of sepulture, thickly stocked with the remains of many generations; but of all these thousands whose dust heaves the surface, a few only are saved from immediate oblivion upon tablets and urns; while the many are, at present, utterly lost to knowledge? Nevertheless each of the dead has left in that soil an imperishable germ; and all, without distinction, shall another day start up, and claim their dues.

CHAPTER VI.

THE FIFTH AND SIXTH HYPOTHETICAL PREROGATIVES OF THE SPIRITUAL BODY.

WHAT is true of the memory, is true also of the law of mental suggestion, or, as it is called, the association of ideas; namely, that it depends, in a very intimate manner, upon the functions and condition of the brain, and of other vital organs. That unintermitted current of thought which constitutes the staple of our consciousness, and upon which the mind exerts its voluntary power at intervals, and which it partially controls, receives its determining guidance, in each mind, from the peculiarities of the temperament, and the habits, and the original dispositions. The reason why such an idea follows such another, in each mind, is to be sought for in the conformation and actual condition of each, including very much that is merely physical, and proper to the animal organization. And yet this involuntary and constitutional suggestion of ideas, as is well known, has a most extensive influence in regulating the operations of the higher and the more active faculties. The decisions we come to in common life, the style and subjects of our ordinary conversation, the creations of the imagination, and even the severest processes of the reasoning faculty, are all modified, and are often originated, by the arbitrary law of association, such as it is, in the mind of the individual; and this, again, results in part from the peculiarities of the animal organization. No one accustomed to retrace and to analyze, with philosophic curiosity, the stream of his involuntary ideas, can have failed to notice the paramount influence of merely animal sensations over them. Especially during sleep, when the accidental association of ideas is entirely freed from the control of reason, each function of life, and each organ, takes its turn in the production of images and emotions. It seems as if in this movement and succession of ideas incessantly going on, sleeping and waking, nature was at work, mingling the heterogeneous elements of the intellectual and the material worlds, in preparation for the higher processes of the rational and moral life: for, in fact, there is always going on a mental assimilation, or amalgamation, wherein the species of the external universe are being blended with the materials of reason, and with the emotions. This involuntary process is a concocting of that upon which the mind is afterwards to nourish itself.

Throughout the period of infancy and childhood, the involuntary suggestion of ideas takes its course, almost uncontrolled; and it again flows on at random in seasons of debility, delirium, or insanity, and also through the closing years of senile decay. But the mental and moral advancement that distinguishes youth and manhood, consists in the gradual (or partial) substitution of a rational for a fortuitous law of suggestion; or, in other words, of a voluntary, instead of an involuntary series of thoughts. A vigorous mature mind is one in which the real relations of things, and not their accidental connections, bring them forward, and determine either their continuance, as objects of thought, or their speedy dismissal. It is easy then to imagine a state wherein the organic and accidental suggestion of ideas should wholly disappear, and be succeeded by a law of association purely rational; so that each successive state of the mind should be the true and just consequence of its preceding state, and of its actual impressions, and always according to the rule of abstract fitness. Thus analogy would come in the place of contingency, and truth be substituted for accident.

Constituted as we are at present, the body, with its ever-varying conditions, with the fumes of its laboratories, with its appetites and its ills, sways the mental being; and it is only at intervals that the mind asserts its proper supremacy. But the future spiritual body, as we may safely assume, will be the instrument—and the mere instrument of the mind, and in every respect will be subordinate to it. That more excellent corporeal structure, whether it be dense or ethereal, whether tangible or not, is not destined to lead, or to give law, in any sense, to the intellect: it will not either suggest ideas, or infuse emotions: it will not whisper its own interests to the soul; for it will have none apart from those of the mind; nor will it steal an advantage upon reason, to insinuate its desires. Reason and moral sentiment, in full vigour, will pursue their course, and be liable to no interior disturbance—to no privy conspiracy—to no silent and insidious attraction. Our present state is one of alternation between the active and passive faculties, the latter chiefly prevailing; but the future being will, as we suppose, be active only, and always so. The human mind, now, may be compared to a lake among the mountains, exposed to gusts and eddies from every ravine that opens upon its margin; and troubled too by guggling springs from beneath. But the same mind, in its future state, may more resemble a river, profound and copious, which, with a steady movement, pursues its way in one direction, and with a force that clears all obstacles, and bears along whatever floats on its surface.

The supposition we are now entertaining deserves a little further consideration. That the mind is itself inert, or is disposed to subside into a state of torpor, is what we should be slow to believe; and it is better to attribute its apparent sluggishness to its connection with animal organization than to think it inherently inactive. It is certain that no intellectual process can be carried on apart from a concurrent evolution of the cerebral organ, which of course, because it belongs to the animal structure, can be sustained only for a time, and soon generates fatigue, and a sense of pain. Thinking, therefore, like every other voluntary animal function, has its brief period of excitement, and its consequent season of exhaustion. Thus the mind is subject to lassitude, because it cannot act except with the consent, and by the aid of the body, which is essentially inert, and which demands stimulants to move it at all. Perpetual mental activity therefore is not possible in the present state. But now let it be supposed, and the supposition implies very little that is purely conjectural, either that the future spiritual body, as more refined, and less, if at all, dependent upon stimulants, shall perform its office in the mental processes without any sense of exhaustion; or (and this is equally easy to imagine, and it is consistent too with some actual facts) that the corporeal part of mental operations shall be effected in a manner analogous to the mechanism of the involuntary animal functions, such as the pulsation of the heart and arteries, the peristaltic motion of the intestines, digestion, and the several secretions, all which go on with continuous regularity, and are not attended by any conscious effort, nor produce any fatigue. A small change, perhaps, in the arrangement of parts, and in the functions of the brain, might suffice for effecting this important enhancement of our mental economy. Thus it is but the opening, or the keeping open, of a foramen between the right and left auricle of the heart, that enables an animal or man to live without incessant respiration; and thus too, as we may fairly conjecture, the branching off of nerves, higher or lower, from the brain, or the altered location of some cerebral gland, might, even in the present animal body, allow of perpetual intellectual activity, without exhaustion, and without any conscious effort: but how vast would be the power so obtained! The mind, in some such manner set free from the chain that forbids it to move faster, or further at a time than the pulpy substance, which fills the cranium, can bear, would instantly assume its essential vitality, and would work, day and night, regardless of rest. Under the present constitution of human nature, the mind might be compared to an Arabian escort, attending a caravan, which, with its cumbrous bales, and its sick and infirm, drags its weary length a stage or so daily; but only release this escort from its charge, and it starts off, nor can hardly the winds overtake it.

A change, such as this, in our mental economy, would not merely incalculably augment the mind's power and its means of advancement, and accelerate its operations; but would exclude, perhaps entirely, the many illusions, and false judgments that steal upon it, like a thief in the night, during its seasons of inertness. Such a new conformation of the corporeal-mental system, by allowing to the mind its essential and constant activity, would leave no room for that fortuitous suggestion of ideas which now comes into play amid the alternations of mental activity. The involuntary series of ideas would cede to voluntary and rational conceptions; and how much of the fatuity and caprice that attach to human conduct, would be shut out, by this substitute merely! Not indeed that the supposed change would of itself render men wise and virtuous; but it would at least enable the wise and the virtuous to hold on their course with a more steady consistency. Under such an economy, it is probable that the good would be much better than now they are, and the bad perhaps much worse; we may therefore readily surmise the reason of the actual constitution of human nature, in this behalf, as fitting mankind for a state wherein neither good nor evil is to reach an absolute and unmixed perfection. Were such a *lusus naturæ* possible, as that a human being should be born, in whose brain the mental process, instead of being connected with that portion of the organ which acts by occasional incitements, should attach to that portion which keeps the involuntary functions of life in movement—such a man (ought we to call him a monster or seraph?) would, if otherwise eminently endowed, reach, in early life, the *acmé* which other men do not attain till life begins to wane, and, in the first years of manhood, he would be master of all sciences—teacher of all wisdom, and director of all affairs.

Those who steadily addict themselves to the pursuit of truth, in any line of thought, are well aware of the disturbance and the disappointment that arise, notwithstanding their utmost efforts to the contrary, first, from the incessant intermixture of ideas foreign to the subject of which the mind is labouring to make itself master, and which take their rise from the principle of association; and then, secondly, from the mere spending of the force of the mind, that is to say of its *organic force*, just at the moment when abstract notions are coming into an intelligible position, and when their correspondence is about to be perceived. The same process, taken up at another time, is not found to present precisely the same elements, or not in precisely the same proportions; the results therefore differ in the issue, by a little; and so we fail of the satisfaction of ascertaining truth. In such instances it is as if the furnace of the chemist, upon the continued intensity of which the success of a difficult experiment wholly depends, were supplied only with a niggard allowance of fuel, which is almost always burnt out before the ingredients in the crucible are completely assimilated.

And it is thus too that so few arguments, orally conducted, reach any useful result, even where there are no motives of prejudice, interest, or personal feeling to pervert the judgments of the disputants. One of the parties in the controversy (and perhaps both) is thrown out of his track, at almost every step, by the fortuitous suggestions that spring from sounds, terms, and allusions; and his opponent, either weary of bringing him back to the line, or taking advantage of his erratic course, abandons the question, and thinks only of triumphing in the personal combat. Or, as frequently happens, even if the antagonists are equally sincere in their pursuit of truth, and pretty evenly matched too in intellectual power, yet the *organic power* of the one fails much sooner than that of the other; and the more infirm party, to conceal his conscious exhaustion, and to cover his retreat, betakes himself to sophistry and evasion.

In fact, it is only on the ground of mathematical science, where the steps of every process of reasoning may be infallibly recorded, so that the whole can be taken up and laid down, without damage, at different times, that the disadvantages we have specified may be warded off.

Again; and to come to our sixth supposed prerogative of the spiritual body; the mental power, both in its extent and in its kind, depends very much upon the ability (possessed by one mind in a far greater degree than by another) of carrying on several operations simultaneously. In truth, there are certain difficult complex speculations which can be pursued only by the few who possess this peculiar ability in an eminent degree; and here, as in the last-named instance, a new construction of the corporeal-mental system may be hypothetically assumed, such as would at once enhance immensely the intellectual power. We need not here stay to decide the preliminary question, whether the power of the mind to carry on several operations simultaneously is apparent only, or is actual and real;—that is to say, whether, in the strictest sense, the mind be capable of complex acts, or only applies itself, with inconceivable rapidity, in turns to different objects, so as to *seem* to attend to several at once. This obscure question we may leave in the rear, and take up as sufficient for our present purpose, the plain fact, loosely stated, that the human mind does, without conscious difficulty, carry on two, three, or more operations within one and the same mental period. Thus, for example, there are few who cannot with ease read aloud, and with due care and emphasis, while a train of thought, wholly unconnected with the subject of the book, is entertained. Or a conversation may be carried on with our neighbour, on the right hand, in company, while we attentively listen to that which is passing between those on our left. Or a piece of music, of difficult execution, is performed, and at the same time schemes are meditated, or powerful emotions indulged. By the means of this same faculty, extemporary speakers not only deliver themselves with propriety and energy, while the subsequent portions of their argument are being digested and arranged, but note, and turn to their advantage, the varying emotions of their auditors, nor lose a smile, a frown, or a sneer, that shows itself on the sea of faces before them.

Now this power, actually possessed and exercised by men in the present state, whether it be precisely what it seems or not, may easily be conceived of as enlarged in its compass, when the same mind comes to be lodged in a body that has more appliancy and a higher finish. And yet this obvious and probable enhancement of our power of attention is not all that may reasonably be looked for, as likely to result from a more refined corporeal constitution. Let it be considered then that the cerebral part of the mental process is, as we have already said, like every other voluntary operation, attended with a sense of fatigue, and that it is followed by lassitude. Thinking, therefore, even in the most vigorous minds, has its limits and its seasons; nor are these limits to be overpassed without injury or peril to the brain. A single process, or a process that is homogeneous and simple, may however be carried on more easily, and longer, than a complex process, or than one that exercises different faculties, and involves heterogeneous subjects. Indeed, any high degree of complexity soon brings on a confusion of ideas, and a collapse of the mental energy. In fact, very few minds voluntarily undergo any such difficult labour; and most make their choice of some single object, and addict themselves thereto in compliance with the natural bent of the mind, or with accidental interests, and wisely turn to the best account the special gifts which nature may have conferred upon them, whether of reason, imagination, or moral sentiment. The habit of simple and single intellectual action soon fixes itself in a definite form, and men become mathematicians, logicians, experimenters, poets, artists, moralists, and thus learn to entertain every object of thought in a technical manner. Hence result those partial apprehensions of general truth which limit the advancement of each mind within narrow bounds; and hence too comes that division of labour in the world of mind, which although productive of advantage on the whole, and in relation to ordinary pursuits, and to the secular sciences, yet bars the advancement of philosophy in its wider range, and is peculiarly disadvantageous in its bearing upon the elevated themes of theology, which, because they are in the most absolute sense universal, are not to be apprehended by any single faculty of the mind, but stand in such a manner related to our entire intellectual and moral constitution, as that it is only when every faculty, in harmonious and simultaneous exercise, is actively engaged upon them, that they can be really embraced. The metaphysician, let his analysis of abstract notions be as exact as it may, still misapprehends the Divine nature, inasmuch as the analytic habit of his mind, and his peculiar mental conformation, tend to abate the moral and conceptive faculties; it is therefore only one set of relations which he discerns; and so the poet, and even the man of acute moral perception, alike misapprehend the supreme excellence. On his high and arduous ground we fail, not merely because the infinite transcends the finite, but also because, by inveterate habit, we go on to divide, and to distribute, and classify that, the very essence of which is, that it is indivisible and ONE.

But inasmuch as the human mind, even now, goes some way, when employed upon lower and more common objects, in carrying on diverse operations simultaneously, it is very credible that, in the future spiritual body, this power, depending, as it appears to do, upon the corporeal structure, should be greatly extended. And this extension may take place either merely by a higher degree of refinement in the corporeal-mental mechanism, such as should allow more activity with less effort; or else, which is the preferable supposition, that the mental process, so far as dependent upon the body, should be placed in analogy with the involuntary animal functions, and so be free to move on without expending the organic force. In either case the mind, feeling itself released from a confinement that had heretofore impeded its progress, would at once bring the complement of its faculties to bear upon whatever engaged it:—it would henceforward fill out its circle of thought and emotion, instead of passing from part to part, and of relinquishing one, while it grasps another. The mind, thus advantaged, would combine itself with every element of knowledge and feeling; and while having more to do with synthesis than with analysis (which at present, from the limitation of its faculty, it chiefly affects) it would, not the less, discern in their distinctions whatever really differs in nature. The mind thus set at large, would probably lay aside entirely its habit of attending to things by turns, or in succession, or as if it were traversing *a line*, and would, if we might use the figure, bring a broad percipient surface into contact with broad surfaces, and would act and feel at all points at once. It must be in some such manner, if ever, that the human mind will attain a comprehensive knowledge of the highest and most momentous truths:—it is thus, if at all, that it will become qualified to reason satisfactorily concerning the principles of the divine government; and thus, if ever, that, instead of building up and pulling down, with fruitless labour, its systems of theology, because something essential is always found to have been omitted, that it shall build, and bind what it builds, and so make some real progress in knowing the Infinite Perfection.

CHAPTER VII.

THE SEVENTH PROBABLE ADVANTAGE OF THE FUTURE LIFE.

THERE is yet a mental advantage, highly desirable in itself, although but moderately enjoyed at present by the human mind; and it is one which may reasonably be anticipated as likely to accrue from a more entire subserviency of the corporeal economy to the intellect. What we mean is, an intuitive perception of abstract truths, even of a complicated kind, and whether they be mathematical or metaphysical.

There is, we grant, an intense gratification, as well as a credit, resulting from the successful, though laborious prosecution of abstruse principles, through circuitous and intricate paths; and if we were to adduce, as a single example, that process of reasoning which has brought our modern astronomy to its present state, and if we think of the steady resolution, as well as grasp of mind, and the intrepidity which have been brought to bear upon the subject, a just exultation on account of the powers of the human understanding may be felt; and we might be almost ready to decline any imagined advantage, such as should supersede these arduous and ennobling labours. Nevertheless it must be confessed that, inasmuch as it is truth, and nothing else, which is the ultimate object of philosophic reasoning, and, as it is the *result* rather than the *process* for the sake of which so much labour is undergone, a direct mode of attaining any truth cannot be otherwise than preferable to a circuitous one. The illustrious men who have earned immortal fame on the fields of modern science, would unquestionably, any of them, have gladly foregone their individual reputation in exchange for a natural faculty of discerning instantaneously, the entire chain of relations, which, in fact, it cost them the labour of their lives to demonstrate. The traveller prides himself upon his achievement who, at the jeopardy of his life, and with incredible efforts, has climbed a peak of the Andes: but would not that same adventurer relinquish the credit he has so won, if, instead of it, he might take the wings of the eagle, and hover at liberty and leisure above the snowy summits?

In a mathematical or a metaphysical proposition it is affirmed, that two or more quantities, or beings, or conditions of being, though dissimilar in form, or expression, are equal, or are identical; or that they bear such and such a relation, the one to the other. The subsequent process of reasoning, which is to exhibit this affirmed equality, or this identity, consists in nothing but in tracing and naming, one by one, all those intermediate relations, each of which is so simple or obvious that it may instantly be perceived, and will certainly be assented to. But there is always room for some considerable diversity of method in presenting such demonstrations; and this diversity has respect to the acquirements, the intellectual habits, and the native powers of the minds to which they are to be addressed; for while, in dealing with one mind, it may be necessary to insist, slowly and patiently, upon every intermediate step, and to express in form the very simplest relations, with other minds any such minuteness would be both superfluous and repulsive, inasmuch as these are well able to take in at a glance a wide range of related truths, and are accustomed, with safety and assurance, to advance by great strides, where the less expert must grope their way. It actually belongs then to the human mind to discern intricate and remote relations; and yet this can be done, even by the strongest minds, only within certain limits.

There are, moreover, very many abstract relations, such that, with our present faculties, we fail to trace them at all, in a direct manner; and they become known to us only by an inference, drawn from the absurdity of admitting any contrary supposition. In fact a considerable portion of abstract science stands under this condition, and is assented to, rather because the denial of it involves some impossibility, than because the truth itself can be brought to stand out clearly in our view. The *reductio ad absurdum*, how useful soever it may be, and indeed necessary, with our present limited faculties, is a method of reasoning that would never be resorted to by minds enjoying a wider range of thought; and the use of it may be taken as a sure indication of the confinement and imperfection of our intellectual faculties.

Those who, either from an original perspicacity, or as the fruit of acquired facility, are able to grasp complicated abstract relations, may be supposed to do so by the means of an unconscious rapidity in running through all the intermediate relations; or perhaps, and this seems the more probable supposition, it is by a peculiar power of discerning, at once, what may be called the *entire nature* of the subject, with all its relations, so that the particular truth affirmed in any one proposition concerning that nature, stands out as a necessary part of the whole, or as plainly involved in some more comprehensive proposition. Now this ability, whether it consists in the power to pass in an instant along a chain of truths, or in the faculty of grasping truth in its universal and most abstract forms, does in fact belong to some human minds; and when we come to ask what it is which prevents inferior intellects from exercising this power in any sensible degree, and what it is which puts a limit to the power, even in the most highly gifted minds, we shall be led to believe that the limitation arises from the condition of the cerebral structure, or from its pathological state, and that it consists in some organic confinement, or from a sluggishness of the brain. That the cause of this difference between one mind and another is corporeal, may reasonably be inferred from the fact, that those variations of power of which every one is conscious in himself, spring from the state of the brain; as when, from circumstances unquestionably of a physical kind, such as the condition of the general health, or the state of the atmosphere, or the influence of stimulants, or the condition of the stomach, the ability to grasp abstract truths is very greatly enlarged, or is as much contracted. No one mind, it is true, can be made conscious of the individual facilities, or of the difficulties that attach to another; nevertheless each may scrutinize the variations that affect itself, and may, with some degree of distinctness, trace the operations of whatever affects the body, in depressing or elevating the intellectual vigour. Thus analyzing our personal consciousness, and taking our happiest moments as a gauge of the original power of the mind (for no man ever outstretches his actual powers) we may feel a strong persuasion that what we need, is only to be still a little more disengaged from *organic* imperfections and impediments, in order to our being able to seize, as by intuition, the most remote and intricate abstract truths. The conjecture then is hazarded, and its reasonableness is referred to those who are addicted to the pursuit of abstract science, that a corporeal-mental constitution, either more refined than the present animal organization, or entirely disengaged from the organic mechanism of vessels, circulating fluids, and secretions, would admit of the intuition of principles, which are now ascertained by laborious calculations, or by difficult and indirect processes of reasoning.

It seems safe to affirm, in relation to what may be abstractedly possible to the human mind, that, whatever it has at any time actually achieved, under favourable circumstances, or whatever effort it may, for a few moments only, have sustained, the same, to say no more, it might at all times perform, and might continue to perform, if it were but exempted from those causes of embarrassment and exhaustion which are felt to arise from the imperfections of the animal organization. If indeed we are calculating, in any instance, what it may fairly be expected that men, such as they are, will achieve, we must reckon only upon the average amount of their powers—bodily or mental. But if the question be—What might the human mind achieve, set free from the infirmities and disadvantages that attach to individuals, then it is not the actual *average* that is to be regarded; but the actual *maximum;* and the rarest and most admirable performances of a favoured few, who have far outdone their competitors, are to be assumed as the real measure of the abstract powers of the human intellect. And even this measure ought to be regarded as probably too low, inasmuch as there is reason to suppose that the most vigorous human mind still labours under some considerable disadvantages of a corporeal kind, and would be capable of far more, were it wholly exempted from all the obstructions and obscurities that attach to the animal brain. Now there are well-authenticated instances (and that of

Newton is enough for our argument) of the possession, to a great extent, of the very power we are speaking of, namely, the ability to discern, at once, and without a process of proof, the remote relations of number and figure. Something of this sort comes within the reach of most minds, addicted, by original taste, to mathematical science. Such, on frequent occasions, step on beyond the formal methods instituted to exclude any affirmation contrary to the one set forth in the theorem; and in a moment perceive that this theorem is only a special statement of some more universal truth, which truth is already intuitively known.

What then would be the consequences, and what the practical value of such an emancipation of the intellect from the trammels of calculation, and the subtilties of logic? With a view to finding a reply to this question, it must be kept in mind that the reasoning faculty is in itself nothing more than an instrument—a means to an end—a power, subordinate to higher purposes: it is for the truth's sake and nothing else, if the mind be ingenuous, that we reason or calculate. The necessity we find ourselves under, at any time, of putting this engine in operation, and of keeping it in play through the course of a long and difficult process, cannot, *in itself*, be deemed a perfection. It is indeed well that we possess such a power, and that we are able at any cost, to ascertain remote and abstruse truths; but surely, no one would refuse to accept the same results, obtained in a readier manner. We do not construct steam engines for the sake of working them, but for producing the accommodations of life; nor would a furnace be kindled were we permitted to wield the magician's wand, and could at will surround ourselves with every luxury.

As it is, we have time, in the present life, to do little more, in relation to abstract truths, than just to find them out; or at most, to apply them to some few practical purposes. But let it be assumed that, in another stage of our existence, we shall be freed from the operose methods of calculation and reasoning, and be endowed with the power of intuitively perceiving all the properties and conditions, as well of mathematical as of metaphysical entities:—the mind, not made indolent by this advantage, would start forward, as from an advanced position, and move on with rapidity toward new and higher ground. Master of all actual and possible relations, affecting space, time, matter, number, and abstract being;—relations it could not consent to leave unknown in the rear, the mind would proceed to inquire concerning the perfections of the Infinite Nature, toward which all virtuous intelligences must be tending with an irresistible impulse, when once it is directly opened to their meditations. In the present world we pursue the inferior order of abstract truths, because these comprise the only species of absolute perfection that comes within our range; but when a still higher, and a vastly more excellent species of truth—truth combining all intrinsic attractions, and all practical inferences, shall invite our inquiry, then must it take the supremacy that belongs to it; and we shall feel the advantage of being able to dismiss, as familiarly understood or discerned, all inferior principles.

CHAPTER VIII.

THE EIGHTH PREROGATIVE, ACCORDING TO OUR HYPOTHESIS, OF SPIRITUAL CORPOREITY.

A social economy, with all its happy and momentous consequences, and apart from which scarcely a half of human nature could be brought into action—a social economy demands at once a power of individual seclusion, and a faculty of communication. The corporeal lodgment of the mind, fencing it from intrusion, provides, as we have assumed, for the first of these purposes; and in doing so, that is to say, in preventing what might be called the immediate contact of minds, or their free intermixture, reduces them to the necessity (at least in the present state) of employing some system of external notices of thought; or, as they are termed, signs, whether representative and real, or arbitrary, as language.

Nor is language important to us merely in our social relations; for although it can hardly be supposed that a mind absolutely insulated would, in its solitude, have originated language, or could have felt the want of a means of expression, nevertheless, as language has actually become a part of our intellectual constitution, the employment of it exerts an influence over the whole of our mental operations; and while it facilitates them, in one sense, does also, in another, impede and limit the play of our faculties; and especially of the highest of those faculties. The constant presence of words in the mind slackens its curiosity, by leading it to believe that it knows what in fact it does not know; and it renders also its perception of all abstract truths obtuse and confused, in so far as the rude symbol of each idea is taken in the stead of the idea itself, and carries with it its concretions—its excess, and its defect, and its accidental associations. The substitution therefore of some new and more direct, or *real* means of communication between mind and mind, would not merely place the social economy on a more sure, elevated, and happy ground; but would, by its indirect consequences, involve very important advantages to the mind in its own operations. Every thing would come before us as fresh, and real, and substantial, if our imperfect and artificial symbols were displaced by a means of expression essentially true and perfect.

Language belongs, in the first instance, to the ear, and is afterwards, by a transfer of associations, conveyed to the eye. Nevertheless, when once the written and visible system of symbols has become as familiar to the mind as the audible symbols are, the one connects itself with its associated ideas quite as rapidly as do the others; nor do we, in reading, attain the meaning of the words circuitously, by first thinking of the sound for which they stand, and then of the meaning of that sound. The two species of symbols, therefore, the visible and the audible, are to be regarded as on a level when presented to the mind, though not entirely so when language is mentally employed, as a vehicle or medium of cogitation, for when so used, it is the sound, rather than the written sign, that is thought of. On account of this difference we must at present be understood to speak of language oral and audible.

Language, consisting as it does of arbitrary signs, is manifestly a rudiment of the material system; it is a fruit and consequence of our corporeity, and might, with some propriety, be designated as the point of contact, where mind and matter artificially, yet most intimately blend, and reciprocate their respective properties; the first—namely, mind, imparting to the modulations of sound several hundred thousand distinctions, which nothing less than the boundless refinements of its own conceptions could, to such an extent, multiply and fix: while, on the other hand, the second, namely matter, imposes upon the first its own limitations, and generates innumerable errors, consequent upon its essential rudeness, and its inferiority, or imparity, as related to the mind.

Every machine and instrument is an adaptation of some existing power, or principle, conferring upon the intelligence that has devised, and that employs it, a special advantage, in carrying on some operation which otherwise would be barely practicable, or not at all so. But whether or not the particular work so performed could be achieved without the instrument, still the mind which invents and employs it, is always immeasurably superior to its own instrument; and whatever refinement of workmanship, or intricacy of construction may belong to the latter, both are less than the skill and intelligence whence they proceed, and less too than the bodily powers to which they render aid. What is the staff or the hammer to the hand and arm that wield them? what the lens or telescope to the eye?—or again, to the mind that reasons on the facts they disclose; or what the sculptor's chisel to the taste and skill that direct it?—or what the lyre and its chords to the soul of melody that trembles on the fingers of the performer? Now of all the instruments or artificial combinations which man employs, there is not one at all to be compared with language;—there is not one nearly so elaborate in its construction, or so copious in its materials, or so nice and appliant in its evolutions.

The vocabulary of a highly civilized people, as that of the Greeks, Romans, Italians, Germans, English, including the inflections employed in its combinations, and including also technical terms, and proper names, must, at an average, be estimated as comprising two hundred thousand distinguishable arbitrary signs; and a large proportion of these are susceptible, in construction, of very many variations of meaning, so as in fact nearly to double the number of sounds to which distinct ideas are attached. And yet this vast apparatus, taken in its most refined form, is found, in relation to the occasions of the mind, to be scanty, inexact, and poor!—it is nothing better than a material machinery; and matter must fall vastly short of being commensurable with mind. Whether regarded as the instrument of silent thought, or as the medium of communication between mind and mind, language proves itself so inadequate to some of the purposes to which it is applied, as to forbid the hope that those sciences will ever reach a permanent and indisputable state, which depends upon it as their only means of expression. Mathematical truth, happily, has formed for itself a language adequate to its purposes; a language real, and which is liable to no ambiguity or variation; but then this is because mathematical science is conversant with the properties of matter and its relations; and therefore the instrument of its conveyance, being homogeneous, is sufficient. But how far otherwise is it when we have to do, either with metaphysical abstractions, or with the heights, and depths, and refinements, of the human passions and affections! On this ground how does it want compass, nicety, power! Language well and truly conveys all those notions that are its own creatures, or that are more modified by it, than they modify the medium of their expression. After having vulgarized and enfeebled our conceptions and our sentiments, language then sufficiently represents and recombines what it has first reduced to its own level. Meanwhile every profoundly impassioned and sensitive mind, and every mind accustomed to hold language in abeyance, during its processes of analysis and abstraction, is painfully conscious of the inferiority of any actual medium of expression that is at its command. In the recesses of the human soul there is a world of thought which, for the want of determinate and fit symbols, never assumes any fixed form, such as might beneficially constitute a part of the intellectual and moral wealth of the species, or even much augment the wisdom and virtue of the man.

Or, if we needed another sort of illustration of the vast superiority of the mind, as measured against its instruments of expression, we might refer to the facility with which three, five, or even ten or twelve different sets of symbols are held in readiness, and used, almost indifferently, for the conveyance of thought. What a proof is this of the grasp, and of the elasticity of mind, that it can, with a sovereign ease, and just as a man lays down one tool, and takes up another, so lay down and take up at pleasure this or that voluminous machinery of signs! Let it be supposed that each language of five familiarly commanded by any one, comprises not more than twenty-five thousand words; then does the mind hold each of these sets of signs, with all the special rules that affect the construction of each, unconfounded and distinct, so as in a moment to be able to detach its passing train of ideas from one of these systems of signs, and to affix it to another! Now this wonderful facility in so playing with these operose and cumbrous engines, and in so shifting instantaneously the entire system of intimate mental associations, is by no means to be considered barely as a proof of great ability in the individual, or of the reach of the memory; but rather as a tacit, yet sure indication of the immeasurable, not indeed infinite, inherent power of the human mind, to which such operations may become so familiar as to be performed almost without any consciousness of effort. Of what then might this same mind be capable, if it were furnished with an engine of expression homogeneous with itself, plastic in quality, and commensurate with its faculties!

Now there are two suppositions, either of which may, with some reason, be entertained relative to the means of communication in a higher economy; the first of which is, that, in the stead of a system of signs adapted, as all our signs are primarily, to sensible objects, and derived from the material world, and transferred by figure to things abstract and intellectual, there should be constructed a system primarily adapted to things abstract and intellectual, and drawn from the world of mind, and therefore strictly proper to notions of this class, and neither more, nor fewer, nor other, than those notions are; nor in any such way convertible as to give rise to ambiguities of expression, and confusions of thought. Such a medium of communion, it is manifest, being the mind's own creature, and its commensurate power, would, in all its applications, both as an engine of cogitation and as a means of communication, transcend the most perfect of our mundane languages, as far as any one of our languages transcends the mute signs and awkward grimaces resorted to by men not understanding each other's tongue. With a real language of this kind at command, and which would be a true reflection of itself

—a just and clear image of thought and emotion—the mind would feel as if the broad light of day pervaded its inmost recesses, or as if its very self were repeated in every expression; the likeness of the mind and soul would be such as is returned of the person by the most highly polished mirror; or to adduce the most complete illustration of the advantages of an intellectual language, such as we have imagined, we must again refer to the instance of the language of mathematical science, which, because homogeneous with the truths it conveys, is faultless, infallible, and liable to no loss or change in the lapse of ages: it is exempt from the caprices of fashion, and superior to the individual errors and infirmities of those through whose hands it is transmitted. Now a language formed by the mind for itself, and after it has become fully furnished with abstract ideas, and after the purely intellectual part of its circle of notions has gained a due prevalence over sensible images, such a language, consisting of symbols of abstractions, not of the symbols of the symbols of those abstractions, would be to the mind, and to its operations, what the language of geometry and algebra, and of the modern calculus, is to the truths thereby conveyed; and the consequence of employing this homogeneous and perfect medium would be the superseding of all fluctuating systems of metaphysics, and theology, and morals, and the exclusion of endless and fruitless altercations on such subjects, and the gradual accumulation and consolidation of an ABSOLUTE PHILOSOPHY.

Our modern philosophy, in all its branches, has now been about twenty-five centuries in growing; and during the last five of these centuries, a solid and permanent advancement has been made in all those sciences which command a medium of expression adapted to their nature, and exempt from ambiguities and fluctuations. Meanwhile abstract intellectual philosophy (putting out of the question the general rectification of sentiments and notions accruing from the influence of Christianity) remains what and where it was, in the bright times of Grecian intelligence. The preliminary work of fixing the sense of terms, and of advancing axioms, has still to be done anew by every professor of these studies; and his labour is scarcely completed before it is broken up and cast aside by his successors. This incertitude appears to admit of no remedy.

The second supposition that offers itself in relation to the future communion of minds, is this, namely, that the method of expression by arbitrary signs should be altogether superseded, and that, in the place of it, the mind should be endowed with a power of communication, by a direct conveyance of its own state, at any moment, to other minds; as if the veil of personal consciousness might, at pleasure, be drawn aside, and the entire intellectual being could spread itself out to view. "If there are tongues," says the apostle, "they shall fail;" and it may be intended, not that the various languages of earth shall be exchanged for the one language of heaven, but rather that language itself, or the use of arbitrary symbols, shall give place to the conveyance of thought, in its native state, from mind to mind. The conveyance of emotions, by the varying expression of the countenance, and which is understood as if instinctively by infants and by animals, gives us a faint indication at least of a mode of communication much more intuitive and immediate, than that of language: nor is it very difficult, by the aid of this instance, to carry forward our conceptions so far as to grasp what we are now supposing, namely, an instantaneous and real unfolding of the thought and feeling of one mind, by an act of its own, to other minds. We say by an act of its own, for the purposes of a moral economy, and the preservation of individuality of character, seem necessarily to demand the seclusion of each mind, except so far as it may choose to discover itself. This seclusion and individuality appear also to be involved, as we have already remarked, in corporeity.

Of the same kind with the expression of feeling by the countenance, is the conveyance of the fine distinctions of thought and emotion by the means of the modulations of the voice, which in fact amount to a *second power*, superadded to the conventional value of language. What is conveyed by emphasis, and still more by tones, often far surpasses what is contained, or could be contained, in the words as written. This language of tones is a *real* language, suffused, if we may so speak, over the mass of arbitrary signs, and serving to give them a double force; it is a vital energy, informing an inert body. Those who have had much to do with children, must have observed that they slowly acquire their knowledge of arbitrary terms, and especially of abstract phrases, in a great degree, by the aid of their *instinctive* apprehension of the meaning of tones, and of the expressions of the countenance. It seems as if this real language were implanted in all minds, and being understood without teaching and without induction, is made the means of acquiring that which can be known only by instruction and habit. In this fact have we not an indication of a future means of communion, more real and immediate than that of arbitrary symbols? The intellectual power of music furnishes another, and an analogous instance of the conveyance of emotions, with distinctness and force, by means more natural than that of conventional signs. Melody and harmony have a fixed affinity with the several emotions of our moral constitution; and they awaken, with unvarying certainty and precision, this or that sentiment or passion. In this instance we have an example of the corporeal conveyance of the states of one mind to other minds, founded upon the original conformation of mind, as combined with matter. And this mode of communion may easily be conceived of as much extended and improved.

Whether we prefer the first or the second of the above-named suppositions, the consequences must be nearly the same; for an arbitrary language, if absolutely perfect, and framed from intellectual, not from material types, would perhaps fall very little short, in accuracy or power, of an immediate revelation of the inmost mind, as a mode of intercourse; and in either case, the interchange of knowledge and feeling would be incalculably promoted, and at the same time the mind, in its solitary operations, would be freed from the thousand illusions that take their rise from the ambiguous and impliable languages of the present state.

There is, however, a point of difference between the two suppositions which deserves to be noticed, and it is this; that whereas the use of language let it be as perfect, as it may, makes it necessary for the mind to tread always upon a single line of thought, at a time, and to divert from that line as often as it would give utterance to feelings or ideas of another class—on the contrary, if the mind were able to unveil itself independently of any medium of expression, and if, as we have before supposed, a more refined corporeal structure should enable it to pursue, simultaneously, several distinct trains of ideas, then would the intercourse of minds fill a vastly wider circle than otherwise it could; and in fact those complex truths, and those mixed impressions, might be conveyed which, on the very account of their complexity, are not at all to be communicated in their real nature or their full force, so long as it is necessary to sunder them, and to dole them out piecemeal. It is easy to understand how happily this advantage must bear upon the advancement of the junior members of a vast social economy, in their intercourse with those who have long ago scaled the heights of divine philosophy; for although the infant capacity of the learners, as well as other reasons, might put limits to the communication of knowledge, yet whatever it was judged expedient to convey, might be conveyed in its genuine form; it would be truth entire, although truth in part; whereas, at present, we learn little, if any thing, and especially in relation to things spiritual, that is not so conveyed as to give birth to many errors of apprehension, and so as to confirm such errors, by intermixture with unquestioned truths. Language, or the symbolic conveyance of thought, is but a melody, sweet yet simple; but a full utterance of the soul, such as we have here imagined, would, in comparison, be a swelling harmony, as of many voices and instruments.

CHAPTER IX.

THE NINTH POINT OF ADVANTAGE BELONGING TO THE CONTRAST BETWEEN ANIMAL ORGANIZATION AND SPIRITUAL LIFE.

THE present animal body, although justly considered as the auxiliary of the mind, is very far from being merely such; for, on the contrary, it has its proper interests, and its peculiar impulses and instincts; and these are of so peremptory a sort as often to prevail entirely over those of the mind. But now we assume it as probable that the future corporeal structure, whether it be ethereal or palpable, shall be the INSTRUMENT OF THE MIND, and nothing else, and that it shall have no purely organic welfare to provide for; and in a word, that it shall, in the strictest sense, be the servant of the intellectual and moral nature; just as the hand, the foot, or the eye, is the servant of the body.

The serious, and too often fatal disadvantage, which we undergo in commencing life as animals merely, and in having the interests of the animal nature secured by habits, and by powerful impulses, before the higher welfare of the soul, or of the intellect, comes to be thought of, is a trite subject of fruitless complaint, and one not necessary here to be insisted upon. This order of things is no doubt unavoidable, and properly belongs to the initial stage of our existence; but it is easy to conceive of a very different economy, and one that, while it should afford all the benefits derivable from a corporeal union of mind and matter, would be exempt from the dangers and degradation thence accruing in the present state.

The animal body is not only mechanically divisible, and destructible, and easily injured; but it is also incessantly preying upon itself; and it speedily dissolves, unless sustained by assimilative materials. This liability to dissolution, and to external violence, necessarily involves keen sensibilities and powerful appetites; and it also demands an instinctive dread of death. Now these various pleasurable sensations and desires, and these sensibilities to pain, and these instinctive fears, are generally paramount, and unremitted, and therefore take the lead of every other impulse, and give law to, or virtually overrule, the course of life, and to a great extent countervail what, abstractedly, we should say, was the intention of nature, rendering the rational faculties, and the emotions, subordinate to the preservation and pleasures of the body. The rational faculty has indeed its tastes, and the moral faculty has its impulses; but these principles are neither incessant, nor of absolute and imperative necessity: they therefore learn to give way to that which will not give way. To a great extent it must be granted that the body serves the soul, only in order that the soul may the more effectively serve the body; as if a brute held a man in bondage, whom it compelled to lend it his superior intelligence, and whom, for its own purposes, it would cheerfully carry and help at bidding.

Instead of all this, let us imagine a corporeal frame, indestructible and indivisible; vital without waste, and therefore needing no pabulum, or none but such as might be supplied in a manner analogous to that in which the animal body derives support from the atmosphere, and from light and heat. Such a body would need no dread of dissolution;

nor would it have its cravings, its appetites, or its sensual propensity; or to say all in a word, it would have no welfare of its own to care for, or to assert. Instead of an importunate controversy, never well adjusted, and never brought to a conclusion, between body and spirit, there would be, on the one side, the sheer passivity of a tool, or engine; and on the other side, the unchecked supremacy of a superior nature. There would be one class of interests only to be thought of, and only one class of occupations to be followed. The body, with its complement of powers, applicable to its congenial element—matter, would be to the spirit, precisely what now the senses and the muscular system are, while in a healthy condition, to the animal will. Not only do not the eye, and the ear, and the hand, ever repugnate, or plead for their particular interests; but they are almost, or entirely, forgotten, while the animal will is eagerly employing them to effect its purposes. And thus, as we may imagine, the spiritual body shall be so purely the instrument of the master power, that it will barely, if at all, enter into the consciousness, as a separate existence. Perhaps beings who have never been subjected to the conditions of animal life may, although actually corporeal, need to be informed of their corporeity; or they may know it, rather by reflection and inference, than by immediate consciousness; and we may conceive of an insulated race of spiritually embodied beings who, although really conversant with an external and material world, would have recourse to circuitous deductions, when required to show that any thing except mind existed.

This sort of absolute subordination, or sheer instrumentality of the body, is, we say, readily conceived of; and it is clearly a condition of being which is abstractedly possible, and such as may in fact be now the prerogative of the most exalted natures. There are, however, reasons for doubting whether, in the full sense, as above stated, it is intended for man, or at least in the *next* stage of his existence; and it is separable from those other advantages which, in the preceding chapters, we have ventured to assign to the future spiritual body. This body may indeed be immortal, indivisible, and exempt from the necessities of aliment and clothing; but in so far as it is still assimilated with the material world, percipient of the properties of matter, and therefore so far passive, the mind, by this alliance, may yet be susceptible of pleasures, not proper to pure spirit, and such as may give occasion to the continued exercise of self-command; and it may still be bound to use abstinence, and to cherish nobler counteractive tastes. Then again, as is quite obvious, whoever, by alliance with matter, is open to sensitive pleasures, is likely to be liable, nay, we should say, is necessarily liable, to the suffering of pain, from exposure to other properties of matter, as, for example, to the intensity of fire. This point well deserves attention; nor is the chain of inferences on which our reasoning depends circuitous. Corporeity is, by its definition, an amalgamation of mind and matter, in consequence of which the former exerts certain powers over the latter, and in turn becomes passively conscious of its properties. Of these properties it is conscious, first, in the way of mere distinction; and secondly, in the way of gratification and of suffering—of pleasure and pain. Now it is hardly to be admitted as possible, that a corporeal structure—the vehicle of mind, should be open to the one class of sensations and not to the other: in fact, the one is often nothing more than an excess of the other; and it is as easy to think of the mind being conscious of light and colours, but unconscious of their absence and their opposites, darkness and blackness, as of its percipience of sensitive pleasure, while incapable of sensitive pain. It is true that the mind may be removed from the actual occasions of pain; or it may be shielded from it; but yet it must, as we suppose, be essentially liable thereto, if it be at all passive in relation to the properties of matter.

Moreover, as there appears to be a *physical* connection, or necessary correspondence, between the one class of sensations and the other, so likewise are we compelled to suppose that there is a *moral* relation between the two; or a necessary connection, arising from the constitution of free and accountable agents. For all the analogies at present within our reach, tend to confirm the opinion that those higher and purer motives in which virtue essentially consists, demand, as their support, the concurrent influence of certain lower and more cogent motives;—those, namely, which spring from an abstract liability to corporeal misery. And if the mind is to hold converse with matter pleasurably, this accession of the means of enjoyment is probably to be balanced by such a liability to pain as may effectively check the too eager pursuit of a lower and dangerous species of felicity. Is there not reason in the supposition that the two kinds of passivity are necessary as antitheses, the one of the other, as well in a moral as in a physical sense? If man, in a future and higher stage of his existence, is to exult in the brightness and beauty of a fair and new creation, and is to delight himself in contrasts and agreements of colour, glowing amid a universal effulgence; if he is to perceive all sweets and perfumes, and to be ravished with forms, melo dies, and harmonies, can this corporeal bliss be tasted on any other condition than that of its being *possible* for him to endure the anguish of fire, the vehemence of frost, the distraction of discord, the horror of deformity, and the pungent corrosion of acrid poisons? And again, if the most elevated and the purest sort of happiness—that most proper to the spirit, is to be softened down, attenuated, blended, by taking its turn with pleasures of an inferior kind, and if in this manner complex sentiments are to be generated, (which in fact appear necessary to the harmony of the intellectual life,) if this is to take place, then must not those who are thus open to what we must call the seductions of corporeal enjoyment—must they not have in recollection, as a silent dread, the abstract possibility, at least, not merely of moral and intellectual degradation, and a loss of the noblest tastes, but of exposure to the terrible wretchedness of continued corporeal pain?

As a leading hint for meditations of this sort, let it be remembered that no expectations we are able to form, on the ground of physical analogies, such, for example, as those that have occupied the preceding pages, or any others which to the reader may seem more probable, throw any light upon the momentous question, whether, in the next stage of our existence, we shall find ourselves MORE HAPPY, or less so, than we are at present. There are, indeed, the strongest reasons for supposing, revelation apart, that human nature is destined to expand its actual powers, and to occupy a wider sphere of action and of knowledge, than it does in the present state; but then this future advancement, like some advancements of the present life, may rather expose us to heavier cares and pains, than augment our enjoyment, or secure our peace. The actual condition of mankind, taken at large, will by no means warrant our confidently assuming that a physical and intellectual progression must imply an increase of happiness and virtue; nor, when the moral state of a large proportion, or of the mass of mankind is duly considered, can we, on the strength of abstract arguments, drawn from the divine attributes of benevolence and wisdom, deduce with safety the inference that the millions of our fellow-men are moving forward on the road to goodness and felicity. On the contrary, appalling facts that force themselves on our reluctant notice, in relation to the habits, usages, and propensities of several races of the human family, wear the most grim and gloomy aspect, and are such as to suggest forebodings as painful as any the mind can admit. Individually, indeed, we may entertain a cheerful and rational hope concerning the future life; but then the grounds of it must be drawn altogether from another quarter—namely, from the specific inferences of our belief as Christians. But to this subject a little more attention is due, before we advance to the second portion of our theory of another life.

CHAPTER X.

THE BALANCED PROBABILITY OF HAPPINESS OR MISERY INVOLVED IN THE PHYSICAL THEORY OF ANOTHER LIFE.

In reviewing the several particulars of this first portion of our physical theory of another life, it may be well to advert, for a moment, to each singly, with a view of showing more in detail, that each of these points of supposed advantage—each conjectural prerogative of the spiritual body, stands evenly balanced between happiness and suffering, as a means of augmenting, indifferently, the one or the other, as thus:—

By the senses of sight and hearing, by the excursive power of the imagination, and by the far-stretching deductions of science, we now take mental possession of a vast extent of the visible world; and the power of actually traversing the fields of the material universe, we may, with some show of reason, anticipate, as intended for a being to whom already so much has been granted. Does it not seem that, at present, while some of the faculties, corporeal and mental, greatly exceed others in the range or sphere that is allowed them, there is an incompleteness, or a want of balance, in our constitution? We are tenants of a spacious house; but although we have the run of certain apartments, we are only permitted to look into the halls and the saloons. But shall not these restrictions be at length removed, and man find all doors of the palace thrown open to him? Man, who now possesses the faculty to comprehend, and the taste to admire, the divine works, shall at length, as we may infer, enjoy the liberty of following the Creator, wherever order and beauty are displayed. The mind shall find itself competent, corporeally, to every labour, and to every adventure which its high rational desires may impel it to attempt; nor, in the mere destitution of the mechanical means, shall it be left to sigh, and to confess that its noblest ambition is frustrate; and that, although endowed with a seraph's intelligence, and excited by an insatiate thirst of knowledge and desire of action, it is gifted only with a locomotive power fit for the brute that grazes in a meadow! The complement of the human faculties shall, may we not confidently say it? be at length filled up, and the body be put in symmetry with the range of the mind.

But then every faculty has its impulse, which when repressed, becomes a wrestling uneasiness; and this species of agony bears proportion to the inherent energy of that faculty. And if now, when the locomotive power has but a very narrow range, and when the exercise of it, although pleasurable at first, very soon produces fatigue and pain—if now, we say, corporeal restraint and imprisonment be one of the most intolerable of bodily ills, what shall imprisonment be when the locomotive energy is a thousand times more vehement than at present, and when the exercise of it is attended with no conscious effort, and is followed by no lassitude, and when the widest and the fairest fields shall lie in prospect before it? The chain of the captive is galling, in proportion, or nearly so, to the captive's animal vigour and elastic spirit. Let it then be imagined that the future man, new born to his inheritance of absolute mechanical force—the inherent force of mind, and finding himself able at will to traverse all spaces, should, in the very hour wherein he has made proof of his recent faculty, be stopped, either by malignant superior powers, or by the dread ministers of justice, and on account of forgotten misdeeds, be seized, enchained, incarcerated! Might we not, with a rational consistency, and in conformity with some of the actual procedures of the present social system, imagine, for example, the merciless tyrant who in cold revenge has held the innocent in his dungeon through long years, or the ruffian slave-dealer, just bursting from the thralls of mortality, and proudly careering through mid-heaven, but only to encounter there some stronger than himself, and more fierce, who, with mockery showing their warrant, shall grapple with his young vigour, hale him to the abyss, find there a chain strong enough to bind him, and rivet him to the rock, where he is to chafe, and taste the retributive miseries of captivity, and the fruitless strivings and writhings of a power sufficient, if it were not bound, to bear him from star to star! All this is so credible abstractedly, and may be so readily conceived of, on the ground of common facts, that one can hardly think of it otherwise than as actually true.

Many similar conceptions, which often break upon the mind uncalled, and which, even when strictly examined, refuse to be dismissed as mere dreams—many such conceptions which, whether or not they have their archetypes in any region of the universe, are at least reasonable enough to answer the purpose of convincing us that those enhancements of our powers which are to be expected in a future life, may be either the means of enjoyment, or the means of misery, according as our moral condition, and the great rules of the divine government shall determine.

Or let us take up another sort of alternative; and in order to conceive the more distinctly of the happy part of it, imagine the instance of a spirit, which, in the initial period of its existence, has been secluded from the material universe, and acquainted only with intellectual abstractions, and with pure moral emotions: such a spirit, already capable of reflecting upon, and of comprehending the change it is passing through, we suppose gradually to awake to a consciousness of the properties of matter, one by one: hitherto totally destitute of ideas and sensations, it is now slowly born into corporeal existence; it is becoming conscious of solidity, and it gropes its way along extended surfaces, and in learning the power of resistance in these surfaces, it learns its own new power of originating motion, and of traversing space. It begins then to grasp the external world, and seems to itself to have taken possession of a foreign nature, and by the aid of the contrast, thence arising, it comes to think, for the first time, of its own spiritual nature, as a distinct being; by the knowledge of *another species*, it comprehends and reflects upon its *own species*, which we may suppose to have been abstractedly impossible so long as one kind of being only was known. Thus the spirit's birth into the world of matter, is almost equivalent, perhaps quite so, to a new birth into the world of mind.

But other sensations follow in their turn. This solid extension, with which it has just become conversant, is perceived to be not of uniform quality; for besides its mechanical properties, its hardness, softness, roughness, and weight, it affects the sensitive faculty by its chemical properties, in all their variety:—its pungencies, its flavours, its perfumes; and each new property, as it comes to be perceived, enlarges, so far, the mind's circle of conscious existence. Then next the vibrations of sound call it to enter a new world; and melody and harmony, breaking suddenly upon the soul, cause it to feel as if another spirit had been added to itself; or as if another being, happy, impassioned, and ecstatic, had come to be blended with it, and to double its power of enjoyment. Recollecting its primitive state of mere intellectuality, it now feels itself to be three or five times more than it then was. But the range of perception still goes on enlarging, and this mind, in the course of its gradual birth into the material world, becomes alive to warmth—genial and pleasurable sense, and yet an ominous sense also. Has it not now reached the boundary of sensitive existence? no, for in the next instant light breaks in upon it with a sudden amazement, and the universe, with all its beauties and glories, and its immensity, stands revealed! We said, that the first perception of sound and harmony was as if another spirit, rich in sensations, had been added to the individual consciousness; but this new perception of light is nothing less than the having the individual consciousness, heretofore gathered about a centre, expanded without a bound, and made capable of a sort of ubiquity. To see, and in seeing, to converse with all forms of grace and grandeur, is to have the life multiplied a million times; and it is to stretch existence and enjoyment to the height and width of the universe. Thus far we have followed the new-born mind to the limit of those sensations that are actually enjoyed by ourselves; but there yet remains all that further consciousness of the properties, and of the internal constitution of the material world, which lies beyond the reach of human organs of sensation;—all that which is too subtile, or too intense, or too remote, to be admitted or sustained by the animal brain and nerves; and this yet unknown portion of the properties of matter, not improbably, vastly exceeds the portion which our animal life allows of our perceiving: and we are free to suppose that, when a more refined and an imperishable corporeity shall be inherited by man, the means of knowledge, and the faculties of sensitive enjoyment shall be augmented tenfold; so that its future new birth into the material universe shall quicken and amaze the human spirit, as much as we have imagined the pure spirit to be awakened and delighted, in passing from mere abstract intellectual life, to sensitive life, such as we now actually possess it.

Yet all this, manifestly, is only the favourable side of an alternative; for our daily experience teaches us, that sensations which are pleasurable within a certain limit, become first uneasy, and then painful, beyond it; so that agreeable sensation may be called the delicious *initial* stage of a process, the *last* stage of which, if it comes on, is an intolerable anguish. Every species of sensitive enjoyment needs a stay; and it is *enjoyment* so long only as it is moderated: in other words, the mind, in becoming conscious of the properties of matter, is laid open to the extremes of pleasure and pain; and it may endure the one as soon as enjoy the other: the most thrilling delights are but the a, b, c, of insupportable torments. What, for example, is an extreme case of neuralgia, but a point at the lower limit of the very scale upon which are marked the nice degrees of animal felicity? Only let the inherent sensitive faculty of the mind be entirely excoriated, if we might so speak, and itself be turned out upon the material world, to feel and to taste, without abatement, the whole stress of all its properties, and it must suffer anguish in a thousand modes. In the present animal body the mind's sensitiveness to light, for instance, is sheathed and restricted; how small is the optic expansion, and how is this small surface curtained and provided with triple means of seclusion! The mind converses with light in a very jealous way, and much as the besieged hold a parley with the besiegers, when the latter are ten thousand to one of the former; that is to say, a few of the enemy only are admitted within the gates at a time. Fully exposed to the vibrations of light, the mind, even at the dimmest twilight, would suffer an agony of excitement; and under the beams of noon must be maddened with torment. Need we go on to speak of heat, of which the feeblest degrees only are pleasurable, while a slight augmentation of its intensity totally vanquishes the fortitude of ordinary minds; and none perhaps could retain self-command longer than a few minutes if left to feel its extremity. And let it be remembered that, although the animal texture, the muscular fibre, the nerve, and the vessels, are presently dissolved, or consumed, by the action of fire, and so the animal anguish quickly reaches its end, yet that we assume far too much if we conclude that the sensitive faculty of the mind is itself liable to any such dissolution. Fire reduces to vapour or to ashes that which, by its nature, may exist indifferently in a solid and organized, or in a gaseous, or a pulverized form. But is the mind susceptible of vaporization, or can it be reduced to powder? We suppose not, and therefore believe it might sustain, undestroyed and undamaged, the utmost intensity of heat: nor is it certain that every species of corporeity must give way, and be dissipated by this element.

There is room for the same statement in relation to every property of matter, which we find intensely to affect the sensitive principle; such as the corrosive poisons; and perhaps we owe it, at present, to the insensibility of our animal organization, or to its neutralizing inertness, that the material world does not, in a thousand modes, affect us as do arsenic and oxalic acid when taken into the stomach. Enough we know to be sure, that, apart from considerations of a religious kind, the probabilities of enhanced pleasure or pain, in coming more fully into contact with matter and its properties, are evenly balanced.

Again:—a discernment or intuitive knowledge of the interior constitution, and of the occult forms of the material system, we have named as likely to be enjoyed when the mind enters upon its state of spiritual corporeity, and we have conjectured that this immediate perception of the mechanism of nature, besides the pleasure it may directly afford, will involve a higher advantage, inasmuch as, by disengaging the attention from those physical truths, which now principally excite curiosity, and employ the reasoning faculty, it shall send the mind forward, with its insatiable thirst of knowledge, toward the more excellent and sublime mysteries of the spiritual economy, and of the divine nature. But then this advantage demands certain moral conditions in the mind itself, or it must become the occasion of an enhanced misery; and that in two ways; as thus:—

The pleasures, organic and mental, arising from objects of sense, are, to a great extent, as we well know, dependent upon our being able to keep entire many illusions, and certain natural exaggerations, which at once conceal what might awaken disgust, and impart to these enjoyments a fictitious importance. All gratifications of the senses, and all the pleasures of taste, and all the excitements of worldly pleasure—all the pride, and all the pomp of life, demand largely the aid of artificial lights and glare, or, in plain words, of *deception*, to eke out their essential poverty, and to render them what the mind can, and will, care for. Every day we stoop to be cheated and delighted with what we should scorn or loathe, if it were offered to us in its naked value. But, by the law of habit, a long course of exclusive regard to factitious gratifications of this sort, brings the mind into a state in which, at length, it ceases to recollect that an illusion is an illusion—ceases to reclaim its native superiority, and becomes the passive victim of the sleights and tricks of worldly pleasure. The soul is at last smothered in the trumpery of its vulgar and sensual delights. Now to a mind thus wedded, by inveterate habit, to all that is false and unreal, the new faculty of seeing through forms and semblances, and of keenly and clearly discerning the unadorned mechanism of things material, must at once strip it of its all, and reduce it to a pitiable destitution. The gold will no longer shine, the diamond no longer sparkle; the plumed pomp of rank will be a nothing—set about with quills; and this plump world, sleek with delicacies, is at once shrivelled to an atrophy; and the material universe, lately so gay and blooming to the idolatrous eye of its devotee, starts to view, as a gaunt skeleton, barely knit together with its sear sinews.

Or we may look at the natural consequence of this supposed intuition of the occult construction of the material system on another side. If the entire nature of things material were once seen, and seen without a shadow of uncertainty, and all were known at a glance which it is the glory of our physical sciences to discover; then the mind, by the necessity of its constitution, would be thrown forward toward higher objects, and its inherent curiosity would be fixed upon the next range of unknown principles. But what must these principles relate to? Unquestionably they must involve, if they do not exclusively embrace, the awful verities of the Divine Nature. It is these truths that must stand forward *next*, after the material system has been understood. And yet, while this physical necessity of moving forwards impels the mind irresistibly to approach the Ineffable Perfection, perhaps its own moral condition, and its confirmed impure tastes, are of a kind that would lead it to escape, and to hide itself from the brightness of eternal truth. We may imagine an insufferable conflict, rending the soul perpetually, and urging it at once vehemently to penetrate a mystery, and to learn that which, when actually known, must inflict upon it the tortures of self-contempt, remorse, and despair.

Or again:—A very obvious train of thought, and one by which we need not be here detained, will lead us to admit that the boon of a plenary memory, or a perpetual and perfect consciousness of all that has, in any period, belonged to our corporeal and mental existence, could prove a blessing only to those whose whole constitution, moral and intellectual, were in harmony; but a curse to any within whose bosoms vehement and malign passions were at variance, and all at war with the unalterable principles of virtue. Memory, what is it but the fuel of remorse to the guilty? and how intensely must that fire burn which shall be supplied with its material in a hundred-fold proportion to what it is in the present life! But on this topic the reader's meditations can need no prompting.

Then a similar train of inferences may be pursued in relation to the supposed substitution of a real and rational association of ideas, in the place of an accidental and organic succession of thoughts and feelings. The bliss of folly, and the laughing infatuation of vice, are sustained, in great measure, by the aid of that whimsical and irrational series of images which ordinarily diverts the mind from the consideration of its real condition and its welfare. And these fantastic images become continually more and more blended with the actual moral tastes, and therefore more and more enchain the attention, and exclude truth and reason. The dissipation of these dreams would be, to a mind enthralled by them, a sad and terrible awakening. On the contrary, if the mind has really set forward on the road of virtue and wisdom, and intently desires truth—the highest truth, and nothing else, then nothing so propitious, or so happily exciting, could happen to it, as to be exempted, and for ever, from the tyranny of merely organic suggestions, and from the brute despotism of fortuity, within the sacred precincts of its meditations and emotions.

The very same alternative presents itself, if we think of the probable consequences, either of an enlarged power of attending simultaneously to various objects, and of carrying on various operations, or to the faculty of perceiving abstract relations at a glance. For each of these advancements, whilst it liberates the wise and sincere from mental embarrassments, and frees them from occasions of error, will strip the unwise and the false-hearted of those means of illusion which, with a half-conscious perversity, they have been wont to employ for the purpose of maintaining their self-esteem. To rational natures, illusions must be temporary; but it is not certain that a cordial and happy admission of truth, and a submission to its practical consequences, will immediately, and in all cases, follow the dissipation of error; for between the mere intellectual perception of any principle, and a yielding to the inference thence resulting, there intervene, not only contrary desires and inveterate habits, but the sheer stubbornness of the will; or that energy of pride which is seen to be the firmest element of human nature, and the one which, least of all, and last of all, is open to the influence of considerations of personal welfare; nor are instances rare, wherein, with a clear and distinct choice, personal welfare—self-interest entire, has been held in contempt, and has been for ever thrown away, for the saving of pride, and for the preservation of a stubborn purpose. Now that which happens (we may say ordinarily, or often) in the present state, may be reckoned upon as likely to happen also in a future state; and it may then be seen that intelligent beings, under the full glare of the eternal principles of truth and virtue, will nevertheless spurn to confess the application of these truths to their own individual case, and will choose rather to endure the worst consequences of persisting in a false position. There are few, perhaps, who, if they would look closely into their hearts, might not find the indications, at least, of feelings which, under certain circumstances, would impel them to act in the obdurate manner we have here supposed.

There is, however, this difference to be noticed, namely, that, in the present state, let truth be brought home to our convictions ever so clearly, at certain times, there is yet always left behind a reserve of sophisms, or of specious exceptions, or evasions; there is always a mistiness and a dimness, to which, after a little while, the mind may revert, and so may fondly persuade itself that things are not really as they have been represented. But this refuge of lies must, as we suppose, be entirely broken up with the breaking up of that animal organization of the mind whence chiefly illusions arise; nor could these fallacies ever again be resorted to, after the faculty of discerning intuitively the abstract relations of things had come into play. The mind would then incessantly have in view the unalterable verities of moral order and goodness, just as we now apprehend the simplest mathematical propositions, and yet would (or might) wrestle against the plain consequence, as applied to itself, with an unabated determination never to confess it—never to bend, or to say, "I have sinned, and am in the wrong." Such a struggle between the intellect and the will, going on while the personal welfare was dismally sacrificed, cannot be conceived of otherwise than as involving utter wretchedness.

Nor should it be forgotten that, although at present, owing in part to the extreme indistinctness and variableness of language, in part to the organic imperfections of individual minds, and in great part too arising from our want of immediate communication with the spiritual world—owing, we say, to these causes, even the simplest elements of moral truth never force themselves irresistibly upon our assent; whereas, when these obscurities and ambiguities shall have passed away, moral truth, probably, will be the simplest and most certain, and the most irresistibly convincing of all kinds of truth, not excepting mathematical axioms; so that the mind, if it be not happily in harmony with these principles, shall be crushed under their weight, and be totally unable so much as to raise itself into an attitude of resistance, although still repugnant in will. As the most distressing uneasiness to which upright minds are now liable is that occasioned by misgivings and perplexities concerning the great moral system, so, in the future state, as we may believe, shall an intensity of disquiet affect the perverse, the unjust, and the impure, from the glaring brightness and certainty of the principles of that same system.

We have alluded to the benefits and pleasures that are likely to result from the substitution of a perfect medium of communication among minds, in the place of the rude and inadequate symbols which compose our mundane languages. And yet here again this high advantage can be no blessing apart from goodness, integrity, purity, in those to whom it shall attach. All powers and qualities, whether mechanical, chemical, intellectual, or moral, are severally enhanced by the accumulation of numbers;—that is to say, each part or parcel of the mass is raised to a higher value or intensity when it forms one of a heap, than when left to itself; it is so that combustion rages the more that fuel is heaped upon the pyre, and so that minds develop their fullest powers, and so that very sedate sentiments are often exalted to the pitch of a mad enthusiasm. The more complete and immediate is the correspondence of the parts, or of the individuals one with another, the more will this enhancement of the individual, and of the combined force be accelerated, and the further will it go. The present imperfections of language therefore, if on the one hand they operate to bar our advancement in knowledge and virtue, on the other, serve to put a check upon the pestilent circulation of vice. The actual peace and purity of the world are perhaps nearly as much attributable to the shutting in of the horrid secrets of the worst hearts, as to the diffusion of the benign sentiments and happy affections of the best. What would human society presently become, if those mysteries of malice and impurity that are locked within some few bosoms, were divulged to all, so that all might and must catch the infection of blasphemy, hatred, and corruption.

Now, although we suppose that, in the future as well as in the present state, communication shall be voluntary, and that therefore the secrets of the heart may there, as here, be kept secret, yet we know there is actually a motive in our nature, and a motive that expands itself especially in the most depraved minds, impelling such, with a wantonness of horrid vanity, to expose the ulcers of their souls to the eyes of others. That such an ambition attaches to desperate wickedness, none can doubt whose lot has led them to be much conversant with the lost and reprobate of human kind.

This motive cannot fail to be powerfully excited by the consciousness of an increased facility for indulging it. This sort of augmentation attends all the passions and desires. Let then the very worst minds, herding with multitudes ready for infection, find themselves endowed with a faculty —not of dimly, laboriously, and inadequately expressing intellectual and moral notions, but in vividly and copiously setting forth, as it were upon the stall, the rich abominations of their souls, and of attracting and of fascinating all eyes, by the endless novelties of their versatile wickedness: —let such feel themselves able to convulse vast congregations with woe-shaken bursts of laughter, by fresh and fresh exposures of infernal sin; let there be room for this, and what were such a world! and yet in following out this frightful supposition, we invent nothing, we assume nothing out of nature, or which may not be sustained as simply probable by the analogy of actual facts, frequently occurring in the present state.

Once more; let it be considered that, although the absolute subordination of the corporeal faculties to the will and purposes of the mind, and the consequent absence of separate bodily interests, must be felt as a high advantage by those who are conscious that they are steadily pursuing the real welfare of the spirit, and are pursuing it on the true path, the feeling must be the very reverse in any case in which it is known that these real and permanent interests have been desperately compromised, and that the course upon which the spirit is rushing forward is one of madness, folly, damage, and despair. In the present state, we often owe much of the alleviation of mental distress to the constantly recurring necessity of caring for the body; and sometimes even the very sufferings of the body gratefully relieve the heart of the otherwise incessant burden of its griefs: there is a diversion, an alternation, and a relief, arising merely from the shifting of our cares and pains.

But if the body has no longer any wants, and no separate welfare to be thought of; if it have come to be nothing but the mind's passive instrument, and its medium of action and sensation; and if, at the same time, the mind knows that it has fallen far back from the course of hope and happiness, if its well-being has been sported with and thrown away, then must a brooding melancholy and remorse fix themselves without intermission upon the soul, and its misery must become unmixed. Here again we are not dreaming of things altogether unreal and fantastic, but are only imagining this our actual human nature, and our actual modes of feeling, at work in their accustomed manner, under a change of circumstances, and this change too, such as has a rational connection with the known principles of the intellectual system.

Our conclusion then is (as stated at the commencement of this digressive chapter) that although we may reasonably anticipate certain enhancements of the powers of human nature to take place in a future stage of its progress, yet that none of these additions or improvements necessarily involves an increase of happiness, but on the contrary, is in itself as likely to bring with it an intensity of suffering. The question, therefore, whether we are to be MORE HAPPY in another world than at present, or less so, must be determined by reasons that are to be sought for altogether from a different quarter. Any PHYSICAL THEORY of another life must leave this anxiety just where it found it.

6

CHAPTER XI.

PROBABLE POINT OF CONTRAST BETWEEN THE ANIMAL AND SPIRITUAL BODY, IN THE PRINCIPLE OF THEIR CONSTRUCTION RESPECTIVELY.

HITHERTO we have adventured nothing concerning the exterior conformation, or visible structure of the future human body, nor indeed are much disposed to do so, inasmuch as it is not merely a subject of secondary importance in itself, but it is one that comes less within the reach of rational conjecture; and is too of a kind likely to call up the fantasies of the imagination. Nevertheless, before we pass on, let a word be said on this point: yet we shall not stay, either to defend or explain the hint or two we may suggest.

We assume then, in the first place, that the apparent import of some passages and phrases of Scripture tends to suggest the belief that the die of human nature, as to its form and figure, is to be used again in a new world. Partly on the ground of inferences from general principles, and partly on the strength of particular assertions, we suppose that the fair and faultless paradisaical model of human beauty and majesty, which stood forward as the most illustrious instance of creative wisdom—the bright gem of the visible world—this form too, which has been borne and consecrated by incarnate deity—that it shall at length regain its forfeited honours, and once more be pronounced, "very good;" so good as to forbid its being superseded; on the contrary, that it shall be reinstated and allowed, after its long degradation, to enjoy its birthright of immortality.

It is true indeed that the inspired writers put a disparagement upon those adventitious recommendations of the person to which, in our fondness and folly, we are prone to attach an inordinate importance. Nevertheless, while they do so, they are far from using the style of cynics or of stoics; much less do they, like the atheist, throw contempt upon human nature, or spurn the conditions of the animal and social economy, or pride themselves, like the mystic, upon a sovereign disdain of all ordinary motives and affections. Nothing of this sort do we meet with in the Scriptures: on the contrary, not merely the prophets and poets of the Old Testament, but our Lord and his apostles, uniformly treat with a grave respect whatever is part and parcel of human nature:—a respect well becoming devout minds, which are apt to discern, and are prepared to reverence, the Creator in all his works. From the general tone of the inspired persons we might gather the opinion that, in speaking of the human body, they, with a prophetic eye, beheld it as destined to a new and permanent glory, and as intended to stand as the image of God, freed from distortions and blemishes, and exempt from decay.

So plastic are all materials under the hand of infinite intelligence, and so susceptible are natural forms of accommodation to two or more purposes, and so much does the unexhausted skill of the Creator delight to show its resources, that we may readily believe the human body to have been so planned from the first, as that its form might adapt itself to another and a different internal economy. That is to say—while the uses of internal parts and their functions may be changed, yet it will be so as that the new functions and uses of parts shall, without damage, work in with the original contour and symmetry of the form. In this manner, not only shall the first design of the Creator be honoured, but the momentous early history of man upon earth shall be visibly kept in mind, by the perpetuity of the form under which its events were transacted; and so too, shall there be secured a vivid recollection of personal identity and individual character. On this supposition, the human form, whatever splendours may invest it, or whatever energies it may exercise, will carry forward, through ages, a memento of that first stage of life, whence fortunes so high have sprung; in like manner (to compare great things with small) as ancient houses preserve, in their armorial bearings, the symbols of the feats by which the founder of the family won his honours and lands.

But let all this be as it may, meantime there is little hazard in stating the probability that, whatever is to be the type of the future corporeity, it shall not exhibit less of divine skill and benignity than does our present animal organization; rather, as it may well be supposed, this advance in the scale of being shall be marked by a corresponding higher excellence of the mechanism that sustains it; and we may believe that the frame which is to exult over death, shall be even more wonderfully constructed than the one over which death had triumphed. Shall not the very element of that immortal body be more plastic, more refined, and more readily assimilated to mind; so that no contrarieties will have to be reconciled, no repugnances to be overcome, and no compromises to be made?

There is, however, a probable point of contrast in the construction of the present and the future body, which deserves to be noticed; and it may be thus explained. The admirable contrivances involved in animal and vegetable organization may properly be considered under two aspects, that is to say, first, as consisting in the adaptation of the general properties and affinities of the material world to the purposes of life; and secondly, in the adaptation, one to another, of the several members, organs, and viscera of the plant or animal, so as to educe from those elementary principles the intended result. For example, in the economy of a plant, there is first to be noticed, the CHEMICAL and invisible process, through the course of which light, heat, moisture, electricity, oxygen, azote, carbon, and the various metallic and saline substances furnished by the soil are compounded in modes inimitable by human art, for the production of the several specific vegetable substances—the wood, the resins, the sap, the sugar, and the rest. But then in the next place, there is the MECHANICAL adjustment of parts, as seen in the root, and stem, and leaves; in the vessels, the absorbents, the expirents, the flower, the fruit, the seed. And the same distinction is observable in the animal system; that is to say, there is the secret process with its elementary principles; and there is the visible mechanical apparatus.

Now in some beings the *principles* may be few and the *process* simple, while the *mechanism* is complex and the *parts* intricate and many. Or in other beings, on the contrary, the principles may be various, and their interaction highly refined, while the mechanism is of the simplest kind; and then it is easy to conceive of great diversities in the *relative complexity* of these two classes of contrivances;—as for example, in one instance there may be an elaborate structure, and few elementary principles; in another, a harmony of a thousand elements, effected upon an organization that might be understood at a glance. If an illustration of this distinction were needed, we might refer to certain products of human ingenuity, and perhaps should not find a better than that furnished by the chronometer, or by a musical automaton, in both which a very few of the principles or properties of matter are wrought upon; namely, gravitation, elasticity, momentum, friction, vibration; and these few are all of one class, and might perhaps be reduced to two; while the parts of the mechanism and the adjustments which are to produce the required regularity of movement are so numerous, so refined, and so complicated, as to render either of those pieces of workmanship a wonder of skill, science, and practical ingenuity, as well as of manipulative execution. On the other hand, an achromatic lens presents an instance of almost the simplest possible structure, and of the absence of any thing that can be called mechanism or complication of parts, and yet this mere adaptation of two crystal disks, the one to the other, which may be understood at a glance, (while the chronometer, or the automaton, might long perplex even an intelligent eye,) involves, and brings into combined operation, not merely certain abstruse mathematical principles, but several of the mechanical properties of matter, together with the laws of light, and the specific qualities of particular substances: in fact, almost the round of our modern sciences is implicated, directly or remotely, in the construction and use of an achromatic lens.

Now to apply the distinction, as above explained, to our immediate purpose, we assume the probability that the contrast between the present animal body, and the future spiritual body, or between terrestrial and celestial orders, will be found to bear an analogy to the difference thus exemplified; so that while the animal organization of the present human body, although in fact it combines many principles, and brings into concert many powers, yet excites our admiration mainly on account of the complexity of its parts, the delicacy of its construction, and the elaborate adaptation of function to function; on the contrary, the spiritual body shall, perhaps, be absolutely homogeneous in its elements, perfectly simple in its construction, and uniform in its structure;—a pure corporeity. Nevertheless, by a wonderful adaptation of its principles, it shall stand actively related to all, or almost all, the powers and properties, as well of the material as of the immaterial universe; and shall offer an epitome of all being—passively sensible of all qualities, potent toward all—the mirror of whatever exists, and an apt agent in every sort of movement.

In a structure, such as we here imagine, it would be the *harmony of principles*, instead of the *complexity of parts*, that would display the infinite resources of the Creative Intelligence; and moreover, a structure of this sort would leave human ingenuity in the rear, even at a greater distance than do the terrestrial organizations at present known to us; for while the skill of man goes far in effecting delicate and complicated pieces of mechanism, it soon reaches its ultimate point in attempting to harmonize various principles within the limits of a simple structure; nor, in fact, is it easy to name more than two or three signal examples of this kind in the whole range of the arts.

The above-mentioned hypothesis of a simple construction of multifarious principles, plainly implies, if not a higher exertion, yet a fuller display of intelligence than is afforded by an elaborate construction of few principles. Or perhaps the difference in this respect should be thus stated, that, in the former case, the Contriving Mind starts from a higher point, inasmuch as there is presumed a preparatory adaptation of the first elements of the material and spiritual systems; and this species of skill supposes an absolute knowl edge of, and command over, not only all things actual, but all things possible. Man fails in his attempts of this sort, because he has no command whatever over things that might be, but are not; and only a very limited and glimmering knowledge of unreal, abstract, or possible existence. What he finds ready to his hand, he can recombine; and there he stops; but the Creator has devised all elements, material and immaterial, so as at once to admit of certain combinations of them, and to provide for every possible combination which the ultimate, and far remote purposes of his universal government may at any time require. Our hypothesis is then, that the spiritual body, and the future mode of human existence, shall give evidence (not so clearly given in the present world) of an absolute supremacy in relation to the primary laws of the creation, such as affords room for highly complex adaptations of elements and principles within the simplest structures.

CHAPTER XII.

THE TRANSITION OF HUMAN NATURE FROM ANIMAL TO SPIRITUAL CORPOREITY, A PART OF THE ESTABLISHED ORDER OF THINGS.

THERE may be, as in fact we assume that there are, the strongest physical reasons for expecting a new and higher kind of life, as intended for the human family. Innumerable analogies gathered from the processes of the vegetable and animal world illustrate and corroborate this expectation; while the irresistible impulses, or instincts of the human mind—moral as well as intellectual, support it. Nevertheless, for religious purposes, and for bearing the stress of our moral principles, we must always choose to rely upon the direct testimony of the inspired writers. Our faith and hope rest upon the affirmation of Heaven itself; not upon the soundness of philosophical speculations, or even demonstrations, if such could be obtained. It is not as theorists, but as believers, that we look for another life.

And yet there is a particular consequence, resulting from our receiving the knowledge of another life, through the medium of a miraculously attested revelation, which demands to be noticed; and it is this, that the corporeal renovation of human nature, which may properly be regarded as an established part of the great order of the material and sentient universe, or as a NATURAL TRANSITION, comes to be associated in our minds with religious ideas *only*, and so to share the fate of a class of impressions which, alas! with most men are not the most constant or substantial.

The inspired writers have a definite commission to execute, a special purpose in view, and an extraordinary dispensation to carry forward; nor do they ever lose sight of their peculiar office:—their business is, in whatever they may announce or relate, and whether it be in itself natural or supernatural, ordinary or otherwise, to fix the attention of men upon the divine agency, to which they always give a prominence that nearly puts out of view second causes. Mankind looks with eagerness to that which is visible and proximate; but the ministers of Heaven demand devout regard to be paid to that which is invisible, and which, although remote, is yet principal. God is the source of all things, and the disposer of all: and he is so alike of what follows a known and common course, as of what breaks in upon that course. The inspired writers have but one language, the language of piety, for events of whatever order; hence it is that the terms and style of a supernatural narrative run through the account they give of even the most ordinary and natural events: not that they ever affirm miracles where there were none, (a most unworthy supposition,) but that they convey an impression, always just indeed, of the constant presence of the divine power and providence: in a word, they write and speak, as "seeing Him who is invisible."

But there arises incidentally, from this mode of writing, a degree of ambiguity, or we should rather say, a degree of difficulty, in discriminating between what was strictly miraculous, and what simply natural, in some of the transactions recorded in Scripture; for when facts of the latter kind are described as seen from the height of heaven, they may appear to have been what they were not—special interpositions of omnipotence. In truth, the ordinary and extraordinary acts of the divine government differ rather relatively, and as they affect our modes of thinking, than essentially. Rigidly considered, the entrance of a human being upon the world in the common course of nature, is not less really a manifestation of the power and providence of God, in that single instance, than is the exit of a human being from the world in a chariot of fire; there can be no impropriety, therefore, in referring the one event as well as the other to its proper cause—the power and will of God. But yet when, in obedience to the dictates of piety, we have thus acknowledged the supreme agent in relation to the ordinary occurrences of life, or to the events that belong to the history of nations, it may be necessary, and it is useful, to distribute them into classes, as natural or supernatural; and it is the business of the biblical expositor to make this distinction, wherever it may be done, in expounding the inspired histories. Now, unquestionably, what may be done in relation to the accounts of past transactions may also be done in relation to those predicted events that are yet to mark the destiny of the human family; and it will perhaps be found, in some instances, that our conviction of the reality of things future or unseen has suddenly become more impressive, merely in consequence of our having seen reason to think of them as *natural*, or as proper parts of the established scheme of the universe, instead of miraculous interruptions of that scheme.

In such instances, if such there be, it is not that events of the latter class are abstractedly less credible than those of the former; for in relation to omnipotence the two kinds stand on precisely the same level of credibility; but it is merely that, from the constitution of our minds, and from our habits of thinking, we are able to bring the one home to our conceptions in a more vivid and a calmer manner than we can the other. Whatever be the mode in which any great change in the physical condition of man is brought about, that is to say, whether it be in steady and regular accordance with the system of the universe, or as a single and unprecedented act, two things are still true concerning it, namely, first, that such a change must spring from the divine power; and secondly, that if it be future, and if remote also from our ordinary means of information, our positive belief of it must rest upon the divine testimony. These facts established, and remembered, we are then free to consider any future signal event in the history of man in the light either of natural or of supernatural causation, as the reasons adduced in each instance may seem to demand.

With the daily and hourly miracles (so to call them) of the vegetable and animal world before our eyes; with creations, renovations, transitions, and transmigrations innumerable, going on, while yet individuality and identity are preserved, nothing ought to be thought incredible, or even unlikely, concerning the destiny of man which comports with these common wonders, and which in itself is only an analogous transformation. No prejudice of the vulgar can be more unphilosophical than is that which would obstruct, for a moment, our acquiescence in the belief of a future transfusion of human nature, with its individuality, into a new and more refined corporeal structure. The profound resources of the divine intelligence are constantly being developed in our view, not in a thousand modes merely, but in a hundred thousand; and it is perfectly manifest that this Sovereign Intelligence—master of whatever is abstractedly possible, delights in taking the utmost range of diversity, not merely as to fashion, but as to rule and condition, and as to history and circumstance; and if so low a mode of speaking were tolerable, one might say, the probabilities that man, the chief terrestrial animal, and an animal of so complex a constitution, is destined to undergo several transitions, are as a thousand to one to the contrary. Every thing belonging to human nature is mysterious; or rather, bespeaks the existence of powers and instincts *undeveloped*, and which, though they just indicate their presence, do not reach their apparent end in the present state.

It is true, indeed, that many species of animals fulfil (so far as we know) the law of their existence, and reach their highest excellence under one form of life; and then die, as they were born, with no other difference than what belongs to the changes involved in growth and decay. But then none of these species offer, in their organization, any indications of incompleteness, or show the latent types of an expected metamorphosis; whereas, in every case where a transition from one mode of life to another is to take place, the germs of the future being are wrapped up in the organization of the present being; and in every such instance a well-practised naturalist, in examining it (supposing it to have been hitherto unknown to him) during its initial stage, would, without hesitation, announce it to have in prospect another and a higher mode of life; for he would discern within, or upon it, the symbols of its destined progression, and he would find in its habits certain instincts that have reference to a more perfect manner of existence. Now is it so with man? We have already taken this for granted, and the theme is one that has often been touched, and is not a necessary part of our argument, inasmuch as the task we have chosen is not that of proving the truth of the doctrine of a future life, but that of following some probable conjectures concerning it, taken as true, on the authority of the Christian writings. Nevertheless a word or two may be allowed on the subject before we pass on.

The proposition, then, which we assume is this, that the rational and moral consciousness, with the various faculties therein comprised, is to survive the decomposition of the animal structure, and is to attach itself to a new and more refined structure. Of course, therefore, it is not to the *animal organization* that we are to look, as if to find *there* the symbols of a metamorphosis, or the germs of another type of life; for the mere animal is to accomplish its purposes in the present initial era of human existence; and, like other intransitive species, it develops all its parts, and falls into decay without leaving any renascent element. But it is among the moral sentiments and the intellectual faculties, that is to say, within the circle of the proper consciousness of the man, that we ought to find, if at all, the indications of a second birth and of a new economy of life. Now all that has been said, and that may be said, and it is not a little, in illustration of the theorem of the immortality of man, as foreshown by his moral sense, by his expectation of retribution, by his aspirations after a better existence, by the vast compass of his faculties, and by his instinctive horror of annihilation—all these prognostics of futurity, and if there are any other, are capable of being condensed into a single proposition, setting forth the fact—a fact the mere statement of which contains virtually a demonstrative proof of the principle it involves, namely—that the idea or the expectation of another life is a constant element of human nature, or an original article in the physiology of man. Shall any one deny that the human family has harboured the thought of living again after death? or if any one would labour to show that this common expectation is groundless, his very argument, and the stress and ingenuity of his reasoning, affords the best sort of evidence that the instinctive belief of immortality is too general, and is too deeply seated to be easily loosened.

Now let this mere fact, stripped of whatever, by the most severe analysis, we may reject as adventitious, be coldly regarded in a purely physiological light; and let it be put on the ground of analogy with any facts that may seem naturally to comport with it;—as for example, with the preparations that are made by any of the transitive species of animals (whether blindly or wittingly) for their approaching metamorphosis. If an animal—an insect, the history of which, at present, we know nothing of, is observed, at a certain season of the year, to abandon its usual haunts, and to turn away from its wonted enjoyments, and to seek for itself a crevice or secure asylum, fit for affording it what it must immediately need in its new and untried condition; if it is seen to be employed in a manner which has no utility whatever in relation to its present mode of life,—in such a case, we infer, without a shadow of doubt, that the creature is following a sure leading of nature; nor should we deem any thing much more unaccountable or monstrous, than to find that all this forecasting of futurity, and all these prudential operations came to nothing, and that the deluded insect, instead of awaking in gaiety from its transition-torpor, had utterly perished, and that its dust had been irrecoverably scattered by the winds.

What sound principle of philosophy then forbids our looking at the human species as the chief of the terrestrial tribes, and then inferring that the sum of human instincts, impressions, expectations, and opinions, (taken at large,) constituting as they do the elements of our constitution, the parts of our nature, are to be held infallible indications of what awaits the species, and as physically prophetic of its destiny? Our present argument is reducible to a very few words, or to a syllogism that contains its own demonstration. Man, we affirm, is to undergo a metamorphosis, and is to pass on to another stage of existence—because, by the constitution of his mind, he expects to do so.

But we are told that it is among the characteristics of human nature to admit, and to adhere to, many groundless opinions; and if we should deny this, an opponent would say—" You affirm *my opinion* of the futility of the doctrine of a future life to be false; yet it is mine, and the opinion too, of many." In reply, we freely admit this fact, and allow that an adherence to baseless prejudices is a characteristic of human nature; but we must insist upon an important distinction, which is this, that, although any particular persuasion may be unfounded, and any single dogma may be false, and any one chain of reasoning sophistical, yet it must by no means be granted, either that the reasoning faculty in man is in its first principles illusive, or that the abstract import, or condensed value of human belief, taken together, can be at variance with truth and nature; or that the common instincts of the human family are nugatory, and have no end, or final cause. Suppositions such as these are contradicted by the entire analogy of the animated world, as well as that they are abstractedly improbable and repulsive. Thus for example, *any one* of the religions professed by particular tribes of men may be false, in whatever distinguishes it from *other* religions; that is to say in whatever is partial and peculiar; but the religious instinct, and the abstract belief of invisible creative power, is not false; and so any specific expectation of what awaits us after death may prove a dream, but not so the human expectation at large of surviving the dissolution of the body. Those sheer errors of which men individually or nationally have been the victims, are always of a kind that may be traced to artificial and accidental causes, such as the influence of interested impostors or enthusiasts; or they have sprung from the vanity and perversity of philosophers, or founders of sects. But, on the contrary, the common or generic impressions, expectations, and opinions of man, spring unquestionably from the elements of his nature, and how much soever they may be warped, or exaggerated, deformed, repressed, or denied, they reappear, everywhere, and in every age, with unabated force, and with very nearly the same essential properties. These opinions and impressions must be substantially true, if there be truth or harmony at all in the scheme of the universe. Among such physical elements of human nature, the prime is the belief of an Intelligent First Cause, and the second is the belief of a future life and a retributive economy. To impugn, then, the doctrine of immortality, or of another stage of existence, succeeding the present, is to find a species, marked in the most distinct manner with the indications of a future transformation, and yet to affirm that no transformation actually awaits it.

But if a future life does await the human family, and if it be a change involved in the original constitution of our nature, then it must be allowable to speak of it, and of the means and mode of the change, as we might of any other part of the scheme of the universe:—yet always with a becoming modesty and seriousness; and this, notwithstanding the particular circumstance attending our belief of the fact, namely, that our persuasion of it rests upon evidence which has been miraculously conveyed to us; and notwithstanding the fact also, that the renovation of human nature, when brought about, shall be effected in a manner bearing peculiarly upon the religious condition of men, as individually accountable.

Every signal event, affecting the welfare either of individuals or of nations, may, with the strictest propriety, be viewed, either first, as a natural product of common causes, or as an act of the divine government toward the individual or the community, and as carrying with it a special meaning, in relation to the principles of the great moral economy under which mankind personally and in the aggregate are moving forward. Thus for an instance, the first desolation of Jerusalem was in truth what it is represented to have been by the inspired historians and prophets —an immediate judgment of God upon the nation's impiety and infatuation; a judgment long threatened, and, in the destined moment, accomplished. Nevertheless it was the natural consequence, not merely of the personal ambition of the Babylonish monarch, but of the altered relative position of nations within the range of the Chaldean power. In like manner, that visible display of the divine displeasure which marked the second desolation of the Jewish state, by the sword of the Romans, may, without any diminution of our religious sentiments concerning it, be traced as easily and naturally to its proximate political causes, as we so trace the fall of any modern republic. And what is true in reference to things on a smaller scale, is not untrue or irrational in relation to things on a larger scale. No principle of piety—piety well understood, forbids our considering under this same twofold aspect, the desolation of the world by the general deluge, which, while it was in the fullest sense an outbursting of divine wrath, provoked by the boundless wickedness of the human race, was, at the same time, an event attributable, like an earthquake, or the eruption of a volcano, or the inundation of a province, to the working of telluric forces, whether chemical, mechanical, meteorological, or sidereal. If, from an ill-judged fear of giving way to a skeptical temper, we refuse to entertain the physical, along with the religious view of these, and of similar events, we expose ourselves to the danger of being driven altogether from our religious convictions, by proofs, not to be resisted, of natural agency in bringing those events about. On the contrary, a well-digested persuasion of the perfect consistency of the natural and the spiritual economies under which we are placed, at once exempts our religious faith from all jeopardy, and brings our confidence in the certainty of the divine promises and threatenings home to the mind, with the most impressive force and vividness. It is not the lessening, but the enhancing of religious sentiments toward which we are now tending.

In like manner, and in adherence to the same rule, we might find our salutary apprehension of that second, and yet more tremendous desolation of this our planet by fire, which awaits it, to be suddenly and greatly strengthened by our seeing reason to consider it as a physical event, to which, from their very constitution, all the planetary bodies are exposed, and which, under certain conjunctures, must inevitably happen, and which our own planet is always in imminent danger of. If it be the ill chance of a family to occupy the upper stories of a vast laboratory, wherein processes are carrying on, such as would want only the slightest accident to produce an instantaneous and fatal explosion, such a family, knowing the conditions of its tenancy, assuredly should live mindful of what may, any hour, be their fate.

The physical fortunes of our globe (let the phrase be for a moment allowed) have already, as we cannot doubt, included more than one chaotic convulsion; and it has undergone, if not more than one universal submersion in water, at least one fusion by fire. It may then have to pass through another, at some period when, either by collision with some erratic celestial body, or by the gradually advancing vehemence of the central furnace, the pent-up energy of telluric combustion shall get vent, and becoming ungovernable, shall, in the rage of a day, or of a month, leave nothing mundane undissolved that, in its nature, may yield to the intensity of heat.

Such then being the probable fate (if we may still speak physically) of this planet, and perhaps of others of the system, it is what we may be looking for; and as if our position were like that of the occupiers of the vine valleys, on the trembling flanks of Etna or Vesuvius, whom we may imagine to have been informed, or to know on some rational grounds, that, by the slow but incessant enlargement of the fiery abyss beneath them, the entire crust and framework of the mountain must, within some calculable period, fall in, and the vast circuit of its base be converted into a sea of flame and sulphur. On just such conditions, may we say, does the human family tread, from age to age, the soil of their native planet. Now all this, which would happen, and at the very moment when it shall happen, if there were no rational and accountable family upon the earth, shall, when it does take place, come in at the destined hour to accomplish the special intentions of the divine government toward the descendants of Adam. To us men, it will be, in a peculiar sense, as to all mundane creatures, it will be, in a common sense, the terrible day of wrath—a day not by any propitiation to be averted.

It is true that when the present progress and prospects of nations are considered, and when the yet undeveloped powers of nature, in several regions of the earth, are calculated, a strong, or almost an irresistible persuasion is engendered, as if long cycles of centuries were still in reserve for the human family, during which civilization and happiness shall be spreading, until the combined faculties of the physical and moral world shall have produced their utmost sum of good. But then there are other considerations which may well lead us to regard such expectations as extremely fallacious, and as very likely to be disappointed. What we see taking place on a small scale, may possibly take place on a larger scale: as for example,—a district of country, or a few acres only, has been redeemed from the wilderness, and is just beginning to reward the enterprise and ability of a meritorious band of settlers; and we confidently realize, in idea, the wealth, and the thriving population, which within a century, must cover it. But an inundation or an earthquake lays waste the fair territory; its occupiers perish in the catastrophe, or are scattered,. never to be reassembled; and the whole falls back into its primeval savageness. What now is our little planet but a narrow province of a vast empire; and the fate of a district, or of a farm within it, may be the fate of the whole. If a dyke bulges, and lets in the ocean, if a fire consumes a factory or a city—the crust of the globe may bulge, and the central forces of water, or of fire, or of both in conflict, may desolate all continents. None can affirm, while these lesser calamities are matters of frequent occurrence, that the greater shall never happen.

Whether it is to take place in that same day of telluric ruin or not, (which is not our present question,) there is to be, and it is to come in as a proper part of the great economy of the universe, a second birth of the human family, when all born of Eve shall, by the creative energy, live again; and, whether for the better or the worse, individually, shall take their stand upon a higher level of physical existence than at first. This transition, which now we find it so difficult to think of, otherwise than with a sort of incredulous apprehension, as a mysterious article of our Christiàn faith, shall, when it occurs, be felt, however mómentous in its consequences, as a simple fact, and as forming a natural epoch in the history of man, whom we shall then understand to be a creature destined, from the first, to metamorphoses, and to far extended progression.

CHAPTER XIII.

THE SURVIVANCE OF INDIVIDUAL CHARACTER, AND OF THE MORAL CONSCIOUSNESS.

A CERTAIN degree of illusion attaches to whatever is future and untried; and this false colour, spread over our prospects, at one time exaggerates our hopes, and at another, by reaction, damps them as much. If a future change in our condition be of a very extensive and important kind, we are very apt to suppose that, even if our consciousness of identity be not impaired by the event, our ordinary modes of feeling, and our characteristic sentiments and tastes, will none of them remain the same. From previously entertaining these delusive expectations it happens, when we come actually to pass through some such important revolution of our personal condition, that our first emotions are not so much those of surprise at the greatness of the change, as of disappointment at the small extent to which it has affected our usual sensations, and at finding how little our customary personal consciousness has been disturbed. We feel ourselves possessed of the same familiar self—of the same peculiarities of taste; and that the very same moral and mental habits have passed on with us, through the hour of transition, from one condition of life to another; nor can we say that this transition, in itself, has made us more wise or virtuous, or that it has enhanced by so much as a particle our personal merits, although it may have enlarged our range of action, and perhaps have added to our means of enjoyment.

Now we may reasonably imagine that it will be precisely

thus in the moment of our passage from the present to another mode of existence. The several powers of life shall have become more intense in their activity, our consciousness will have been expanded; the faculties will no longer labour and faint at their tasks, or relapse exhausted: life will burn clear and steady, and will need no replenishing; but yet the inner man—the individual—the moral personality—will be untouched:—the remembrance of yesterday, and of its little history, will be distinct and familiar; and we shall come to an instantaneous conviction of the momentous practical truth, that the physical and the moral nature are so thoroughly independent one of the other, as that the greatest imaginable revolution passing upon the former, shall leave the latter simply what it was.

A short season, probably, will be enough to impart to us an easy familiarity with our new home, and a ready use of our corporeal instruments, and a facility in joining in with the economy around us. Moreover, it is reasonable to believe that, whereas, in the present state, the heterogeneous elements of mind and matter, as consorted within the animal organization, are held together as by force, and so as to occasion a vague feeling, coming over us at times, as if we were dreaming, or as if our very life were an enigma, and as if we were held back from actual contact with what is real and substantial;—on the contrary, when the corporeal nature has become nothing else than the instrument and vehicle of the mind, and when the two elements of our existence have come to be perfectly blended, and when, as a consequence, our feelings are all of one sort, and when our several energies and impulses, instead of counteracting one the other, shall flow on always in the same direction, that then there shall attend us an incomparably more vivid sense of reality—that then we shall perceive all things with a sharp intensity, and shall have a bright, vivid, consciousness of life, such as shall make us think of the gone-by period of animal life as if, indeed, it had been a dream. It is so that a man may have groped his way, hour after hour, across a marshy level, veiled in fogs, till he comes to the foot of a steep, where, after some arduous steps, he gains a height, and not only overlooks the mists of the swamp, but beholds a wide illumined landscape, and the clear sky, and the sun.

At the moment of recognizing our personal consciousness, after passing through the future physical transformation, what we must fix upon will unquestionably be our habitual emotions, tastes, and moral dispositions; for it is these that constitute the very core of our being, and it is these that must stand out, with so much the more characteristic distinctness, when whatever that was accidental and adjunctive has fallen off from us. All merely animal sensations will have been superseded; all mechanical and technical habits will have lost their means and occasions; the intellectual furniture will, for the most part, or perhaps entirely, have given place to knowledge of a more direct and substantial kind; but the sentiments we have cherished, and the affections that have settled down upon the mind, and which constitute its character—these now, with a bold supremacy, will make up our consciousness, and compel us to confess ourselves to be the same. Much indeed that belonged to our first stage of existence will, in the retrospect, appear shadowy and unimportant; but not so any of those events or courses of conduct that shall be found to have created or controlled our moral being.

It is plain that, when any order of beings is to pass under a renovating process, the process must be of a kind analogous to the properties which are to be so transformed; thus for instance, it can be nothing but a physical power,

7

and a series of physical transitions, that must translate an animal from one condition of organization to another; and thus, too, it can be nothing else but a moral power, and a moral process, or a working upon the *affections* by *motives*, that can effect a transition from one moral condition to another. It is indeed easy to admit the illusion that, if we were but transported to a purer sphere, and were but exempted from certain evil influences, we should at once become virtuous; but a supposition such as this will not bear to be examined; for although external causes may have had a powerful influence, at first, in producing our present moral dispositions, and so in determining our character, these dispositions, when once formed, possess a fixed continuity of their own, which is by no means destroyed merely by removing the exterior influences whence they arose; and moreover, such dispositions, or settled passions, when actually consolidated, include a reproductive energy; they are living powers; they vegetate, and cover the entire surface of the soul. The moral nature then, or the personal character, far from being open to renovation merely by the means of a physical transition from one mode of life to another, or by a passage from one set of circumstances to another, is not to be rectified, if at all, otherwise than by its coming under the operation of congruous influences; that is to say, it must be wrought upon by moral considerations, and must be swayed by reasons.

An instantaneous change, either from good to evil, or from evil to good, if effected in a sovereign manner, by a foreign power, and effected irrespectively of an economy of motives, would rather be the annihilation of one being, and the creation of another, than the changing of the character of the same being; for it is of the very nature of a change of character that there be an internal process, a concurrence of the will, and yielding of the rational faculties to rational inducements, and also the giving way of one species of desires, and of one class of habits, to another. While, therefore, it consists perfectly with the abstract reason of things, and with what we see around us in nature, to expect that the future transition from the present mode of existence to another, will be effected immediately by the divine power, it directly contradicts, not merely the reason of things abstractedly, but our actual knowledge and experience of the principles of the moral and intellectual system, to hope for any such sovereign renovation of our dispositions, as consequent upon an enlargement of our faculties, or upon a change of scene, circumstance, and society. That the Sovereign Benevolence may indeed, if it pleases, so touch the springs of our motives as to bring about effectively a change of character, is by no means to be denied; and indeed such an act of grace lies at the foundation of that economy of mercy under which we are now placed; but then this exertion of spiritual influence always flows in the channel of moral means and inducements; nor are we entitled to look for it under any other conditions than those explicitly laid down, and solemnly insisted upon by the inspired writers, who strictly confine our expectations of efficacious grace to the present economy, and who, in the tones of awful warning, announce *this* to be the day of salvation, and *this* the accepted season of mercy.

A little consideration may convince us that to indulge an expectation of a sudden and physical restoration of moral soundness, by a sovereign act, in the same way that we may look for a renovation of our corporeal faculties, must directly tend to bring the mind into a state in which nothing less than the most prodigious of all miracles could avail for its restoration. The first principles of a moral economy are immediately nullified when we persuade ourselves that our moral nature does not differ from our animal organization, in relation to the divine power, and that the one, like the other, might be reinstated by a word. The hope, well sustained as it is, of a happy and not a very remote renovation of our bodily and intellectual existence, and of an entrance upon a higher and a wider field of action and enjoyment, does indeed impart a kindling impulse and a much needed energy to the languishing principles of virtue ; but these very principles, upon the force and vivacity of which our future welfare absolutely depends, could only be relaxed, or totally destroyed, by our supposing that, when we wake up in another world, we shall find a miracle to have been wrought unconsciously upon our tempers, desires, and affections—and such a miracle as supersedes the mortifying task of now repressing malign and sensual dispositions, and of cherishing those that are pure and benevolent.

We conclude then that any expectation of an improvement of the moral nature, merely in consequence of a transition from a lower to a higher stage of physical existence, will be found delusive. And yet, though we must not suppose the moral faculties to be renovated by such a transition, we may well believe that it will give scope to a much increased intensity of all emotions and affections of this class, whether they be benign or malignant, pure or sordid. This probable enhancement of feeling in another life deserves some attention; for it is conceivable that the most profound or agitating sensations of which we are conscious in the present state, may seem trivial, when they come to be compared with the corresponding passions and affections of the future life.

Every one accustomed to reflect upon the operations of his own mind must be aware of a distinction between the intellectual and the moral faculties, as to the rate at which they severally move; for while the reasoning power advances in a manner that might be likened to an increase according to the rule of arithmetical progression, and which consists in the adding of one proposition to another, and in the accumulation of equal quantities; it is, on the contrary, the characteristic of the passions, and of all intense sentiments, to rise with an accelerated movement, and to increase at the rate, as of a geometrical progression. Even the milder emotions of love and joy, and much more, vehement sensations, such as hatred, anger, jealousy, revenge, despair, tend always toward this sort of rapid enhancement, and fail to do so only as they are checked, either by a sense of danger, connected with the indulgence of them, or by feelings of corporeal exhaustion, or by the interference of the incidents and interests of common life. Especially it is to be noticed that those of the emotions which kindle, or which are kindled, by the imagination, are liable to an acceleration such as produces a physical excitement, highly perilous both to mind and body, and needing to be speedily diverted. And although the purely moral emotions are not accompanied with precisely the same sort of corporeal disturbance, nevertheless, when they actually gain full possession of the soul, they rapidly exhaust the physical powers, and bring on a state of torpor, or of general indifference.

Now this exhaustion manifestly belongs to the animal organization; nor can we doubt that, if it were possible to retain the body in a state of neutrality, or of perfect quiescence, from the first to the last, during a season of profound emotion, then these same affections might advance much further, and become far more intense, than, as it is, they ever can or may. The corporeal limitation of the passions becomes, in truth, a matter of painful consciousness, whenever they rise to an unusual height, or are long continued; and there takes place then, within the bosom, an agony, partly animal, partly mental, and a very uneasy sense of the inadequateness of our strongest emotions to the occasion that calls them out. We feel, that we cannot feel as we should: emotions are frustrated, and the affections which should have sprung upward, are detained in a paroxysm on earth. It is thus with the noblest sentiments, and thus with profound grief; and the malign and vindictive passions draw their tormenting force from this very sense of restraint, and they *rend* the soul because they can *move* it so little. Does there not arise, amid these convulsions of our nature, a tacit anticipation of a future state, in which the soul shall be able to feel unboundedly, and to take its fill of emotion?

Except among the insane, no emotions are permanent, or invariably uppermost; but in surrendering a powerful emotion, or in allowing it to be displaced by interests and feeling of a more common class, we confess the present inferiority of our nature, which will bear so little; and we silently console ourselves by the instinctive belief that a time will come when the passions shall take their high course, without pause or restraint. It is with a somewhat analogous feeling that, when the desire of knowledge is thwarted, we remand this appetite of the soul to a future life. The necessities of the body, and its appetites, are the ruling powers of the present state; while the passions and affections are accessories only, which must not have more than their seasons of indulgence; and they must take a subordinate place, for this very reason, that it is their essence, if freely indulged, to absorb the soul, and to exclude every other object and pursuit; whereas an indulgence of the intellectual tastes may be made to consist much better with some regard to the ordinary interests of life. Now this characteristic exclusiveness of the moral sentiments and passions, ought to be regarded as an indication of that supremacy which belongs to them, and which they must ultimately acquire. Those powers of our nature which now are to be repressed, and confined to moments, because, if let loose, they would become masters of the soul, in a manner incompatible with our bodily and social welfare, will, we cannot doubt, at length reach their rightful ascendency, and give law, in an irresistible manner, to the active and intellectual faculties. These latter are but means to an end—the highest reason is no more; and the time shall come when what is instrumental shall give place to what is supreme and final.

And when the sovereign faculties of the soul—its affections, shall have gained the sway that belongs to them, they will no doubt put the instrumental faculties into a state of much more energetic action than they ever reach at present, while impelled in an inconstant and irregular manner, and often by motives of an inferior class. Far from supposing that, in a higher region, where the affections shall be more intense and more permanent, nothing shall be done or thought of, but to indulge these profound sentiments, or that an invariable, inactive, unproductive ecstasy, is to fill the endless circle of ages, on the contrary, we assume it as certain that every active faculty, corporeal and rational, shall then come into play at a vastly enhanced rate, and with much more fruit and advantage, than at present:—the impulse being greater and more uniform, the movement shall be proportionably accelerated.

CHAPTER XIV.

CORRESPONDENCE BETWEEN THE PRESENT AND THE FUTURE EMPLOYMENT OF THE ACTIVE PRINCIPLES OF HUMAN NATURE.

If once we relinquish the principle of analogy, as applicable to the divine operations and government, we abandon all the means we have of extending our knowledge, and we are left in a state of distressing incertitude, in relation to the most momentous subjects. But if the rule of analogy may really be relied upon, and if it be safe to conclude that a practical correspondence of means and ends connects the training we are subjected to in the present life, with the employments of the life to come, and if the present is indeed to be regarded as an education for the future, then does it appear certain that an initiatory course, of which, when it is auspiciously passed through, the product consists in forming habits of patient and strenuous exertion, of order, of self-denial, and constancy, and in cherishing the spirit of enterprise and courage, and in bringing both mind and body into a state in which the utmost possible may be done and borne—we say such a course will be followed by another that shall demand, and bring into exercise, these very same qualities and habits, and shall put them to work still more intensely. Can we believe that the precious and costly fruits of a long and painful culture, in the present state, are all to fall to the earth, and perish, just as they are ripened?

But it may be asked, What scope can there be for the exercise of the strenuous virtues, or what room for patience, constancy, courage, in a world of peace, love, and absolute security? Now in replying to this natural inquiry, it might be allowable first to sift a little the evidence on which our common notions of the future life are founded; and perhaps it might appear that in this, as in so many other instances, the *entire* scriptural evidence comprises some counterpoised statements, from a comparison of which, and not from any one portion of it, our belief ought to be derived; but waiving any such Biblical investigations, a little attention to the subject will enable us to conceive of such a substitution of one operation of the moral powers, for another, as may give exercise to the bold and arduous virtues without implying either positive suffering or personal danger. Let us make this attempt to conceive of what we may call—TRANSMUTED MORAL QUALITIES.

We may begin with that main element of terrestrial virtue—pious resignation to the divine will, and a calm fortitude, under circumstances of privation, disappointment, and suffering. How then, it may be asked, can any such habit of the mind, together with the sentiments that attach to it, find place in a region of felicity? With the view of finding a satisfactory (or at least a sufficient) solution of this difficulty, we should ask ourselves on what ground it is we conclude that the principles of the divine government, and the actual administration of those principles, shall all be spread open to us, under a full light, at the moment of our entrance upon the upper world? No such supposition can in fact be made good, and on the contrary, reason may be shown for thinking that those practical and temporary trials of our implicit confidence in the divine rectitude and benevolence with which here we are exercised, are in truth, preparations for some far more difficult acts and habits of silent reverential submission, than are as yet called for. The lesson we learn in surrendering, for instance, the darling joys of life, one after another, may seem a mere schooling—an unreal play, when we come into a position of nearer concernment with the vast movements of the divine government; and then, even although we should not be exposed to personal sufferings or losses, yet with the more intense sensibilities belonging to a higher mode of existence, and in view of transactions of which here we think little, or know nothing, we may be thrown back with force upon our already acquired sentiments of loyal and devout acquiescence in the measures of absolute wisdom and rectitude, and we may be compelled to confess that the habit of mind which had been forming on earth, was far from being superfluous in relation to the events and duties of our after life in heaven.

A due consideration of the essential, and therefore the *unalterable* disparity which separates finite and dependent minds from the Infinite Mind, will lead us to perceive that no future advancements, whatever, that may be made by the former, in knowledge or goodness, or intellectual power, can in any sensible degree lessen the interval between the Creator and his creatures, even the most exalted of them. It is very true that a humble class of beings may at length overtake and outstrip a higher class; and yet the highest shall never feel themselves to be approximating to the Supreme Perfection. It is at once mathematically and metaphysically certain, that the finite can never measure the infinite; and inasmuch as it does not either measure or grasp it, the symmetry of the infinite can never be seen, or be otherwise than hypothetically assumed, and devoutly confided in. The attributes of God must therefore always surpass the comprehension of his creatures; and if his attributes are incomprehensible, the visible acts too, which are the products of those attributes, can be but imperfectly understood. At least it must happen, in certain critical conjunctures of the universal scheme of things, that insuperable difficulties will present themselves, and that, as often as great epochs give place one to another, an abyss will be opened, into which not the most exalted minds can dare to look with a steadfast gaze, and from the brink of which such will retire trembling.

We may indeed sometimes have persuaded ourselves, in the fondness of speculation, that certain inveterate difficulties are now at last cleared up, and that the scheme of the moral universe lies all outspread before us, as in a map. But the wise speedily surrender any such conceit, and return gladly to the only ground on which either men or seraphs can feel a footing—the ground of implicit submission to the Infinite Nature. It is indeed highly probable that certain *particular difficulties* which embarrass our speculative theology, and which now afflict us by their formidable aspect, may utterly vanish at the moment when we reach a higher and more advantageous point of view; and we may then wonder at the slenderness of those modes of thinking, which could allow of our being staggered in any such manner. But then at the very same moment in which we clear the mists of mortality, the mysteries of heaven will open upon us; and these, we may be sure, will involve difficulties of a firmer texture, and such as shall try, to the utmost, the silent fortitude of the soul. It is not the vapours of earth, but it is "thick clouds of the sky," that surround the throne of the Almighty.

Yet we must by no means imagine that this new call upon the religious fortitude of loyal minds will induce a comfortless or distracted state of feeling; for as, in the present state, that very same spiritual acquaintance with God, which gives occasion to our perplexities, supplies us also with sufficient means for holding them in abeyance, so that they do not smite the soul with dismay and despair, in like manner doubtless, shall still fuller discoveries of the Supreme Excellence and Goodness abundantly sustain our confidence, animate our constancy, and give spring and warmth to our communion with Him, who, though "past finding out," is nevertheless always glorious in benevolence and wisdom. We see it to be thus, even now, with the pious, who, although they may be exercised as they advance in their course more and more severely, still grow, not merely in fortitude, but in peace and joy. And thus it is in common life, that the youth contemns the troubles of childhood, while he cheerfully encounters the more real difficulties of his entrance upon the world; and again, that the man forgets the smaller cares of his youth, and bears up beneath the multiplied anxieties of ripe age:—each new period, in relieving us from one burthen, imposes another, and a heavier, and calls into play whatever fortitude we had acquired in our preliminary course, and yet does not forbid our continued enjoyment of existence.

Again: a passive fortitude is not the only virtue which the training we are under tends to cherish; for there is a manifest purpose in the construction of the moral and social system, to call forth the more active excellence of courage and the spirit of enterprise; nor need we exclude (properly understood) the stirring sentiment of ambition. Can we doubt that He who, in his word, is "calling us to glory and virtue," and who by the same channel enjoins a manly and vigorous discharge of our parts, is also, in the actual circumstances through which we are led, preparing the intellectual and moral powers for what they are to perform in another sphere. In the case of certain individuals, this apparent purpose occupies the principal place in the scheme of providence toward them. It is clear too, that the noblest and most generous tempers—the very choicest minds, make the readiest proficiency in learning this lesson; while mean and inert souls—the selfish, the diffident, and the pusillanimous, although they may acquire something of the *passive* virtues, almost totally fail in regard to the *active*. Adhering then to the rule of analogy, and confiding in the principle that a rational consistency, and an adaptation of means to the end, runs through the divine proceedings, we conclude that the future life shall actually call into exercise a bold energy, and intrepidity, and ambition too;—an ambition not selfish or vain, but loyal.

In assuming so much as this, we are by no means obliged to suppose that those who, in the present state, shall have gone through their probation, and won immortal glory, are anew to become liable to loss, injury, or jeopardy of happiness. Without admitting any such supposition, we may readily conceive of a state of things in which there may be services to be performed, enterprises to be undertaken, and a promotion to be aimed at, such as none but the bold and the strong shall be equal to, and none but the aspiring shall dare to attempt. These services may involve encounters with powerful and crafty opponents; or they may demand sudden exertions of intelligence, and a ready recurrence to resources, under circumstances that would amaze and baffle all but the calmly courageous. Moreover there may be high advantages to be snatched by the few whose flight can be long sustained, and is the most steady; there may be dominations to be exercised which those shall secure to themselves who can prove, by service done, that they are equal to the weight of the sceptre. It is surely a frivolous notion (if any actually entertain it) that the vast and intricate machinery of the universe, and the profound scheme of God's government, are now soon to reach a resting-place, where nothing more shall remain to active spirits, through an eternity, but recollections of labour, anthems of praise, and inert repose. No idea can do more violence to all the principles on which we reason than this does.

Not less unreasonable is it to imagine that the future government of God, instead of being carried forward, as now, by independent and intelligent agencies, shall proceed by the interposition of his immediate power, while the creatures stand aloof, as idle spectators of omnipotence. Some such baring of the arm of the Almighty may indeed mark particular epochs of the moral system, and may come in to terminate one cycle of government, and to introduce another; but to suppose that the ordinary movements shall be of this kind, is a notion devoid of probability, and derogatory, as we must think, to the divine wisdom. If the two schemes were hypothetically stated, namely, that of a government by immediate interpositions of omnipotence, and that of a government the ends of which should be secured by an all-pervading adjustment of the free agencies of intelligent beings, as well good as evil, the latter scheme must at once be preferred, as the best adapted to display infinite wisdom, and so to compel all at length to acknowledge and to bow to the Sovereign Excellence, which, out of the refractory and chaotic materials of the moral world, has educed, not merely a predetermined result, but a good result—a result worthy of wisdom, rectitude, and benevolence.

It would not be very difficult to show in what way, probably, every one of the active qualities, moral and intellectual, which are now in training, may come into exercise within a future system, even although that system should exclude the necessities and pains of the present state. All the practical skill we acquire in managing affairs, all the versatility, the sagacity, the calculation of chances, the patience and assiduity, the promptitude and facility, as well as the higher virtues, which we are learning every day, may well find scope in a world such as is rationally anticipated, when we think of heaven as the stage of life that is next to follow the discipline of earth.

Thus far we have thought of the future exercise of the active virtues, in relation chiefly to personal interest. But if we duly consider the force, and the probable issue of those intense emotions of good-will to others, and of compassion towards the wretched, which are now at work within generous bosoms, and which yet are very slenderly or partially brought into play at present, we shall be impelled to think, nay, confidently to conclude, that these dispositions are, in this world, only bursting the husk, and germinating, underground, in preparation for free expansion and fructification in the beams of a warmer sun. With no other indication of the destinies of the universe than what may be furnished by those swelling emotions of pity that are now working, pent up, in tender and noble hearts, we should hardly fear to err in assuming that a sphere will at length open upon such spirits, wherein they shall find millions needing to be governed, taught, rescued, and led forward, from a worse to a better, or from a lower to a higher state of life.

With the material universe before us, such as we *now* know it to be in extent, our conjectures need not be put to much difficulty in imagining what may be wanting to fill out our idea of a future economy, where, what now we so ardently long to do, but are baffled in attempting, shall be practicable, and shall offer itself to our hands, on the largest scale, and where the utmost which the most ambitious charity could desire shall actually be granted. In admitting suppositions of this kind, we are not compelled to trench at all upon any article of our Christian belief, or to bring into question any of our serious convictions concerning the firmness of the divine administration of human affairs. All we do is, on the strength of the principle of analogy, to conclude that a preparation of feeling shall find its expansion, and that a commencement of moral qualities shall have its end and completion. If the instinctive yearnings of the human mind after immortality are allowed to furnish a strong presumptive evidence (revelation apart) of the life to come, so assuredly must the instinctive and vehement desire of the noblest minds to diffuse truth and happiness, and to relieve misery, be allowed to foreshow what is actually to be the employment of such minds. If there be any soundness in the one sort of argument, there must be an equal force in the other. For it is quite as easy to suppose that the Creator should have imparted to human nature the notion and the desire of immortality without intending to realize it, as that he should have instilled a boundless benevolence, which is to have no more opportunity to express itself than it may chance to meet with in the present state: and how often are such opportunities almost wholly withheld! Some there are, who would barely care to live at all, if they may have no sphere of charity, and whose notion of substantial happiness consists mainly, or entirely, in the idea of wide and successful beneficence.

We conclude then, first, that the substitution of spiritual for animal corporeity leaves the probabilities of increased happiness or misery evenly balanced; secondly, that the transition of human nature from one mode of physical existence to another shall not *of itself* affect the moral sentiments or personal character; thirdly, that emotions and passions, whether benign or not, shall probably be far more intense in the future state than they are at present; and fourthly, that the active principles of our nature, and our intellectual habits, such as they are now in training, shall, in the future life, come into actual use.

CHAPTER XV.

INTRODUCTORY TO SOME CONJECTURES CONCERNING THE RELATION OF THE MATERIAL TO THE SPIRITUAL UNIVERSE.

The above-named conclusions bring our theory of another life to its intended issue, so far as it is to be drawn from a consideration of the present structure of human nature, bodily and mental; but it remains (if there be grounds for doing so) to pursue the indication of facts and of analogies, bearing upon the great scheme, material and spiritual, in the midst of which this, our human nature, is evolving its destinies. In other words, we now wish to give some sort of hypothetical consistency to the several elements of our conceptions, in thinking of a future life, as related to the theatre upon which it is to take its course.

Allusion has been made above to the extent of the material universe, and to our actual knowledge of its vastness; nor perhaps is it to be avoided in the present state of astronomical science, that we should desire, in some manner, to connect our belief concerning the destinies of the human family, with our conceptions of the great system, in the midst of which we are moving. None need apprehend ill consequences as likely to result from such endeavours, who have well learned the prime principle of sound philosophy, namely, never to allow even the most plausible and pleasing conjectures to unsettle our conviction of truths which have been established independently, and which rest upon positive evidence. If there are any who will frown upon all such attempts, as not merely fruitless, but reprehensible and dangerous, they would do well to consider that, although individually, and from the particular constitution of their minds, they may find it very easy to abstain from every path of excursive meditation, it is not so with others, who, almost irresistibly, are borne forward toward the widest fields of contemplation—a region from which the human mind is not to be barred, and which is better taken possession of by those who reverently bow to the authority of Christianity, than left open to impiety.

Fully persuaded of the certainty, and the awful reality of the Christian revelation, and prepared, always, to surrender whatever can be shown not to comport with its decisions, and kept in check by those methods of reasoning which the modern physical logic supplies, we advance a step or two, in anxious curiosity, as if to survey the vast realm of the universal King, and to ask what may be the relation in which we stand, or are ultimately to stand to our fellow-subjects of this unbounded empire

Is it for no purpose that the human eye is permitted to traverse the immensity of space? or is it with no moral intention that, now at length, and after five thousand years of labour and conjecture, a true notion of the material universe has been attained, and has become diffused among all ranks, in every civilized community? At last, and in these times, man knows his place in the heavens, and is taught to think justly of the relative importance of the planet which has given him birth. During a long course of centuries it was to little purpose, or to little in relation to man, that the emanations of light had passed and repassed, from side to side of the universe; for until of late, that is to say, the last three centuries, it was not certainly known whether this earth (itself unexplored) were not the only scene of life, and whether the sun, the stars, and the planets, were any thing more than brilliants, floating in an upper ether.

A revolution in the intellectual world, affecting our notions and modes of thinking on many subjects, has been gradually produced by the discoveries, and by the full establishment of the modern astronomy;* and it may well be conjectured that certain momentous consequences of this advancement of science have not as yet been developed. Minds unfriendly to all religion, and to Christianity especially, confidently anticipate the shaking of popular belief by this very means; and it is just possible that a course of conduct on the part of the adherents of revelation, analogous to that which was pursued by the Romish church toward the first promulgators of true notions of the universe, might produce very lamentable effects upon the religious convictions of many. But that any such course should actually be adopted is barely to be supposed; on the contrary, it may be expected that, by the turning of thoughtful minds, again and again to the subject, a happy coalescence of all great truths —physical and religious, will at length be brought about, and such a combination of them effected as shall tend powerfully to enhance the serious influence of the latter, and accelerate the general prevalence of piety—the piety of the Scriptures.

When once religious principles have taken full possession, as well of the understanding as of the moral faculties, we may with perfect tranquillity pursue speculations of any kind that seem likely to enlarge our conceptions of the sys-

* The eloquent and important Astronomical Discourses of Dr. Chalmers ought here to be named, as having given as well an impulse, as a direction, to religious meditation, in connection with subjects of this class.

tem within which we are moving. Such speculations can never either rob us of our firm property in the highest truths, or disturb our enjoyment of them; but they may serve to deepen, tenfold, our ordinary impression of the awful import of those truths. Christianity is not endangered, but it may be the more forcibly impressed upon all minds, in consequence of the converging of truths, from all sides, upon the one practical inference, which should impel us, without delay, to conclude friendship with the Creator and Ruler of all worlds.

All truths shall at length be one; there shall be one philosophy, and one religion, nor is it difficult to trace the actual progress of the human mind toward this desirable consummation. Would it not be unbecoming for religious men to attribute to chance those signal improvements in the mechanic arts which have given certainty to our modern astronomy? Without the aid of the elaborate instruments of observation, now in use, the calculations and theories of abstract science could never have been put to the proof of a comparison with facts, and therefore could never have possessed the authority of actual science. Far from being inclined to boast, in these instances of the skill and sagacity of man, we devoutly admire that providence of God, which, after delays so long, has at length conferred upon mankind the means of obtaining a just, though incomplete knowledge of his vast dominion! and we now look with confidence for such further extensions of our philosophy as are needed for bringing all our notions from whatever source derived, into a happy unison.

The moment chosen for imparting Christianity to the world, was that in which learning and civilization, in all kinds, had reached their highest point, and were more widely diffused than at any preceding time; nor is it unreasonable to suppose that the happy moment predestined for the general promulgation and triumph of this same Christianity shall be that in which the substantial and well-ascertained sciences, having passed their season of debate and conjecture, shall be advancing, not as heretofore by revolutions and shocks, but by continual accessions; and when, having reached the popular mind, all men shall be prepared to admit, and to feel the force of, the great moral inference that is yet to be drawn from them. This sort of coalescence of great principles is not indeed to be expected to take place in a moment, or as the consequence of the discoveries or reasonings of any one mind; but it may draw on by insensible means, and be promoted by this, that, and the other, unnoticed agency. In expectation of it, we may be feeling our way onward a little, in advance of our actual position; and this must be done by entertaining such hypotheses as seem consonant with known facts, and which hypotheses will open up untrodden ground, and enable us to improve every new indication of things as yet unknown.

And in this place again, the author must urge the reader always to bear in mind what are, and what are not, the legitimate uses of hypothesis, in philosophical pursuits. An hypothesis then, however plausible, is never to be ranged along with truths; or to be classed with things proved; nor suffered to fill a vacuity in our systems, until it may be displaced by a better theory, or by ascertained facts. This was the fallacious practice of the ancient theorists; but it is now exploded. Hypothesis is *a preparation for reasoning*—a preparation which saves time, and prevents the overlooking of any facts that may hereafter present themselves, and which, should they occur, will instantly be noted and turned to the best account, as tending either to confirm, or to explode the supposition already advanced. To use a familiar illustration, well-devised hypotheses are labelled drawers, always ready for the reception of facts fortuitously presented. In those branches of science which are open to experiment, it is hypothesis that leads the way, in every instance.

In relation to our immediate subject, namely, the connection between the scheme of the material universe, and the destinies of the human, and of other rational orders, it may be stated as *possible* that some of those revolutions and catastrophes which have, not unfrequently, in the course of ages, been observed to take place in the remoter regions of the heavens, such as the sudden combustion of stars, and their extinction, or the appearance of new stars, may, any day, take place nearer home, and within such distances as should allow of their being distinctly observed. Now, on the supposition of such an event, it is possible that new views of the constitution and destinies of the universe might be thereby suggested; and in that case, the having entertained more than one hypothesis on the subject, would be a preparation for turning the actual facts to the best account; and would also quicken and animate our observation.

There are two facts, each of which is significant in relation to our present subject, and of which the first has long been understood, while the latter (only of late ascertained) is every day receiving new illustrations, namely, That our planet is, in no sense, of primary importance in the general system, or entitled, by its magnitude, or by its position, or by its constitution, to be considered as exerting any peculiar influence over others. This knowledge of our real place and value in the universe is a very important consequence of our modern astronomy; nor should it ever be lost sight of, in any of our speculations. But then it is also now ascertained that the great laws of our own planet, and of the solar system to which it belongs, prevail in all other, and the most remote systems, so as to make the visible universe, in the strictest sense, ONE SYSTEM—indicating, beyond a doubt, one origin, and showing the presence of one Controlling Power. Thus the law of gravitation, with all the various conditions it implies, and the laws of light, are demonstrated to be in operation in regions incalculably remote; and just so far as the physical constitution of the other planets of our own system can be either traced, or reasonably conjectured, it appears that, amid many diversities of constitution, the same great principles prevail in all. Hence it appears that our further conjectures, concerning the existence of sentient and rational life, in other worlds, are borne out by every sort of analogy, abstract and physical: and then this same rule of analogy impels us to suppose that rational and moral agents, in whatever world found, and whatever diversity of form may distinguish them, would be such as that we should soon feel our selves at home in their society, and able to confer with them—to communicate knowledge to them, and to receive knowledge from them. Neither truth nor virtue can be local; nor can there be any wisdom and goodness in one planet which is not wisdom and goodness in every other.

We must believe that rational and moral intercourse would be practicable, even where physical correspondence might be impossible; for while our animal organization demands a specific temperament of the elements, and can act only within a very narrow circle, the intellectual faculties, on the contrary, and the moral emotions, are capable of adapting themselves to every imaginable variety of circumstance, and can always embrace, and coalesce with, universal principles. Hence it might well happen that, in worlds where we could neither respire, nor stand upright, nor endure the heat, or the cold, in worlds where our bodies would instantly congeal, or would as suddenly be evaporized, we might yet, if freed from these accidental organic difficulties, make ourselves one with the rational tribes of those worlds. For the purpose therefore of bringing all such tribes into correspondence, and of blending them in a social economy, nothing would be necessary but to give them, severally, a corporeal constitution independent of all telluric peculiarities of temperature, density, and atmospheric influence.

Our involuntary impressions that other worlds differ vastly from our own, in the modes of life they support, is so strong that, perhaps, if transported to some neighbouring planet, we should feel more amazement in meeting there with beings precisely like ourselves, than in encountering the strangest and most grotesque forms that have ever been dreamed of. Yet, whether brethren in figure and countenance, or not, it is not possible to doubt that all, in all worlds, who are capable of reason, and who are open to moral affections, are tending, though at different rates, toward the same eternal truths, and are made amenable to one law, and are submitted to one principle of government.

But shall not those who are brethren come some day to be companions, or at least to know of each other's existence and well-being? Many reasons may be adduced, strongly tending to suggest the belief that all races, holding to the same principles of reason and virtue, shall at some, perhaps remote era of their existence, be brought to compare histories, and so to receive severally the benefit derivable from their common experience. The present construction of the material universe is plainly marked with the intention to prohibit intercourse; but this vast framework is a means only to a higher end; and in the twinkling of an eye, it may give place to another order of things; or another order of things may, even now, although to us occult, be actually in play, as we shall presently have to state.

The principle of insulation may long prevail, and yet may at length give way to a higher and better principle—that of communion, and of free intercourse. Such a change has actually come about within the human family. During many centuries the several tribes of men—remote in position, knew little or nothing of each other, nor did they maintain any extended or useful correspondence. Extensive empires remained secluded, during their long terms of wealth and power, and passed away, leaving barely a memorial of their existence. But now, at length, all nations are drawing close the bonds of brotherhood: there are no longer any vast unexplored regions, imprisoning their inhabitants; commerce, the spirit of adventure, and the spirit of benevolent enterprise, are fast connecting all with all; and it is now within the prospect of the human family to constitute—not indeed one political structure, but one family, cherishing peace from a sense of interest, and from a sense of justice, and mutually promoting the advance, one of another, as the surest means of prospering severally. Intercourse and combination must be the ultimate condition of those who are by nature capable of society. Insulation and variance are unnatural, and must be temporary.

Species that are incapable of entertaining abstract notions, and which therefore are incapable of generalization, and of adapting themselves to any new order of things, and incapable, for the same reason, of progress, can have nothing to gain, either from intercourse with any other species, or from intercourse with new masses of their own species. To such, the results of individual experience can never become additions to a common stock of knowledge or of skill. But herein the human species stand immensely above the level of all the tribes of earth. Except by correspondence with his fellows, man knows nothing, and can do nothing; but by the aid of this correspondence a common fund of intelligence is formed, which does, or which may, constantly increase, and increase without limit. And how much of improvement and of advancement may spring from the residence of an individual only, belonging to a more civilized community, among a less civilized community! Such a visit, made under auspicious circumstances, may have the effect of raising the nations of a continent from semibarbarism to the highest pitch of refinement.

So far as we see or know, correspondence and interchange of knowledge, among races that have made unequal progress, is the one and only means of advancement which the great principles of the intellectual system admit of. The Ruler of all worlds does not *immediately* instruct any in what it most concerns them to know; and because it does not consist with the laws of his government to afford any such direct information, tribes of men remain ignorant, from age to age, of the simplest and most necessary truths. But it *does* consist with these laws to allow the better informed to mix with the ignorant, and to diffuse the benefits of their acquirements.

It may reasonably be doubted whether the highest and the most occult truth are in any way at all to be apprehended and made intelligible, except as they may slowly be gathered, in the way of induction, from a copious acquaintance with facts within the circle of which those abstruse principles may be seen to work themselves out. The history of only any one rational family cannot, probably, in the nature of things, carry us further than to the extent of a very partial knowledge of the laws of the moral universe. But the history and experience of *one other* such family, would doubtless serve to expand vastly our conceptions, and to place the whole of our previously acquired moral notions in a new light, or to bring them into a new relative position. If permitted to take our standing at *two* distant points, in the great circle of the social system, we should gain a parallax, and thenceforward should have the means of measuring the distance between ourselves and the centre of all with some certainty.

The advantage accruing from correspondence with *one* other race would no doubt be proportionately multiplied in extending our acquaintance with many others. And yet even this accumulation of knowledge might long fall short of its consummation, and we might be conscious of a want of symmetry in our notions without the power to supply the deficiency. But in some remote quarter of the universe, and perhaps in some obscure world, there may have been a train of events going on, altogether peculiar, and such that this single history would serve to develop the MASTER PRINCIPLE of the divine government, and would supply the the key to all difficulties. Until this one race has been conversed with, and its history perused, all races, perhaps, might vainly ponder the reasons of the procedures of the Supreme Power; nevertheless the actual publication of this clearing instance may depend (as we speak) upon an accident, and may be delayed, through cycles of ages.

Our general (and hypothetic) conclusion is this, and it may be expressed in two propositions, namely, first, That as beings endowed with the faculty of abstraction and generalization are thereby made capable of indefinite improvement through the means of intercourse, individually, and also species with species, such intercourse is to be regarded as probably coming within the ultimate intention of the divine administration towards them; for otherwise these intellectual powers would fall short of what is plainly their highest use; and secondly, That, as a comprehensive knowledge of the principles of the moral system is probably not to be obtained in any other manner than through a process of extensive induction from actual facts, even the most virtuous and rational minds must for ever remain bewildered and distressed, in relation to the divine government, unless intercourse at large with other races of moral beings should be allowed in a future stage of our existence.

We have then before us, on the one hand, the very strong abstract probability that a race capable, by the faculties conferred upon it, of indefinite advancement, and of rising to the very highest range of generalization, shall at length come into correspondence with other rational orders, and perhaps with all. On the other hand, we have, not merely the instinctive expectation of another and a higher mode of existence, but the divinely authenticated assurance that the rational universe comprises a lower and a higher species of corporeity, and that a transition from the lower to the higher actually awaits the human family. Now when these two principles are combined, it is almost inevitable that we should indulge some conjectures concerning the material universe, considered as the theatre of a great intellectual economy, and as framed mainly, though not exclusively, for the purpose of giving effect to the laws and ultimate intention of the moral world.

The various conjectures which offer themselves to our choice on this ground, seem reducible to three distinct suppositions, each of which is sustained by its own degree of probability; and, perhaps, after stating them in order, we may be inclined to think that a combination of the three is more likely to be near the truth than any one of them by itself.

CHAPTER XVI.

THE FIRST CONJECTURE CONCERNING THE MATERIAL UNIVERSE VIEWED AS THE THEATRE OF AN INTELLECTUAL SYSTEM.

Having before us the assumed, and indeed the attested fact, that there are now in the universe two great classes of rational beings, both corporeal, but the corporeity of the one dissoluble, while that of the other is incorruptible; and then taking a glance at the great sidereal economy, consisting as it does of two classes of bodies, the one subordinate to, and wholly dependent upon the other; and this other apparently adapted to a much higher mode of existence than the former, the supposition offers itself that, while the planets are the places of animal and corruptible organization, and the schools of initiation to all rational orders, the sun, of each such system, is the home of the higher and ultimate spiritual corporeity, and the centre of assembly for those who have already passed their preliminary era upon the lower ranges of creation.

The supposition that the sun of each system is the mere lamp and hearth of the planetary band, or only the swivel of its revolutions, is surely not to be admitted. This were much the same thing as if, in viewing from a hamlet on a mountain side the distant metropolis of an empire, the gilded domes of which are refulgent in the beams of noon, one were to imagine that the great world is not in that metropolis, but in the dozen of shepherds' huts, among which one stands.

Recent discoveries make it more than barely probable

that the solar surface, shrouded from the vertical rays of the upper and phosphorescent atmosphere, by an intermediate nebulous stratum, dense enough to moderate the intensity, as well of light as of heat, may sustain life not less readily than the surface of Mercury; perhaps more so; in fact, the temperature may be lower on the former than it is on the latter. But even this probability is not necessary to our conjecture, inasmuch as the assumption that any intensity of light and heat, beyond a certain degree, must be incompatible with life, is altogether gratuitous.

But we must not fail here to point out one circumstance in which the solar surface is distinguished from the planetary surfaces, considered as adapted to the support of corporeal life—a circumstance so highly significant and remarkable, as almost in itself to involve the very points of difference which we have supposed to distinguish animal from spiritual corporeity; and it is this—That whereas the surfaces of the planets, and all the vegetable and animal species thereon subsisting, are liable to an alternation of heat and cold, of light and darkness, and therefore live through returning periods of *excitement* and of *repose*, and this both diurnal and annual, the surface of the sun, with the species it may support, is uniformly exposed to its maximum of heat and light. That is to say, the solar tribes, vegetable and animal, instead of passing, at regular intervals, from stimulus to exhaustion—from activity to rest, sustain (if we should say *sustain*) an equable impulse, from the external elements. But stimulus and excitement are conditions of existence which imply inertia and decomposition; and where there is no such alternation of action and inaction, we may reasonably assume that there is neither a spending of forces nor a dissolution of structure. The *physical idea* of solar life, followed out on the principle of the unintermitted intensity of light and heat, and implying also the constant action of all powers dependent thereupon, will amount to little less than to a conception of incorruptibility and immortality.

To exclude objections against our present hypothesis, it should be stated that, by the revolution of the sun upon its axis, and by the inclination of its axis, all parts of its surface are exposed to our observation; while at the same time, by the frequent breaking out of spots in all parts of its equatorial zone, the physical constitution of the whole is, to a certain extent, laid before us; nor is it hardly possible to suppose any thing else than that the solar surface, although there may be, and probably are, *irregular* variations of temperature upon it, arising from the accumulation or the dispersion of the intermediate reflecting stratum, is yet everywhere, and always, acted upon by so much of the phosphorescent fluid as penetrates that stratum; nor can it be believed that there is any thing resembling a regular alternation of light and darkness—of cold and heat. The variations may be such as we are conscious of during a summer's day, but not such as distinguish midnight from noon, or winter from summer.

The permanence, or incorruptibility of vegetable and animal life, on the solar surface, might indeed be inferred, by contrast, from a consideration of what we see to be involved, as it respects both kinds of organization, in the diurnal and annual alternations of light and temperature. An argument of this sort can here be only very briefly stated, and must then be left with the reader, to admit or reject it as he may please. The supposition may be placed on different grounds, as thus:—It is certain that a perpetual day, and a perpetual summer (other consequences not now regarded) would very quickly exhaust the forces of all terrestrial orders, both vegetable and animal, and must bring all kinds of life, as constituted on this planet, to a speedy close. Life, constituted so as to endure an unvaried intensity of light and heat, must be framed on a principle the very opposite of that which here prevails; and is this opposite principle any other than that of incorruptibility, and of an internal force, not dependent upon excitements, or renewable by an extraneous pabulum?

Or thus—and to confine our attention to the human system: The relative forces of the mind and body, or what may be called the corporeal equipoise, is such, as that the voluntary animal functions are never found to be commensurate with the mental activity; and the disparity between the two is made up by imposing upon the mind a long, and a frequently recurring season of inaction, in sleep, during which, being restrained from making any demand upon the corporeal mechanism, the latter replenishes its stock of excitability, which again, and very soon, is to be spent. There is therefore at present a want of balance between the two combined powers—a want supplied by means of the collapse or confinement of the power which would outrun its colleague. But an essential inequality of this sort can never be so exactly adjusted as that the one force will not, by a little, surpass the other; and this daily increment, small as it may be in each instance, must at length overthrow the equipoise entirely;—so that the defective power will at last give way, and be broken up. We consider it as certain that death must ensue, sooner or later, in the case of any being whose constitution combines two unequal forces, the inequality of which has to be adjusted by imposing frequent cessations upon the stronger of the two. The life therefore of all planetary species, that is to say, of all species exposed to the alternations of light and darkness, and which, in conformity with this alternation, live by turns, waking and sleeping, is a life necessarily tending to dissolution. But the solar species are not exposed to any such alternation, and as they live without repose, they may be, and probably are—immortal.

Yet let this incorruptibility and immortality be thought of apart from those religious associations which the words are apt to call up. Incorruptibility and immortality we are used to think of only in connection with the Christian hope of a better life, as the reward of the good. But the exemption of life from corruption and dissolution may *now* be enjoyed, as a common thing, within the limits of the system of which our globe is a member. Disorganization and death are accidents of life—accidents, unavoidable indeed upon the planetary surface; but not so perhaps upon the solar: and upon the latter it may be as unnatural to die, as upon the former it is unnatural long to live.

Moreover, as we seldom if ever think of incorruptibility and immortality except as the inheritance of human nature, and of the higher orders of beings, we may be led, by a conjecture such as the one now in hand, to enlarge the range of our conceptions of the material universe, and to indulge the bright and happy supposition of fair fields of life and bliss, in all gradations, from the lowest species to the highest; and all freed from the law of preying one upon another, and of death. With these ideas before us, and on the belief that solar life, as compared with planetary life, is of this better and higher sort, let the universe be contemplated, and let us admit the exhilarating conception that the millions upon millions of suns filling the immensity of space, are spheres, not only of perpetual day (as is manifest) but of undecaying life! During this our planetary stage of existence, we have our lodging in the murky suburbs of creation; but yet a distant view of royal palaces and gardens of delight is afforded to us, nor are we left without significant indications of what is there to be found.

There may be those perhaps, who would resent it as a trivial and unworthy supposition, that a heaven can be any thing except a grave convocation of rational worshippers, convened in perpetuity upon ethereal clouds, and occupied for ever in one and the same ecstatic manner. But having this mundane portion of the creation under our eyes, we are impelled to conceive very differently of the universe and the principles which will be found to prevail throughout it. Is it not the style and mode of the Supreme Creative Intelligence to take the widest range, and to include endless varieties and interminable gradations of power and faculty in the circle of his works? Nothing of that stern pursuit of single purposes which belongs to ourselves, when intently moved, seems to attach to the creation. Man is absorbed in his immediate object, if that object be important in his view; but God is always at leisure, and while accomplishing the stupendous purposes of the moral and spiritual scheme, finds time and means for replenishing the elements with insect life, and for decorating all surfaces with gay vegetation.

How very far is it from being true, for example, within the vegetable kingdom, that no ends are kept in view beyond the mere subserviency of each order and species to the uses of the orders next above it! On the contrary, there is everywhere a free exuberance, a copiousness, a versatility, and an unchecked love of embellishment and beauty, such as put shame on the supposition that the rule of a dry utility has been followed as the law of the creation. In truth, the *uses* which any one species may be thought to subserve appear, most often, to be rather adjunctive than principal, and seem an accidental circumstance, thrown in upon the main design. But if a rule so rich and free be indeed the law of the Creative Power, it will show itself in all worlds; and most of all in those warm and resplendent spheres where the elementary conditions are such as peculiarly to favour its development.

The prejudices (not perhaps very culpable) of a somewhat morbid spirituality, might perhaps lead us to distaste the animated world around us, as God's work,* and impel us to be scandalized at some of its conditions; and thus it is conceivable that the realities of the upper world, when first they open upon minds imbued with prepossessions of this kind, may excite a recoil and an amazement, such as may try the principles of piety. Let it just be conceived of that spirit, born and trained in some pure ethereal region of reason and love, and where no orders of creatures inferior to itself had ever been seen or heard of, and where the attributes of Deity, in the most abstract mode of their expression, had alone been contemplated; let it be supposed that such a spirit were told it should be taken where the Creative Power had put itself forth in quite another manner; and then that it should be brought, without further preparation, to this planet of ours, and be placed in the depth of a teeming wilderness of the torrid zone, and there left to examine, not only the luxuriance and beauty of the vegetable orders, but the forms, instincts, habits, of the insect tribes, and of the reptiles, the birds, the quadrupeds,

* The ancient Manichean doctrine gave a bold and distinct expression to this order of prejudices; and it was plainly avowed, by the authors of that system, that they could not admit the present world, with its animal species, to be the work of supreme benevolence, wisdom, and purity. Nothing is more dangerous than to indulge notions which tend to make us think our tastes and principles more refined and elevated than those of the Creator and Ruler of the universe. Something of this infatuation very commonly besets ardent and abstracted minds.

which people the sultry forest. Now although ourselves, with the preparation we have gone through, are in a position to admire these various orders, and in fact to derive from this very source, a main portion of the evidence of our natural theology, may it not readily be imagined that, to a pure spirit, such a one as we have here supposed, the effect of the exhibition, and of all its details, would be to generate a sort of wonder, not unmixed with perplexity, or even distress?

Something perhaps analogous to this may await the human mind when, after having entertained abstract notions of the Divine Nature, and in forming which we have consulted our own narrow conceptions of what *ought to be*, rather than coolly considered what *is*, we are introduced into another domain of God's universal empire, where, instead of the meagre and colourless outline which had stood before our poor imaginations, we behold the rich and various products of the Infinite Intelligence; all indeed bright and good;—but good in a sense related to infinite, not to finite reason. Now the products of infinite power and absolute wisdom not merely surpass our powers and our notions in *dimensions*, but in *kind* also, and in their leading principles. That is to say, the universe is not only more vast than we can measure or conceive of; but it is probably more various than we are apt, or willing to imagine; and moreover it involves and exhibits motives or reasons of procedure, such as would by no means have occurred to us, as natural, or as abstractedly fit, considered in relation to what we assume concerning the divine attributes.

Now to revert a moment to our present conjecture, concerning the construction and intention of the visible universe, there are some perhaps, who, in the loftiness of their religious conceptions, would resent, as totally unworthy and grovelling, the supposition that the sun of our own system, and that each sun of each system, is a home and heaven to its planetary tribes, and that this solar heaven is stocked with various orders of sentient beings. Let then the supposition be discarded by those who distaste it; and assuredly no value is attached to it, otherwise than so far as it may serve a purpose which is in some degree important, namely, that of tending to bring our religious conceptions into definite alliance with the real world, and with nature, and to break up, a little, those vague and powerless notions which place our religious expectations at a dim remoteness from whatever is substantial and effective. Let us try to persuade ourselves that the future and unseen world, with all its momentous transactions, is as simply natural and true, as is this homely world of land and water, trees and houses, with which we have now to do.

The opinion has been often advanced, and seems to be gathering strength, that the sun and other stars, that is to say, the entire celestial system visible to us, is in actual movement, in one direction; or that it is revolving around a common centre. But who shall calculate the dimensions of a central mass such as may be adequate to sustain the revolutions of all suns and worlds? This opinion is just named in this place, that we may point out its relation to our present conjecture.—If each sun be a place of assembly, and a home of immortality to the rational planetary tribes of its system, the vast world around which all suns are supposed to be revolving, may be the home of a still higher order of life, and the theatre of a still more comprehensive convocation of the intellectual community.

There remains however one point of geological and mathematical speculation which ought to find a place in our present conjecture. It is then believed, on the ground of a calculation of forces, that our own planet, and others, are not solid globes, but hollow spheres, or spherical shells, including a perhaps irregular, but vast cavity, and this cavity occupied by some elastic fluid or gas. Does then this inner cavern subserve any purpose connected with the destinies of those who are treading, or who have already trodden the surface? or has the dim abyss sentient tribes of its own? We do not propose to pursue the conjecture; but yet we must just place it in apposition with that very ancient, and, may we not say, Biblical classification of all intelligent orders, under the three heads of celestials, terrestrials, and subterraneans; or, as they are designated by St. Paul, the *ἐπουράνιοι*, the *ἐπίγειοι*, and the *καταχθόνιοι*.*

This classification of intelligent beings, it must be confessed, by no means corresponds with the distribution we are most accustomed to think of, namely, that which arranges all rational beings into the three classes of the inhabitants of heaven, holy and happy—the inhabitants of earth, who are on their probation—and the condemned and infernal spirits. For, on the one hand, certain classes of the

* Philippians ii. 10; where the universal sovereignty of the Son of God is distinctly stated as including the three great orders of the intelligent economy—the heavenly, the earthly, and the subterrene. This passage should be compared with Romans xiv. 9; where the course passed through by the Saviour of men is declared to have had a reference to the due exercise of his destined sway over the dead and the living: or, according to the opinion which the apostle may be held to adopt and sanction, over the inhabitants of the superficial world, and of the abyss, or central cavern. Again, we should refer to Revelation v. 3 and 13, where (which is especially to be noted) the designation of the *καταχθόνιοι* is varied, and they are described as those who are *ὑποκάτω τῆς γῆς*, and where, moreover, they are associated with those who gladly render "blessing and honour, and glory and power, to Him that sitteth on the throne, and unto the Lamb."

celestials, the ἐπουράνιοι, are spoken of by St. Paul as being in open opposition to the divine government,* while, on the other hand, the infernals, or the inhabitants of the nether region, or of hades, are represented as the subjects of the Messiah's kingly function; and also (as in the passages mentioned in the note) as joining with the celestials and the terrestrials, in an anthem of praise, to God and the Lamb.

This, however, is not the place for pursuing any Biblical, or properly theological question. All we now attempt is just to state the fact that there is an apparent correspondence between the Biblical classification of the intellectual community, and our hypothesis concerning the three modes of existence which seem to be provided for in the structure of the material universe. If we rightly understand the affirmations and the intimations of the inspired writers, man is destined to pass through three stages of life; the first, upon the surface of the earth, and subject to the conditions of animal organization; the second, if we do not mistake the apostolic words, "under the earth," and in a transition-form, of attenuated and inactive corporeity; and the third, and ultimate, in a region of power, incorruptibility, and full activity. This our first conjecture then, concerning the material universe, considered as the frame of the intellectual economy, brings the visible and the invisible worlds into conjunction in that manner which, at a glance, offers itself to our acceptance as obvious and natural. Nevertheless, whatever may be the pretensions of this hypothesis, we advance it as nothing more than a conjecture; and go on to state another, which may equally well consist with what we are bound to believe, on better evidence.

* Ephesians vi. 12.

CHAPTER XVII.

THE SECOND CONJECTURE.

But we are now to hold in abeyance, or altogether to exclude the hypothesis above stated, concerning the material universe, as apparently adapted to sustain three orders of intelligent beings; and on the contrary, shall assume that planets and suns alike, and all worlds, visible and palpable, are the theatres of animal life merely; and that whatever species may inhabit these spheres, they are all subject to decay and corruption.

This supposed; then our second conjecture is—That, within the field occupied by the visible and ponderable universe, and on all sides of us, there is existing and moving another element, fraught with another species of life—corporeal indeed, and various in its orders, but not open to the cognizance of those who are confined to the conditions of animal organization—not to be seen, not to be heard, not to be felt by man. We here assume the abstract probability that our five modes of perception are partial, not universal means of knowing what may be around us; and that, as the physical sciences furnish evidence of the presence and agency of certain powers of nature which entirely elude the senses, except in some of their remote effects, so are we denied the right of concluding that we are conscious of all real existences within our sphere.

Something must presently be said with the view of loosening the firm natural prejudice which impels us to conclude that nothing *corporeal* can elude our senses; but first let the conjecture now in hand be itself distinctly stated.

There prevails, throughout the system of nature, a pervading of the dense elements by the less dense, or the fluid, or the gaseous. Thus all solid bodies are penetrated, either by humidity, or by the elastic gases, or by the imponderable elements—light, heat, electricity, magnetism. Again, fluids are, in like manner, pervious to other fluids, with which they may combine; and also to elastic gases, and to the elements just named; and in its turn, the rarest gas is traversed by, and commingled with, other elastic bodies, and by light, heat, electricity, or magnetism. In some cases the pervading element affects the element pervaded; thus heat expands metals, and at a certain point fuses them; and so galvanism puts into activity the chemical affinities of many solids and fluids. But in other cases the pervading element takes its course through the pervading body without giving any indication, *upon that body*, of its presence, or of its passage. Thus electricity may pass, unnoticed, through a perfectly conducting substance; and the magnetic attraction takes its way through intervening bodies, which in no sensible manner it disturbs; and thus too does the power of gravitation take effect at the greatest distances, without rendering itself sensible in any other manner than that of effecting an approximation of masses.

But is this constant principle of the visible world, showing itself as it does, in a thousand modes around us—is it exhausted and done with, in the instances which our modern physical discoveries have brought to light? We should confidently assume the contrary, and believe nothing less than that it has a still further and higher play in relation to the sentient and intellectual universe. That is to say, we insist upon the abstract probability of the existence, on all sides of us, of an invisible element, sustaining its own species of beings—some perhaps as slenderly endowed with rational faculties as are the insect tribes of earth, and others, in gradation, rising to the highest pitch of intelligence and moral dignity :—some accountable and immortal; others ephemeral, and prompted only by instincts.

Our present conjecture reaches to the extent of supposing that, within the space encircled by the sidereal revolutions, there exists and moves a second universe, not less real than the one we are at present conversant with; a universe elaborate in structure, and replete with life—life, agitated by momentous interests, and perhaps by frivolous interests; a universe conscious perhaps of the material spheres, or unconscious of them, and firmly believing (as we do) *itself* to be the only reality. Our planets in their courses do not perforate the walls of this invisible creation; our suns do not scorch its plains, for the two collocated systems are not connected by any immediate relationship.

The fact is before our eyes, that the Creator works on a scale which, in a mathematical sense, is greater than can be computed or imagined; and it is evident too that he advances toward the infinite in both directions; that is to say, toward the infinitely great, and the infinitely small. We see also that the utmost range of variety, both in principle and in form, is taken in the construction of the sentient system; and that the physical capacity of our own world for sustaining life is indefinitely enlarged by the suffusion of element upon element, and each peopled with its animated orders. We are therefore almost compelled to entertain the belief that the very same law goes on, as far as it can go on; and therefore must suppose that the invisible orders are not less numerous than the visible. Our sight and hearing and touch make us acquainted with a certain stage of the creation, informing us of whatever is moving upon that stage; and there they stop. But is it to be thought that the eye of man is the measure of the Creator's power?—and has he created nothing which he has not exposed to our senses? The contrary seems much more than barely possible;—ought we not to think it almost certain?

In stating the conjecture that the two worlds, the visible and the invisible, may coexist within the same space, and yet be unconscious of each other, and not related by any affinities, we assume what is abstractedly possible; but we should unquestionably consider as more probable the supposition that the two orders of existence, whether consciously or not, on *both* sides, are, nevertheless, really related one to the other, and that in fact the one is an after-stage to the other. Here again we have recourse to the aid that is furnished in so many cases by actual analogies.

Let it be considered, then, that while among many of the terrestrial orders there is seen a tendency to advance from a lower to a higher mode of existence, and in all a progression from the germ to the bud, and from the bud to the fruit, and from the embryo to the perfect animal; and while the human mind plainly indicates this same law in its desire of advancement, in the general sentiment of hope—the most permanent impulse of our nature, and in its aspirations after immortality;—while, we say, there is this upward and onward tendency in the sentient and rational world, the desires and propensities of all orders impel them also in the contrary direction, and lead all to seek their support, and their gratification, rather beneath than above the level of their natures respectively. This downward tendency is in none so remarkable as in man, who is always seen (powerful corrective influences apart) to seek his happiness in the lower range of gratifications. Man may indeed be destined to rise on the scale of existence; but his actual disposition is to descend. In truth, even when most alive to the elevating motives of intelligence and piety, he is still, by his constitution, and by the necessities of his nature, compelled to converse chiefly with things of a lower order, and to be employed in affairs little accordant, apparently, with his high hopes.

Now something akin to this habit of attachment to things beneath us, may be imagined to affect the invisible orders; and they may, while in progress upward *by destiny*, yet, by actual instinct and impulse be looking downward: they may crowd around the solid masses of the material universe—as birds in migration alight upon the sails and masts of ships in the mid ocean; they may concern themselves with the interests of the planetary tribes, and make themselves parties in the affairs of the lower world. All this may be, without supposing that such supernal beings are actuated by motives altogether unworthy of their rank; for, as we see, entirely apart from any degrading sentiment or sensual taste, the human mind delights itself in the order and beauty of the animal creation, and explores too the constitution of the inanimate world, and finds its recreation among the humblest varieties of the vegetable and animal species, and especially draws the most refined gratifications of its rational tastes from the pursuit of the mere relations of extension and number!

We would not wish to take up a too abstruse idea, and yet are inclined to believe that the very law of dependent natures, which, apart from the constant energy of the Divine will, would reduce them to nothing, actually operates so far as to produce a sort of *intellectual gravitation* of all rational beings toward the lower ranks of existence; so, as that, while there are impulses which are bearing us upward and onward, there is also a uniform tendency downward toward that nihility out of which we sprung.

The conjecture concerning an invisible, sentient, and rational economy, coexistent with the visible universe, and occupying corporeally the same field, comports well enough, as we shall presently see, with the intimations of Scripture regarding the spiritual world; and it consists also with every analogy of the physical system, as understood by modern science; for it has been ascertained—that ponderable elements pervade one the other—that the imponderable pervade all—that different kinds of emanations or vibrations are always passing and repassing, in the most intricate manner, through the same spaces, without in the least degree disturbing each other; and finally, that the most powerful agencies are perpetually in operation around us, of which we have not the faintest perception, and which we detect only by deductions from circuitous experiments. Nevertheless our present conjecture, although so far sustained by various analogies, infringes, we confess, upon certain natural prejudices, which impel us, contrary to the discoveries of science, to assume that when we perceive nothing, there can be nothing near us; or that our senses bear upon, and reveal, all species of corporeal existence that come locally within their range. But a little attention to the subject will suffice to show that this confidence in the extent of our perceptions is nothing better than a prejudice; and that it ought to be set off entirely from our philosophic speculations—it is in fact wholly destitute of foundation in reason.

Nothing is easier than to conceive of human nature as destitute of some one of its faculties of sensation; and in truth the instances are frequent in which one of the senses is totally wanting. Now in such cases the mind is cut off from a possible and real relationship to the material system, and it goes about conversing with the exterior world, utterly unconscious of those properties which should affect the sense it is deprived of; and in such a case, this individual mind, unconscious of light, or of sound, or of taste, or of odours, is in a position precisely analogous to that in which we assume all human minds, within the limits of animal organization, to be; that is to say, surrounded by properties or powers of which they have no kind of perception, and of which they can form no idea.

In relation to smell and taste, which are the least constant, or the most *occasional* of the senses, and the least extensive in their range, we may readily conceive of ourselves as destitute of them; and we may also easily grant that there may be many properties around us, analogous to those made known to us by the gustatory and olfactory organs, of which we have no perception. We never deem it incredible that there may be effluvia, or sapid substances, such as altogether escape detection by the smell and taste; on the contrary, the existence of some such unperceived qualities or substances is very frequently assumed as probable. We are perhaps somewhat less ready to imagine that there may be modulations of the atmosphere of a *kind* which the tympanum does not catch; although it may be proved that the undulations of sound, like other undulations, may so intersect, as to annul each other. It is therefore credible, not only that there may be sounds too delicate to affect the human ear; but also that there may be sounds of a *species* of which the auditory nerve is insensible. Sound is conveyed, not by the atmosphere only; but by every other elastic body; and by some much more rapidly and perfectly than it is by the air: as for example, by water, ice, and timber. In fact, the atmosphere, although the most usual, is one of the most sluggish of the conductors of sound.

With these facts in view, our conjecture comes near to be verified, when we suppose that there may be an elastic ether, susceptible of sonorous vibrations in a still more delicate manner, and capable of conveying these vibrations much further, and more instantaneously, than any of the bodies actually known to us. Or we might go a step further.—The sensation of light is now believed to result from the vibrations, not the emanations, of an elastic fluid of ether; but why may not this same element be capable of another species of vibrations? or the electric, or the magnetic fluids may be susceptible of some such vibrations; or an element, as universally suffused as light, through the universe, may be the medium of sonorous undulations, equally rapid and distinct, and serving to connect the most remote regions of the universe by the conveyance of sounds; just as the most remote are actually connected by the passage of light. Yet the sonorous vibrations of this supposed element may be far too delicate to awaken the ear of man; or in fact they may be of a *kind* that is not perceptible by the human auditory nerve.

We refuse to allow that a conjecture of this sort is extravagant, or destitute of philosophic probability; on the contrary, we must consider it as borne out by the discoveries of modern science. Might we then rest for a moment upon an animating conception (aided by the actual analogy of light) such as this, namely, that the field of the visible universe is the theatre of a vast social economy, holding rational intercourse, at great distances? Let us claim leave to indulge, a while, the belief, when we contemplate the starry heavens, that speech—inquiry and response—commands and petitions—debate and instruction, are passing to

9

and fro: nor need it be denied to us to imagine the pealing anthem of praise, at stated seasons arising from worshippers in all quarters, and flowing on, like the noise of many waters, until it reach the courts of the central heavens!

But the natural prejudice which stands in the way of these, our analogical conjectures, is firmer in relation to the objects of sight, than in the instance of any other of the senses. The vastness of the field over which the faculty of vision gives us a command, the precision and permanence of this class of our perceptions, and especially the constant relation subsisting between the senses of sight and touch, (in themselves the most constant of the senses,) so that whatever affects the latter, does, or may, affect the former, and the converse—we say these conditions of the visual faculty, impel us almost irresistibly, to suppose that nothing corporeal can escape it, and that where NOTHING IS SEEN, NOTHING EXISTS.

But now is this instinctive persuasion at all better founded, in relation to sight, than we have admitted it to be in relation to the other senses? We are compelled to grant there may be properties analogous to those which are the objects of taste and smell, and which entirely elude our powers of perception; nor can we deny the probability of there being sonorous vibrations inaudible (in degree or in kind) to the human ear. What then are our perceptions of colour and form, but the consequences of the emanations, or the vibrations of a certain elastic element, just as the perceptions of smell are the consequences of the emanations of another elastic element? These vibrations of light are repelled, or repeated, by all bodies which also affect the sense of touch; and by this double means we assure ourselves of the presence—the forms, the distances, of solid and fluid bodies. Meantime, by other means, we ascertain the presence of some elements that are not perceptible by the touch, and of some that are not perceptible by the eye; and we have moreover indirect, or inductive evidence of the presence of some that are in *no way* immediately perceptible, or otherwise to be known than by their ultimate effects. Thus the presumption that the eye sees whatever is material, utterly fails when we come to examine it; nor can we, with reason, allow it to influence our conclusions or conjectures.

The magnetic influence or stream is not palpable, as is a current of water, or of air; nor is it visible, like the former; nevertheless it proves its reality plainly enough by giving a regular figure to loose particles of iron, and by sustaining a mass of steel in contact with the magnet. In this instance touch and sight go no further than to make us acquainted with the remote product of an occult power. On the table before us a needle, nicely balanced, trembles, and turns, as with the constancy of love, towards a certain spot in the arctic regions; but a mass of iron placed near it, disturbs this tendency, and gives it a new direction. We assume then the presence of an element universally diffused, of which we have no direct perception whatever. Now let it be imagined that the sheets of a manuscript, scattered confusedly over the table and the floor, are seen to be slowly adjusting themselves, according to the order of the pages, and that, at last, every leaf, and every loose fragment, has come into its due place, and is ready for the compositor. In such a case we should, without any scruple, assume the presence of an invisible rational agent, just as in the case of the oscillations of the needle, we had assumed the presence of an invisible elementary power.

Now although, in the one instance, we are thinking of nothing but what is natural and ordinary, while in the other, we must attribute the facts supposed, to a supernatural agent, and are therefore more startled or perplexed by the one, than we are by the other, is there any ground whatever for considering the one as abstractedly incredible and impossible, while the other is known to be real and ordinary? It is true that the one has never happened to ourselves; and that the other frequently, or constantly, occurs; but if the senses, all of them together, totally fail to detect the magnetic power, until, by the accident of a balanced needle it makes itself known, in one of its effects, may not these same senses also fail in detecting a sentient and rational power, near to us; and whether or not this rational power shall give us any palpable evidence of his presence? Our conclusion is that our instinctive persuasion of the non-existence of that, concerning which none of the senses afford us any intimation, is a prejudice, not entitled to any respect, when it stands in the way of a belief that is sustained by independent reasons.

But the possibility and the probability of the existence, near us, of invisible sentient beings, may be stated in another manner. Sensation may be considered as the product of two powers, combined, and acting one upon the other: that is to say, on the one side there is the material property— the emanation or the vibration of ethereal and elastic elements; and on the other side there is the percipient faculty, or the power of being wrought upon by these material vibrations. Now it is only fair to suppose that these correlative powers are so far analogous, or similar, as that if the one be invisible, impalpable, and imponderable, the other may be so too. If it be a fact that the exciting principle, although present and active, may elude detection, in every way, except that one in which it affects the single sense; why may not the percipient principle be equally invisible.

and impalpable? To adduce a familiar illustration, the scent of musk, powerful as it is, may fill a chamber, and yet it is totally imperceptible by the eye, and the touch, and the ear, and the taste; nevertheless it is a very energetic influence, although attenuated in a degree inconceivable; for it will remain attached to walls and apparel for many years after the substance of the perfume has been withdrawn. Why then should not the olfactory sense itself be capable of existing in an equally impalpable and invisible condition? or why may it not be attenuated in an equal degree, and yet retain its power and reality? The scent emanates indeed from a solid and tangible substance, and the sensation also is attached to a solid and tangible organ; but as the actual emanation is invisible and impalpable, so may be the perception and the perceptive being.

The readiness with which we admit the belief of a sentient and rational universe, existing on all sides of us, although unseen; or the reluctance we feel in admitting any such supposition, will be affected by the notion that is entertained of the mode in which the mind occupies, and operates within, the animal organization; and especially by our opinion concerning the functions of the brain, and of the nervous system. The hypothesis which has been briefly stated in the third and fourth chapters of this volume, concerning the muscular power, and the limitation of perception in the organs of sense, is open, as the author is well aware, to objections on the ground of the commonly received theory of the generation of muscular motion, and of the office of the sensorium; and he is aware too, that a full explanation of his own views on these subjects—to do any justice to them, and to set them clear of apparent difficulties, would demand, not merely ample space, but an elaborate examination of the animal structure, such as might place the two theories on a ground of fair comparison. But neither do the limits of the present essay admit of any such discussion, nor would it well comport with the general strain of the work; nor indeed could it easily be made intelligible to readers not conversant with physiology. Nevertheless a concise statement of his opinion seems almost necessary to sustain the author's conjectures and assumptions, in more than one or two instances.

The brain is ordinarily spoken of as well by anatomists and physiologists, as by metaphysicians, as being not merely the seat of the mind, and the organ of our intellectual operations, but as the emanating centre of those volitions which precede muscular motion, and as the receptacle of impressions from the several senses. It is only within the brain, we are told, that the mind converses with the notices of the external world, conveyed to it by the nervous chords from the external organ of each sense; and it is also within the brain that the determination takes place to move the limbs, in this or that direction; which determination, when it has been formed, flows down, by the channel of the nerves, to the particular muscles the agency of which is demanded to produce the required line or circuit of movement.

Now it must be granted, in the first place, that, in the above statement, very much more is assumed than can be supported by any sort of proof, and therefore very much which is fairly open to question; and in the second place, that this same theory of sensation and muscular action, instead of its being the involuntary dictate of our consciousness, contradicts our impressions, and our instinctive suppositions, and therefore is not entitled to our assent until it has been established by some satisfactory evidence.

The author must not be understood as intending that our consciousness, whether mental or animal, ought to be received implicitly, as an indication for what takes place in occult processes; for several familiar instances might be mentioned in which it is unquestionably fallacious: nevertheless some degree of regard should certainly be paid to those involuntary impressions that arise from our organic sensations; and these impressions are entitled to be considered as probably just, until proved to be untrue. Now, on the very ground of these spontaneous convictions, let it be granted that the brain is indeed the seat and centre of all purely intellectual operations—the organ of memory, of conception, of imagination, of reasoning, and of moral sentiment, excluding perhaps certain of the emotions, in relation to which our consciousness does not so decisively refer them to the brain.

We may therefore leave the brain in undisturbed possession of its prescriptive honours, as the organ and residence of the mind; but the very reason of this belief that the higher faculties perform their part within the cranium, if it be allowed to influence also our opinion concerning sensation and muscular movement, would lead to a very different supposition; and assuredly it would never suggest the notion, either of our despatching orders from the brain, down the spinal chord and crural nerve, to certain muscles of the leg; or of our feeling the pinch of a tight shoe—not in the toe, but near to where we feel the pinch of a tight hat.

Inscrutable as is the principle of animal life, and difficult as are all questions relating to the connection between the mind and the body, it yet does not appear to be by any means a hopeless endeavour to trace that principle a step further than at present it is known. The doing so, in a satisfactory manner, must involve both a patient examination of the visible mechanism of the body, and a sagacious pursuit of every clue afforded by the innumerable accidents and peculiarities which so often, in an unexpected manner, reveal the long hidden secrets of nature. Meantime different and opposite theories should be entertained, so that we may be in readiness to avail ourselves, at a moment, of any such fortunate indications.

As for instance, let us take a glance at the nervous system, first, with the supposition in view, that it is the medium through which *specific* volitions are conveyed from the brain to the muscular mechanism. Now although it would be unwarrantable to affirm that the conveyance of distinct volitions through a system of interlaced chords, such as we find the nerves of muscular motion to be, is absolutely impossible, yet it becomes in the highest degree difficult to maintain our belief of any such conveyance, while we are tracing the intricacies and examining the actual arrangement of these chords. Let the auxiliary plexus be spread out in its multiform combinations, and the anastomosing branches, and the subsidiary twigs of the leading chords be followed; especially let the peculiar structure of the ganglia, as discovered by the aid of the microscope, be understood. Within the plexuses, and in the very substance of the ganglia, the fibrillæ, constituting the contributory chords, are intermixed in the most intimate and intricate manner that is conceivable; and the entire construction is such as would seem fitted, not for the transmission of volitions in a distinct manner, from the brain to the limb, or for the return of sensations from the limb to the brain, but rather for confounding effectively all such supposed transmissions. Scores of instances might be specified in which, very remarkably, provision is made, as if for commingling and confusing the lines of communication between the brain and the extremities; and it may boldly be affirmed that, if the office of the nervous network were totally unknown and unsuspected, the very last supposition that would be suggested by a view of its structure would be, that it is contrived to convey particular volitions to particular muscles.

If the scheme of the nerves be spread out, and be compared with the scheme of the arteries, or of the veins, exposed in a similar manner, it appears that there is even more in the former, of anastomosis, and more of involution and intricacy, by plexus and ganglia, and by retrograde ramifications, than in the two latter. That is to say, in the former, more than in the latter, provision is made for an uninterrupted transmission of whatever is transmitted at large, to all parts of the extremities, and for its indiscriminate, or *promiscuous conveyance.* It is plainly a matter of secondary importance to the limbs whether they receive the requisite supply of blood through one trunk, or through another; so that it does but come in sufficient quantity, and with a sufficient force; or whether the expended fluid be returned through one, or through another canal. And in like manner, and even more clearly, the main intention of nature in the arrangement of the nervous ramifications appears to be, the affording an unfailing supply of some necessary influence, or ether, to all parts of the muscular apparatus, by any means, and by all means; and so as that if one medium of conveyancy should be accidentally cut off or compressed, the emanation may yet reach the parts by some circuit that is not exposed to the same obstruction.

We assume then that, as our consciousness informs us of no such process as that of the dispatching of volitions to the muscles, so neither does the construction of the nervous system indicate its adaptation to a process of this kind, but the contrary, and in a very decisive manner.

But now let it be supposed (thinking only of muscular motion) that the nervous system, connecting the brain and spinal process with the entire muscular apparatus, serves the purpose of conveying, from the former to the latter, a copious supply of (shall we say) galvanic power, which power it is the office of the cerebral mass to generate. We then consider the muscles, those of the arm, for instance, as consisting only of flectors and deflectors; or we may imagine a single pair of antagonists, of which the one bends, and the other extends the limb. On our present supposition then, the brain, by the medium of the brachial nerves, supplies *both* these muscles, evenly and perpetually, with the contractile excitement, whatever it may be, which shall enable each, whenever called upon, to become dense and tumid in the requisite degree.

What then is volition, but the mental influence, immediately present in the arm, and determining it to bend, or to straighten? The mind is not, as we suppose, the prisoner of the attic story; but is the occupant at large of the entire animal organization, acting in each part of the structure according to the purpose of each:—in the arm and leg, willing the limb hither or thither, by its inherent power over matter;—in the skin, in the eye, the ear, the tongue, the nasal membrane, receiving immediately the impressions of external objects, by its inherent susceptibility of the properties of matter; and, let it be granted, within the cranium, carrying on the processes of thought.

The supposition concerning muscular motion, requires only an adaptation of terms in order to apply it to sensation. Instead, for example, of assuming that the picture falling on the retina has to be transmitted, in some inconceivable manner, by the optic nerve to the sensorium, and that there, undisturbed and unmixed, it delivers itself to the percipient faculty, we imagine that the optic nerve merely supplies the retina with a copious and constant stream of the exciting influence—let it be galvanism, and that the mind, present upon the very bed of the nerve, and where the actual picture, in all its vivid colours rests, converses with it, and that it does so because it is originally capable of conversing with light and colours; although while lodged in the animal body, it is restricted from holding any such converse, except upon the highly excited expansion of the optic nerve.

We must however go a step further, and inquire what probably may be the use, or whence is the necessity of the (galvanic) influence generated in the brain, and thence conveyed to the muscles and the organs of sense. Now our theory involves the supposition that the inherent percipient faculty of the mind (and the same of its mechanical power) is so imprisoned within the solid substance of the animal body as to be totally screened from impressions of the external world, except just so far as this solid substance may be vehemently stimulated, commoved, and rendered impressible by the powerful action of the (galvanic) fluid. The very same irresistible agent which compels earths to yield their metallic bases, and which decomposes what nothing else can move, brings, as we suppose, the animal fibre, and the reticular expansions of the nerves into a state of excitability, such as enables them to correspond to the vibrations of light, or of sound, or to the chemical properties of sapid or odoriferous bodies. All that the mind needs for sensation is that the external material vibrations, as of light, sound, &c., should be responded to by an internal vibration or commotion of the animal substance; but this demands a highly charged (galvanic) condition of the organ of sense. It is as if a stretched wire, which faintly corresponds to a musical note, might be made to do so more delicately and more forcibly, by making it the channel of a galvanic current. It is not that the MIND needs this excitement, but it is the fleshy organ which needs it, in order to its admitting the external vibratory impression.

The powerful (voltaic) apparatus which fills the cranium has relation, as we now suppose, to the inertness and the inelasticity of the animal body; and if the mind were imagined to be corporeally combined with a highly elastic fluid, or an ether, susceptible of the most delicate vibrations, there would then be no more occasion for the galvanic stimulus: a mind thus embodied would need no brain, no nerves, no organs of sense, and no contractile fibres.

The well-known effect of galvanism upon the limbs of a dead animal may, at first, appear not to comport with the theory we are now propounding; for in these instances muscular motion, which we attribute to the directive influence of the mind, resident in the limb, is seen to be produced—*not by mind*, but by the mere electric stream. We however gather a very remarkable confirmation of our conjecture from these very facts, which indeed, on due consideration, can hardly, if at all, be made to consist with the common supposition of the transmission of volitions from the brain to the muscles through the nerves. If the office of the nerve is to transmit the will of the mind, distinctively, to the muscles, we see them, in the case of a separated limb, transmiting something very different from such volitions—namely, a galvanic stream; and yet although the cause is totally unlike, the effect is the same as if a volition had been conveyed.

But upon our present supposition, what happens in applying the galvanic wire to the sciatic nerve of a frog is precisely what we should, according to our hypothesis, expect to happen. That is to say, the nerve, in this case, conveys the very same element or energy which it has been wont to convey during the life of the animal; this exciting agent, namely, the galvanic fluid, is instantaneously suffused through the *whole limb*, and is distributed, in its accustomed proportions, to the entire system of muscles. But inasmuch as the mind of the animal has been withdrawn from those muscles, which, while it was present, either retained them all at rest, or employed one set of them at pleasure, this sudden chemical excitement, acting simultaneously, and *without direction*, upon *all together*, nothing else can take place but that the most powerful muscle of the limb should carry it against the smaller and the feebler; and thus, in the instance of the frog, the limb is forcibly projected from the glass that had contained it. Its leap, is the frog's most powerful muscular action; and therefore, by necessity, the limb, when stimulated to action without the mind—leaps.

An analogous effect follows in all cases of the application of galvanism to bodies recently dead:—thus the rabbit jumps, and the human countenance is frightfully contorted in consequence of the contraction of the *stronger* muscles of the face. If the weaker set of muscles could, in this artificial manner, be acted upon, apart from the stronger, placid and pleasing expressions would no doubt be produced. In the case of convulsive affections of the face, in the living body, the *distortion* arises plainly from this very cause, namely, that there is a suffused muscular excitement, uncontrolled by the mind, and therefore taking effect upon all the stronger muscles; while the weaker, instead of being held in that state of easy counterpoise which the mind, when not disturbed, maintains, yield to an unwonted violence; and therefore do not fill out the general contour, as they do when all are under the command of the will, but give way, with a tremulous ineffective resistance.

Spasmodic or convulsive muscular contractions arise, as we suppose, from the withdrawment of the mind, while the chemical stimulus continues to flow to the parts affected. On the contrary, paralytic distortions we attribute to a partial suppression of the excitement furnished by the brain:—partial, and yet just enough to allow the larger and stronger muscles to act.

That which happens among the muscles when their contractility is stimulated, apart from the control of the mind, may be rendered familiarly intelligible by considering what takes place when a mast or balk, fixed perpendicularly, is supported in three directions by cords, one of these cords being five times the size of the other two together. Then if the three are equally moistened by a sudden shower, the mast is immediately drawn from the upright, by the large rope, while the two smaller, its antagonists, either loosen their attachments, or are snapped. This mechanical effect differs little, as to its proximate cause, from what is observed in cases of epileptic fits, locked jaw, and mortal convulsions; for the directive and commanding influence of the mind having been diverted, or withdrawn, while the contractile galvanic stimulus continues to flow in full stream from the brain to the extremities, it inevitably happens that, in each set of antagonists, the more bulky, or what is equivalent, the more excitable muscles, prevail over their feebler partners, and a rigid contraction is the consequence. Thus the fingers are indented into the palms, and the temporal and masseter muscles, the natural power of which vastly exceeds that of the digastricus and platysma myoides, hold the lower jaw, as if iron-bound, in contact with the upper. But when the mental disturbance is remedied, and the voluntary principle returns to its seat and office, then *this same force* of the temporal and masseter muscles, equal to 500 lbs. weight, and by no means counteracted by an equal force in the antagonists, is held in equilibrio, and in fact is so delicately balanced by the mental authority, as not only to act its part with precision in the mechanical operation of mastication, but to play in with the exquisite movements that govern the modulations of the voice. The part performed by the temporal and masseter muscles, in speaking and singing, might be compared to the service rendered by a powerful and well-trained horse, required to pull within the sixteenth of an inch, and in combination too with the power of a dog or of a child: his whole force is always in readiness; but it is so under control as to reach the precise limit required, and yet not to surpass it.

All the facts connected with the ascertained difference between the voluntary and involuntary muscles readily fall in with the theory that the function of the brain, in relation to the muscular system, does not consist in sending forth volitions, but simply in maintaining a copious supply of contractile excitements, (whether galvanic or not,) that the nerves convey this chemical energy and disperse it *promiscuously* among the muscles, and that the actual employment of this force rests with the mind, present, not in the cranium, but in the limb.

A muscle, the antagonist of which is *another muscle*, comes necessarily within the control of the voluntary principle; for nothing else can command it; and if this be withdrawn, a spasmodic contraction of the stronger of the two is instantly the consequence. But if the antagonist force be merely mechanical, as it is in the heart, the stomach, and the intestines, there will take place an alternation between the two unlike powers; that is to say, the supply of excitement from the brain being limited in quantity, or coming only at a given rate, it will be expended in overcoming the mechanical force, which, for a moment, gains upon it; but during the interval of relaxation, the galvanic excitement has again accumulated, and in its turn overpowers the mechanical resistance, and muscular contraction ensues.

A too long continued exertion of the voluntary muscles produces a painful sense of the overthrow of the natural equipoise of the powers. That is to say, the mind has been demanding motion at a greater rate than that at which the brain, in its ordinary state, can furnish the contractile chemical excitement; and the limb drawing this pabulum, as it can, from the nerves of sensation, and from the surface, a sense of pain follows; at the same time the animal spirits fail. But it is manifest that the mind, as seated in the brain, has a power of rousing it to an extraordinary effort, so as to develop a more than usual amount of the electric element. Thus a powerful motive for continued exertion, as when a man, to save his life, is running from his enemy, disperses for a time the sense of fatigue. Nevertheless this power of extraordinary galvanic development has its limits; and the brain indicates afterwards the violence which it has submitted to, and refuses for a while to furnish even its ordinary quantum of chemical power.

The functions of the brain, in relation to the INTELLECTUAL FACULTIES, is a subject far too difficult and copious to be entered upon in this place; nor is it in fact so nearly connected with our proper subject as is the theory of sensation and muscular motion. In reference to these, we cannot allow it to be hopeless that some satisfactory conclusion should at length be arrived at. The proper path of experiment, it would not be very difficult to mark out; and there are some means of bringing the question to the test of facts which, as the author believes, could hardly fail to decide it. Let it be granted for a moment that the function of the brain, in relation to sensation and muscular motion, is simply chemical, and that it has respect to the inertness of the animal substance, and to its low degree of elasticity; and then the way will be open for readily conceiving of other species of corporeity—impalpable and invisible, but not less sensitive or less potent than *animal* corporeity; on the contrary, more so.

If the functions of the brain be only *conditionally necessary*, in relation to sensation and motion, we may easily believe that they are only conditionally necessary in relation to the more purely intellectual operations; or, in other words, that there need be no voltaic pile where the material vehicle of the mind is *in itself* in a high degree elastic, and is responsive to every kind of vibration. Let it only be supposed that there is about us a fluid, the counterpart of that ether, the vibrations of which give us the sensation of light—a fluid in an equal degree capable of receiving and of transmitting undulations incalculably minute and rapid. Mind amalgamated with such a fluid might be immediately conversant with all the properties of matter, and even much more intimately and extensively conversant with them than it can be while it depends for its sensibility upon the constancy and the amount of the galvanic element.

This imperfect statement of a conjecture concerning the office of the brain and nerves, although it may seem a digression from the immediate subject of the present chapter, is not really so, since it opens the way for our readily conceiving of what, on the ground of scriptural evidence, we have reason to think is real—namely, the repletion of the visible universe with invisible corporeal beings; and it may incline us the more readily to admit the belief that the creation, beside its sentient orders, connected with animal organization, abounds with tribes, sentient and rational, whose corporeity is impalpable and invisible, and who are the tenants of what, in an accommodated sense, may be called a quintessence.

These invisible orders, besides the impulse of their instincts and their interests, may, by physical necessity, and perhaps by their liability to gravitation, (however attenuated their substance,) be gathered around the solar and planetary bodies; so that each world may have its own ethereal nations, as well as its terrestrial, or rather, its *animal* species: each planet, as well as our own, may have its *επουρανιοι*, its *επιγειοι*, and its *καταχθονιοι*.

In collating these speculations with the general tenor and the particular testimony of the Scriptures, it is proper to keep in mind a principle which seems pretty well sustained—That the inspired writers always hold close to *mundane affairs*, and intend to speak only of the history and destinies of the families of earth, seldom, if ever, opening to us any wider prospect. On the strength of this principle, we may then assume the probability that the spiritual beings, good and evil, that are spoken of in the Scriptures, are all, or most of them, of mundane origin; and although some may now have come to move in a wider circle, that they have all sprung from this soil. Are there reasons for supposing that the solid materials of our planet have served purposes in a period anterior to the birth of the Adamic family? Such a belief we do not regard as contradictory to any scriptural doctrine, or to the Mosaic history of the creation. But if so, then these pre-adamic families, like their successors, may have acquitted themselves variously during their term of animal existence, some having broken their allegiance to the Supreme Power, while others have preserved virtue and loyalty. Yet both may (whether constantly or not) attach themselves to the scene of their early history, and mingle themselves with the destinies of the modern race. Hence, perhaps, those conflicts and those commotions, those beneficent agencies, and those malignant influences, to which the inspired writers are so often making allusion. But this great subject, considered as a matter of Biblical inquiry, urgently demands a new investigation, under the guidance of the careful, and yet free principles of interpretation which have lately been coming into operation. This, however, in the mean time, may be said, that, should a rational and laborious examination of the scriptural evidence relating to invisible orders, lead to a revival of the belief of Christians, and to the refreshment of their fading impressions—fading, because, in their original state, superstitious and exaggerated—should this take place, and in connection with a better understood theory of intellectual existence, very important consequences might be the result; and all religious minds, awakened to a sense of the simple reality of the spiritual dangers we are exposed to, as tenants of this haunted planet, would be impelled, with undiverted anxiety, to seek safety where always and only it is to be found.

But we must return upon our path for a moment, and briefly state the bearing of this branch of our general theory upon the notions we may entertain concerning the condition of the human soul upon the dissolution of the animal structure; and concerning the state of that vast congregation which has been swelling, with its new thousands daily, during the course of nearly sixty centuries.

The belief of the survivance of the living principle and consciousness, after the dissolution of the animal organization, the author, for his own part, would always derive from those moral and religious considerations, and from that explicit divine testimony which appeal to our highest and purest sentiments. As to the pretended demonstration of immortality, drawn from the assumed simplicity and indestructibility of the soul, as an immaterial substance, they appear either altogether inconclusive; or if conclusive, then such as must be admitted to apply, with scarcely diminished force, to all sentient orders; and it must be granted that, whatever has felt, and has acted spontaneously, must live again, and for ever. We have the best reasons for the confident expectation of another life; nor are we driven to fortify our convictions by arguments which, if valid, prove immensely more than we can desire to see established, or could persuade ourselves to think in any degree probable.

There is not in the structure, or the instincts, or the tendencies of any one of the inferior animal species, the faintest indication of a renewal of life after the extinction of the vital principle. But it is altogether otherwise with man; and we believe him immortal, not because, as it is pretended, thought and consciousness cannot be annihilated, but because the human intellectual and moral structure is such as to imply an after stage of expansion.

This then, on higher grounds, being granted as certain, that man is to survive his animal body, it is not difficult, in following out the several principles of our physical theory of another life, to conceive of an instantaneous transition of the conscious principle—the LIFE, from the animal body, to a body impalpable and invisible; and yet not at all less alive to the material world, but probably more so. The evidence of the inspired writings apart, it might easily be supposed that the human mind, at death, immediately enters upon its highest and ultimate stage of spiritual corporeity. But we are not at liberty to assume so much as this, if the doctrine of the New Testament on this subject has been rightly understood; for it directs us to look forward to a future and distant epoch as the destined day in which human nature is to put on corporeal incorruptibility; and we are also taught to think of the state of souls as a state, not of unconsciousness indeed, but of comparative inaction, or of suspended energy:—it is, so far as we may gather its conditions from the scattered intimations of Scripture, a transition state, during the continuance of which the passive faculties of our nature, rather than the active, are to be awake; and throughout which, probably, those emotions of the moral nature that have been overborne or held in abeyance, by the urgent impulses of animal life, shall take their free course, and reach their height as fixed habits of the mind.

On this supposition then, if it ought to be called a *supposition*, which rests with little ambiguity upon scriptural evidence, it is plain that a more attenuated corporeity may be held to belong to the intermediate transition state of human nature than shall befit its ultimate condition of full energy and activity. Powers latent do not need a structure which has relation to the exertion of powers upon an exterior world. The chrysalis period of the soul may be marked by the destitution of all the instruments of active life, corporeal and mental. And this state of inaction may probably be also a state of seclusion, involving, not improbably, an unconsciousness of the passage of time.

Suggestions such as these should be made no other use of than that of preparing us to catch, at all points, the evanescent indications of the inspired writers, which, in relation to the spiritual and unseen world, are so given as entirely to escape the notice of those who listlessly read what they have been reading from childhood, under the guidance of notions accidentally formed. It is not until the mind has been quickened by an intelligent curiosity, and has obtained also more than one clue to inquiry, by the aid of hypothesis, that the actual extent to which the unseen world is open to us in the Scriptures, comes to be suspected or understood. Let an hypothesis be utterly at variance with truth, it will yet have rendered us an important service—and a legitimate service, if it shall have prompted us to pursue, assiduously and eagerly, any path of Biblical inquiry. It is on this very ground that the author would rest his apology for advancing the several conjectures that find a place in these pages.

A condition of suspended powers, and of destitution, such as we now attribute to the human soul, through its intermediate period, may very naturally be imagined to involve, perhaps a strong tendency or appetency, toward the open world of power and action :—there may be a yearning after the lost corporeity, or after the expected corporeity :—there may be a pressing on toward the busy frequented walks of active existence. Now let it be just imagined that, as almost all natural principles and modes of life are open to some degree of irregularity, and admit exceptive cases, so this pressure of the innumerable community of the dead, toward the precincts of life, may, in certain cases, actually break through the boundaries that hem in the ethereal crowds, and so it may happen, as if by trespass, that the dead may, in single instances, infringe upon the ground of common corporeal life.

At least let indulgence be given to the opinion that those almost universal superstitions which, in every age and nation, have implied the fact of occasional interferences of the dead with the living, ought not to be summarily dismissed as a mere folly of the vulgar, utterly unreal, until our knowledge of the spiritual world is so complete as shall entitle us to affirm that no such interferences can, in the nature of things, ever have taken place. The mere supposition of there being any universal persuasion, which is totally groundless, not only in its form and adjuncts, but in its substance, does some violence to the principles of human reasoning, and is clearly of dangerous consequence. An absolute scepticism on this subject moreover, can be maintained only by the aid of Hume's often refuted sophism—That *no* testimony can be held sufficient to establish an alleged fact which is at variance with common experience; for it must not be denied that some few instances of the sort alluded to, rest upon testimony in itself thoroughly unimpeachable; nor is the import of the evidence in these cases at all touched by the now well understood doctrine concerning spectral illusions, as resulting from a diseased condition of the brain. There is a species of disbelief, flattering indeed to intellectual arrogance, but out of harmony with the spirit and the admitted rules of modern philosophy. Whether such and such alleged facts happen to come to us mingled with gross popular errors, or not, is a circumstance of little importance in determining the degree of attention they may deserve :—one question only is to be considered, namely—Is the evidence that sustains them in any degree substantial ?

Nor in considering questions of this sort ought we to listen for a moment to those frequent, but impertinent questions, that are brought forward with the view of superseding the inquiry ;—such, for example, as these—What good end is answered by the alleged extra natural occurrences ?—or, Is it worthy of the Supreme Wisdom to permit them ? and so forth. The question is a question first, of *testimony*, to be judged of on the established principles of evidence; and then of *physiology;* but neither of theology, nor of morals. Some few human beings are wont to walk in their sleep, and during the continuance of profound slumber perform, with precision and safety, the offices of common life, and return to their beds, and yet are totally unconscious, when they awake, of what they have done. Now in considering this, or any such extraordinary class of facts, our business is, in the first place, to obtain a number of instances, supported by the distinct and unimpeachable testimony of intelligent witnesses; and then, being thus in possession of the facts, to adjust them, as well as we can, to other parts of our philosophy of human nature. Shall we allow an objector to put a check to our scientific curiosity, on the subject, for instance, of somnambulism, by saying, "Scores of these accounts have turned out to be exaggerated, or totally untrue:"—or, "This walking in the sleep ought not to be thought possible, or as likely to be permitted by the Benevolent Guardian of human welfare?"

Almost all instances of alleged supernatural *appearances* may easily be disposed of, either on the ground of the fears and superstitious impressions of the parties reporting them, or on that of that now well understood diseased action of the nervous system, which, in certain conditions, generates visual illusions of the most distinct kind. But no such explanations will meet the many instances, thoroughly well attested, in which the death of a relative, at a distance, has been conveyed, in all its circumstances, to persons during sleep; nor again to those instances in which some special information, buried in the bosoms of the dead, has been imparted, in sleep, to the living. In these cases the singularity of the facts conveyed, and the impossibility of their coming through any ordinary channel, ought, on every principle of philosophical and of forensic evidence to be admitted as furnishing proper proof of an invisible interference. The time will come when, in consequence of the total dissipation of popular superstitions, and the removal too of the prejudice which makes us ashamed of seeming to believe in company with the vulgar, or to believe at the prompting of fear—it will be seen that facts of this class ought to engage the attention of physiologists, and when they will be deliberately consigned to their place in our systems of the philosophy of human nature. Notwithstanding prejudices of whatever sort—vulgar and philosophic, facts of whatever class, and of whatever tendency, will at length receive the regard due to them, as the materials of science; and the era may be predicted in which a complete reaction shall take its course, and the true principles of reasoning be made to embrace a vastly wider field than that which may be measured by the human hand and eye. A reaction of this kind is likely to be put in progress, or to be accelerated, by the making some bold conjectural excursions beyond the range of animal sensation; the consequence of which may be—not indeed the adoption of any of those particular conjectures as true, but the concentration of philosophic minds upon the fact and the evidence that actually comes within our range of observation.

Without entering upon the field of Biblical criticism, which the author, in this essay, purposely avoids, it would not be possible, satisfactorily, to bring into relation with our theory, the Scripture testimony concerning invisible orders. There is however a particular branch of that testimony to which allusion may properly be made,—namely, that which concerns dæmoniacal possession. Not able in this place to engage in the argument, as a Biblical question, the author assumes, what he fully believes may be made good, that the gospel narratives, in those instances, are of a kind not to be disposed of by the hypothesis of accommodation, but are of a plain historical complexion, such as that if they are rejected as untrue, we are bound to withdraw our confidence altogether from the reporters as competent and trustworthy witnesses of facts.

Taking it then for granted that these narratives actually involve what they seem to involve, and that they imply something totally different from all cases of lunacy, madness, or delirium, we then come into possession of several highly significant facts, concerning a species or order of mundane beings, whom, unless there be other evidence to that effect, we are not to identify with the human race, and whom we are taught, by the careful phraseology of the inspired writers, not to confound with the fallen angelic orders—the colleagues and companions of Satan.

The leading ideas suggested by these narratives are such as the following, and they comport well with the conjectures we have entertained in the preceding pages.

First, there is the familiar and ready intermixture of invisible and impalpable beings with human society, so that, within any given boundary, there may be corporeally present, the human crowd, and the extra human crowd; and the latter as naturally and simply present as the former—the latter as vividly conscious of the material world as the former, and as energetically prompted by interests and passions, by desires and fears. Secondly, it is to be noticed that these beings had not, as it seems, the physical power to make themselves heard, or to give any mechanical evidence of their presence, except while usurping the animal corporeity of another species, namely the human. Thirdly, these possessions seem to give evidence of a principle we have above hinted at, namely, the yearning or appetency of invisible and ethereal natures toward animal organization. It would appear as if, during that era in the history of man in which such irregularities were permitted, that the spiritual species eagerly caught at every opportunity of tenanting the terrestrial species. In the fourth place, we cannot but note, what is not obscure in its expression, however obscure it may be in its import, namely, the horror of these dæmons at the thoughts of being consigned to the nether cavern or abyss. Lastly, the highly significant effect of the adding of mind to mind, within one and the same body, is to be especially noticed. This temporary compounding of intelligences, which (were it allowable on so unusual an occasion to coin a term) might be called a state of mental superentity, discovers itself by multiplying the mechanical force of the muscular system, and as it seems, in some proportion to the actual numbers of the foreign minds. The inherent power of mind over matter, to generate motion, was, in these instances, we might almost say, mathematically exhibited, by showing the accumulated force of several minds, acting, as in a focus, upon a single muscular mechanism.

Whoever feels himself obliged, by every principle of sound criticism and interpretation, to consider the gospel narratives of dæmoniacal possessions as simply true, will find that these extraordinary instances, differing as they do in every sense from the Satanic seductive influence, elsewhere affirmed in Scripture, involve just what has been assumed in the conjectures propounded in the present chapter. On all sides, assuredly, it would be admitted that *one* well attested and distinctly reported instance of the presence and intelligent agency of an invisible being would be enough to carry the question of an invisible economy pervading the visible universe. Are not then the gospel narratives well attested, and are not the circumstances simply and distinctly reported? But if so, they furnish us with all we want for the determination of the general question.

The reader will bear in mind the important distinction, already adverted to, between the Satanic influence, and any case of dæmoniacal possession; the one being purely moral and spiritual, and applying also universally to human nature, and being in no sense naturally sensible, or visible, or distinguishable from the ordinary workings of the mental faculties. The other on the contrary was, in an equally exclusive sense, purely physical or natural, and always made itself known by visible and palpable effects, and was confined to individuals, and came within the range of history, as matter of fact, in the most ordinary sense of the phrase. Happily we have reason to conclude that human nature is no longer liable to the ruffian violence of an impure and reprobate ethereal race; but, alas! we have the strongest reasons for believing that men, universally, and in every age, are exposed to silent malignant seductions, which indeed never trench upon the natural liberty of the mind, much less infringe that of the body, but which too often, like the influence of profligate companions, prevails over the better principles of our nature, and the influence of education.

In dismissing our first conjecture, concerning the visible universe, considered as the abode of intelligent orders, we lightly dealt with it, as a *conjecture merely*, which might be entertained or rejected at pleasure. But we are not free to treat with equal unconcern the general principles involved in this our second hypothesis; for although every thing adjunctive or special in such a speculation may be unreal, these principles, if adjudged to be false, are such as must carry with them a large portion of our Christian faith; and the surrender of them would leave us in possession of only the bare skeleton of religious belief.

CHAPTER XVIII.

THE THIRD CONJECTURE.

In our first conjecture it was supposed that room might be made for the several ranks of being—whether animal or spiritual, not only within the bounds, but upon the open stage of the visible universe. The second, involved the belief of an invisible economy, suffused throughout the visible creation, and constituting that higher system toward which the rational orders of the lower and visible world are tending. But our third conjecture embraces the remote revolutions of time, and supposes (without however denying, what we are not at liberty to deny, namely, the reality of an unseen spiritual economy) that the visible universe, replete everywhere with various forms of animal life, is to fill one period only in the great history of the moral system, and that it is destined, in a moment—in the twinkling of an eye, to disappear, and to return to its nihility, giving place to new elements, and to new and higher expressions of omnipotence and intelligence.

For this our third conjecture, it would be difficult to find a form of expression more distinct, than that supplied by certain well known passages of Scripture, which, whether they are to be understood literally, or in a topical sense only, yet may well serve to convey our present idea of an instantaneous vanishing of one form of the creation and the substitution of another; as thus—"The heavens and the earth—they shall perish; all of them shall wax old like a garment; as a vesture shalt thou change them, and they shall be changed." "And all the host of heaven shall be dissolved, and the heavens shall be rolled together as a scroll, and all their host shall fall down as the leaf falleth off from the vine, and as a falling fig from the fig-tree." "Lift up your eyes to the heavens, and look upon the earth beneath, for the heavens shall vanish away like smoke, and the earth shall wax old like a garment." "Behold, I create new heavens, and a new earth, and the former shall not be remembered, nor come into mind; and the new heavens and the new earth shall remain before me, saith the Lord." "Heaven and earth shall pass away, but my word shall not pass away." "The day of the Lord shall come as a thief in the night, in the which the heavens shall pass away with a great noise;—nevertheless, we look for a new heavens, and a new earth." "And from the face of Him that sat on the throne the earth and the heavens fled away, and there was found no place for them." "Behold, I create all things new!"

Now it may seem that, with predictions such as these before us, there can be no room to speak *conjecturally* of the destiny of the material universe, or of the new creation; and, on the contrary, an explanation may properly be demanded of the sense in which that is treated of as uncertain, which appears to be distinctly affirmed in so many places of Scripture. Let it then, in the first place, be observed, that as the author, in the present essay, abstains entirely from Biblical interpretation, he is not entitled to understand the passage quoted above, in a literal and universal sense, apart from that sort of inquiry concerning the meaning of phrases, and the import of the context, which may fully justify the belief that they ought so to be understood. The theologian, perhaps, would refuse assent to a literal and unrestricted interpretation of these predictions, and would affirm that they are of spiritual import only, or are applicable simply to national and ecclesiastical revolutions.

Then in the second place it must be remembered that, supposing the literal and universal import of these passages were granted to us by the Biblical interpreter, yet, in following out our conceptions, even a single step beyond a bare affirmation of the fact, we tread upon uncertain ground, that is to say, upon the ground of analogical reasoning, not upon that of Scripture testimony; and nothing can be much more important than always to observe the broad distinction between those mere facts, which are matters of religious persuasion, and those enlargements of such facts which may be the fruit of philosophical speculation. This distinction forgotten or contemned, and then philosophical speculation becomes dangerous and pernicious;—remembered and respected, it may yield us a service not to be spurned.

Rejecting, as we must, every modification of the atheistic doctrine concerning the eternity of the material universe, or its inherent independence, and, on the contrary, viewing it as nothing more than the product of the creative will and power, existing, while it exists, only as a means to an end beyond itself, we then gain a position whence with ease we may contemplate this vast and goodly framework, permanent as it seems, as standing only during pleasure, and as dissoluble, in any moment, when its uses are fulfilled. The material universe has no indefeasible rights—has no inherent claim to be perpetuated. Nothing abstract would be compromised by its return to nihility. If it be a stage of life to innumerable species, another stage of life may come in its room; or if an admirable exhibition of the divine power, wisdom, and goodness, those same attributes may shine forth with still more clearness, on the fields of a new creation.

But our natural impressions or physical prejudices offer some resistance to the supposition of the utter and instantaneous dissipation of the solid masses of the material system; and it is only by doing a sort of violence to the mind, that such an idea is admitted. And yet those who distinctly entertain the belief of the *creation* of matter out of nothing, ought not to think the *return* of the same matter to its nothingness at all incredible. We say the return of matter to its nothingness ought not to be regarded as a paradox, even when matter is conceived of according to our ordinary notions of it, which impute to its particles, or ultimate atoms, a real, impenetrable, and indivisible, and insoluble solidity. For, in whatever manner this solidity sprang from the divine will, it cannot be greater than the will whence it sprang; nor possess any principle of permanence not dependent upon that will. It is not to be admitted that God has made any thing which, once existing, exists like himself, necessarily and eternally.

We do not therefore hold it to be at all requisite, with the view of making way for our present conjecture, to undermine (if we might so speak) the reality of the material world. Let it be as real and solid as it may, it is no more than the product of omnipotence, and possesses no permanence, irrespectively of omnipotence, constantly in act to sustain it. And assuredly we should not endeavour to shake the stability of the visible and palpable universe by the aid of the metaphysical hypothesis—or demonstration, which denies its reality, and which allows nothing to exist actually, or even possibly, but Mind.

Metaphysical skepticism as well as material skepticism, renounced, and the premises laid down, that the material world, conceived of according to our natural impressions, as solid and (relatively) indestructible, ought yet to be regarded as dissoluble every moment, by the sovereign word of the Creator; this admitted, it may yet be not altogether useless to analyze a little our notions of matter, and to follow them so far as may serve to show that a genuine belief in the reality of the external world may consist with more than one hypothesis concerning its occult constitution.

Between the idealism of Berkeley, and the scientific theory of Boscovich, there is no real connection or affinity, although, popularly, the two systems may seem to amount to the same thing. The former is as purely metaphysical as the latter is simply physical: the one is a mere adjustment of abstract notions; the latter a statement of assumed facts, supported by reasons and evidence proper to a scientific argument; and if the one hypothesis as well as the other leaves everything where it found it, so far as our concernment with the external world is involved, yet the latter may actually promote the sciences to which it stands related; while the former is, in every sense, a barren speculation.

In now propounding his conjectures concerning the occult constitution of matter, the author would deem it an inexcusable omission not to have alluded to the "Theoria Philosophiæ Naturalis," of Boscovich; and yet in doing so, he must not be understood either as entirely adopting the principles of that ingenious writer, or as pretending to interpret his system. In fact, notions similar to those so elaborately maintained by Boscovich can hardly have failed to present themselves to all minds accustomed to pursue abstruse speculations; and every such mind will give to them a modification of its own.

Our acquaintance with matter, as every one knows, is nothing more than an acquaintance with its properties, or rather with those of its powers which affect our senses. But these properties of matter resolve themselves into so many species of motion—emanative or vibratory, and the motion implied in chemical combination. The resistance offered to the touch by solid bodies may seem an exception to this statement; but it is not so in fact: for the resistance of a solid surface is nothing but a *propulsion*, operating within the minute sphere of that atomic force which prevents the actual or mathematical contact of bodies. We know solid bodies, therefore, *only by the rebound* which prohibits approximation within a certain limit. It is then a species of motion that conveys to us the idea of solidity.

In other words, for sustaining all the phenomena of the material world, mechanical and chemical, we need suppose nothing more than an infinite congeries of mathematical points of attraction and repulsion—attraction and repulsion of several kinds. This supposition fully answers all the purposes that are answered by the notion of hard indivisible atoms. That which is superadded to the very simple idea of a centre of attraction and repulsion, in order to bring it up to the notion of a solid atom, adds absolutely nothing serviceable to it, or even perhaps intelligible, and is altogether superfluous. The hard ultimate atom performs no office which the mathematical centre will not perform. But then these infinite centres are only so many starting points of motion—motion in several directions, or motion of several species.

It only remains then to bring this idea of the material world into connection with the principle that motion, in all cases, originates with mind; or in other words, is the effect of will—either the Supreme will, or the will of created minds. Motion is either constant and uniform, obeying what we call a law, or it is incidental. The visible and palpable world then, according to this theory, is MOTION, constant and uniform, emanating from infinite centres, and springing, during every instant of its continuance, from the Creative Energy.

The instantaneous cessation of this energy, at any period, is therefore, abstractedly, quite as easily conceived of as is its continuance; and whether, in the next instant, it shall continue, or shall cease, whether the material universe shall stand, or shall vanish, is an alternative of which, irrespective of other reasons, the one member may be as easily taken as the other; just as the moving of the hand, or the not moving it, in the next moment, depends upon nothing but our volition. The annihilation of the solid spheres—the planets, and the suns, that occupy the celestial spaces, would not on this supposition be an act of irresistible force, crushing that which resists compression, or dissipating and reducing to an ether that which firmly coheres; but it would simply be the non-exertion, in the next instant, of a power which has been exerted in this instant:—it would be, not a destruction, but a rest; not a crash and ruin, but a pause.

Yet, as we have already said, the supposition of the instantaneous vanishing of the present material universe is not at all dependent upon the theory above stated, which supposes matter to be constituted of several species of motion, springing constantly from an infinitude of points. And indeed, dismissing this theory, the dest'ny of the celestial mechanism might be inferred, with some degree of probability, on the ground of facts that are now generally admitted. Thus, for example, if an ether be a resisting medium, diffused through space, a medium which, rare as it may be, is dense enough to deduct something in each revolution, from the onward force of comets, and so to accelerate their revolutions, and to diminish their orbits, the same retarding, yet accelerating power, is in operation also upon the planets; so that the entire system must be *winding up*, and slowly in progress toward that consummation which the inspired writers speak of as a "rolling up the heavens like a scroll." If such be the actual and inevitable tendency of the planetary economy, we may suppose that the dire catastrophe will be anticipated by an instantaneous changing of the things that are "seen and temporal," and an introducing of the things that are "not seen and eternal."

In connection with our present conjecture we ought to consider what is that all-pervading principle which is the characteristic of the present material system; or at least of so much of it as comes within our means of knowledge—and it is this, namely—That the constitution of nature includes the collision of unlike and unequal forces, so acting one upon another, as that the whole can subsist and preserve its form only by running round a perpetual circle of combination and decomposition, of organization and dissolution. In no department of nature, within our observation, is there, or indeed can there be, a state of absolute rest; for those elements which have reached a condition of repose, by perfect combination, and which, left to themselves, might enjoy that repose, are incessantly acted upon by other elements, which, though they by themselves might also rest, cannot rest in juxtaposition with any compound, but must decompose it. Thus it is that the most solid masses are giving way, slowly perhaps, to decomposition, or to a change of chemical form; while the less solid, or the more *exposed* masses are rapidly running the round of their solid, fluid, and gaseous states;—yielding up their constituents, to be consorted anew in some totally different manner. And thus too, the powers of life, vegetable and animal, which, within so many thousand fixed types, are perpetually gathering to themselves the crude elements, are also, without a moment's pause, passing on toward their stage of decay and dissolution. The balance of forces, in the material world, is of such a kind as that it can be perpetuated only by incessant revolutions and transitions; so we keep a pole perpendicularly on the finger, by giving it a gyration.

But there certainly comes within the range of our abstract notions of what is possible, another sort of counterpoise, namely, one in which either equal forces should be balanced, or unequal, on a principle of adjustment, such as should involve no inequality. In the actual world, light, heat, and electricity, (to look no further,) as they are susceptible of a latent, or a less active state, as well as of a state of irresistible energy, and as, during their latent state, they are embedded in the inert and dissoluble masses, formed by the ponderable elements, it must happen that, as often as they pass from the latent to the active state, these masses are either decomposed, or to some extent affected. But instead of this, it is surely conceivable, either that the energetic principles, such as light, heat, electricity, should be excluded from a latent combination with the inert elements; or that they should not leave that state, and that the inert should retain what they possess, unalterably. In such a constitution of elements there could, as it seems, be no formations, no transitions, no growth, and no decay—no death. A world so constituted would be, during the sovereign pleasure of the Creator, unchangeable and eternal; or if it were allowable to apply to the physical world inspired language, intended probably to apply only to the spiritual world, the scheme of things we have imagined might be described as "incorruptible, undefiled, and not fading away."

Such, as we suppose, must be the consequence of establishing a *real* counterpoise between the active and the inert elements of the material world. In the system around us, three great principles are reciprocating their influences: first, the inert elements; secondly, the active elements—light, heat, and electricity, which however may be so many modifications merely of one element; and thirdly, the principle of life, vegetable and animal, which we assume to be nothing else but MIND. From the interaction of the two former, results the circle of changes within which all bodies are revolving, through their solid, fluid, and gaseous states. From the action of the third upon the first and second, results organization, with its various functions; but organization, in combining these two unequal forces, submits to the inevitable condition of that combination, and begins to decay almost as soon as it reaches its perfection. At present, the principle of life seems to attach itself more intimately to the inert elements, and less so to the active; and therefore it lies exposed to all the power of the one over the other. But let the principle of life take on to the active elements—let it, itself essentially active, be balanced against the active, and be so adjusted therewith as to form a permanent combination, and then life might continue at its point of rest for ever.

Not forgetting the caution, once and again mentioned, we might yet, conditionally, make a reference to those passages, heretofore quoted, which affirm the future dissolution of the material world by fire; and assuming, for a moment, the literal sense of those predictions, (and it is not proved that the literal sense should be rejected,) then it will seem to be intimated that the unequal and restless counterpoise which had so long subsisted between light and heat and the inert elements, shall at last be overthrown; the former breaking through all restraints, and overcoming the latter, and so overcoming it as that it shall no more be capable of retaining the active force in a latent state.

But the principle of life—that is to say, Mind, is not dissoluble by any other principle; nor can it give way before any intensity of a merely material energy; and although doubtless dependent upon the pleasure of the Creator, and immortal only by his will, who sustains that which he has produced, yet must it be thoroughly independent of all coexistent and inferior forces. We may at once be sure, on the one hand, that life will endure only so long as He shall please who is the giver of life; and on the other, that it is a principle standing beyond the reach of all other influences, and inherently superior to every other. Let then the material universe vanish, silent and unnoticed as a dream; or let it melt with fervent heat, and pass away, as in a painful convulsion, with "a great noise;" in either case, all minds, rational and moral, shall emerge from the mighty ruin, and float clear and untouched above the terrors and the tempest of nature's dying day. Mind shall shake itself of the corruptible and dissoluble elements, and shall put on incorruption; it shall lay down the dishonour of its union with the inert masses of the material world, and put on the glory of a purely active and uncompounded corporeity; it shall take leave of death, and be clothed with immortality.

It is nothing else but an anticipation of this rising of mind over the level of matter, that is now going on within the human system. Mind, in its first stage of combination with matter, exercises only the lowest of its faculties, and is long little more than merely passive; but it gains every day upon the conditions of animal life, exerts more and more of its inherent powers, mechanical and rational; and at length, not only governs, in a high spontaneous manner, its immediate body, but so diverts and controls the powers of the material world as to make itself, in a sense, master of nature, and to serve itself of her laws. The arts of life are precisely so many conquests of mind, and so many instances of the yielding of matter to the pleasure of mind. Again, by its powers of abstraction the most abstruse relations of the material world are mastered and reduced to a practical subserviency; and then, by the aid of these same relations, the vastness of the material universe is so far grasped, by our methods of reasoning, as to yield itself in degree to our conceptions, and to come within the range of our calculations. Man, although not yet lord of the visible universe as an adult, is lord of it as an heir, and exercises an authority becoming the minority of one for whom vast possessions are in reserve. This is not the language of empty pretension: modern science and art make good, in detail, all that is here affirmed at large.

But as we go deeper and deeper into the recesses of our nature, and duly consider the dignity and the powers of the moral life, and the vast compass of the affections, we shall feel, in far greater force, the truth—a truth of unbounded import, that the most excellent forms of matter are as nothing in comparison with the worth and destinies of the spirit. The affections of the spirit, and their power of intimate communion with the Infinite Spirit, not only raise the mind immeasurably above the level of the visible world, and carry it clear of the fate of that world, but raise it even above the range of the merely intellectual faculties, so that a state may be conceived of, far better and higher than that of the highest exercise of reason.

In truth, what is it that leads us to attach the value we do attach to intellectual labour and achievement?—not the mere practical result of those engagements; nor the mere labour, in itself considered; but the EMOTION, the sentiment, the moral power, connected with it, and by which it is prompted, animated, and rewarded. Within the entire circle of our intellectual constitution we value nothing but emotion;—it is not the powers, or the exercise of the powers, but the fruit of those powers, in so much *feeling*, of a lofty kind, as they will yield. Now that toward which we are constantly tending, as our goal—that which we rest in when it is attained, as sufficient—is that which shall be ultimate, and shall survive whatever has been mediate, or contributory, or accessory. Every thing short of the affections of the soul is a means to an end, and must have its season; it is temporary; but the affections of the soul are the end of all, and they are eternal. Let the universe perish or be changed—the soul shall live.

CHAPTER XIX.

THE GENERAL GROUND OF CONJECTURAL REASONING CONCERNING WHAT IS UNSEEN OR FUTURE.

THE suppositions we have followed, in the three preceding chapters, although separable and independent, are not irreconcilable; but on the contrary, may well consist one with the other, or may each be true in part. Thus it may be the fact that the widely dissimilar physical condition of the solar and the planetary surfaces, as adapted to the support of living species, may, in our own system, and in others, constitute a broad ground of distinction as to the modes of existence severally found there; and that while the planetary species, of all ranks, are necessarily corruptible and mortal, and are permanent only by reproduction, the solar species may enjoy an individual permanency; and even if liable to transformations, may yet be exempt from dissolution. Or if we scrupled to admit this bold conjecture, in its whole extent, yet it is almost impossible to resist the belief, first, that the father-world of the system, itself, the fountain of light, heat, and vital energy, is vastly more than a desert—a naked and terrible wilderness of tempestuous combustion; and secondly, that if actually peopled with various orders, the physical law of their life is more excellent than that which prevails in the planets. The known and visible physical difference between the sun and the planets, goes near to making it certain that the powers of life in the one, must be more steadily balanced where stimulus is perpetual, than where it is intermittent.

At the same time, and while it is supposed that palpable and visible organization, whether mortal or immortal, makes its home upon the surfaces of the solar and planetary bodies, it may be quite true (nor indeed, without doing violence to the language of Scripture can we believe otherwise) that each world, of every system, includes, or is surrounded by, invisible orders, of several species, ranks, and qualities; corporeal, indeed, but imponderable, and attached to an element not open to cognizance by the animal senses. This belief, considered as a matter of philosophy, and not of religion or of faith, needs only that our notions of the corporeal part of the mental constitution should be defined and cleared up a little more, and it would then take its place among truths imperfectly known, but rationally admitted; and it might receive enlargement and confirmation by means of a more exact attention to innumerable facts, that have been suffered to pass unnoticed. On this subject something will be advanced in the next and concluding chapter.

But while the actual universe, as now constituted, is supposed to include great inequalities of the corporeal economy, and to have its local distributions of life—life corruptible, and life incorruptible, and also to comprise within each locality the difference of palpable and impalpable corporeity, it may yet be true (and the apparent meaning of the inspired writings conveys the belief) that the entire framework of nature has its limited era, and shall, after fulfilling an introductory purpose in the great scheme of the creation, give place to a new and higher order of things, and to a construction of elements such as shall better consist with those ultimate moral ends for the sake of which all things are. "We," according to the divine promise, "look for a new heavens and a new earth, wherein is to dwell righteousness."

Thus may our three conjectures be combined, and made to consist, one with the other. But then, in reviewing the whole, as so adjusted, we owe it to our respect for the divine testimony (each one owes it to his own sense of piety) very clearly to separate from the mass so much as shall seem involved in the language of the inspired writers. This portion, whatever may be its amount, and on this point there will be a diversity of opinion, is to be set off; and then so much as remains is to be accounted conjectural simply, and as such to be dealt with. But then, while taking due care not to confound mere speculation with serious articles of belief, we should also take care not incuriously to dismiss undistinguished the entire mass of what is called—conjectural; for although a portion of this hypothetical matter may be nothing better than sheer supposition, and may be sustained only by some general agreement with what is known, another portion may perhaps claim to be considered with a closer attention, and may justly invite examination, as not unlikely to lead to some real advancements of certain branches of philosophy. On this point also something more may presently be said; meanwhile let us, on broad grounds, endeavour to embody the principles that justify conjectures, such as those that have been above propounded.

Reasoning from analogy is only the assuming that a certain power, or law, or principle, which is seen to take effect, in a given manner, under conditions specified, will also operate in the same, or in a similar manner, *elsewhere*, under conditions nearly the same. Thus whatever is found to belong to the general principle of gravitation, and to motion through resisting mediums, in this earth of ours, is confidently supposed to belong to the same principle, and to motion in other planets and other systems, when once it has been ascertained that gravitation actually extends to those systems, and regulates their revolutions. We consider it as certain that the law is the same, although the effects may be varied by the difference of the conditions under which it operates. As for example, if the density of Saturn, as compared with that of the earth, be not much greater than cork, then, his bulk also considered, the tendency of bodies on his surface will proportionately differ from the tendency of similar bodies on the surface of the earth: or again; the velocity of the equatorial regions of Jupiter being vastly greater than that of the earth's equatorial band, and the bulk of the two planets also differing, the respective variation between the weight of bodies, at different latitudes, between the poles and the equator, in the two planets, will vary accordingly;—the one law holding good *invariably* in both. In drawing inferences of this sort, it would be a false diffidence to call them conjectures; for we tread on solid ground, although the path be far extended.

Now our reasoning is not much less firm in texture, or much less entitled to confidence in its conclusions, when we consider this portion of the universe, which is our home, and with which we are familiarly acquainted, as an exhibition—be it on a very small scale, of the leading principles of the creation, itself the product of unchanging intelligence and goodness. The universe is not the work of chance, and therefore will not be found to contain any boundless irregularities, or mere freaks and inconsistencies of plan and principle. The universe is the work of mind, and the expression of fixed moral attributes; it will therefore, amid all its diversities, keep close to principle and law. We could not indeed, *à priori*, say what these principles must be; nor can we, apart from actual knowledge, fix a boundary upon the scale that measures the extreme instances of diversity; nevertheless we may conclude that, whatever is found to consist with these ruling motives, or to come within the circle of these great reasons, in our own world, must consist with them elsewhere; and moreover, that every single principle which here manifests itself in a copious and unexhausted manner, is probably the display of a universal energy, that must find exercise, not in this world merely, but in all.

Thus for instance it is usual to argue, with confidence, from the fact of the incalculable multiplication of animal life, under so many forms, on the surface of this planet, that an unbounded diffusion of life is the universal intention of the creative power; and then, when we find the heavens to be filled with innumerable worlds, as if in harmony with this very same productive energy, and find too, so far as our observation reaches, that these worlds are all governed by the same physical laws, we conclude, not surely very uncertainly, that all worlds, or most worlds (for there may be single exceptions) are abodes of life; and not less variously or copiously so than our own. If this often-repeated argument from analogy is to be termed (as to the conclusion it involves) a conjecture merely, we ought then to abandon altogether every kind of abstract reasoning; nor will it be easy afterwards to make good any principle of natural theology. In truth the very basis of moral reasoning is shaken by a skepticism so sweeping as this.

To set the rule of analogical reasoning, as now employed, clear of all objections and difficulties, would demand a volume; but at present, taking it as generally received, and using it a little further than can here be fully made good in its details, yet not any further than, as the author believes, might be strictly justified, we apply it to the conjectures lately propounded, as follows:—

The universe, as actually known to us, is very clearly susceptible of being considered in a threefold aspect: that is to say, first, as extended through *space;* secondly, as extended in *kind*, or by diversity of species and modes of existence; and thirdly, as extended through duration, or in *time.* Thus, and without logical refinement, we think of the creation or of any single region of it, as *mathematically* measurable; as *physically* open to description; and as demanding to be *historically* recorded, in respect of its commencement, and the epochs and revolutions it may have passed through.

Now bringing the rule of analogy—analogy, including a belief in the universality of the divine attributes, into its application to the above-named threefold view of the creation, we seem warranted in supposing that there will be a proportion or a symmetry, so connecting these three modes of extension, as that not one of them will immeasurably surpass the others. This assumption may easily be explained, and its reasonableness illustrated, by stating some contrary suppositions, as thus:—

Let us imagine ourselves to have come up to the exterior wall of a vast palace, which already we have seen to cover many acres; but on entering the outer gate, and in passing through its courts, we find that the enormous structure rises only one story from the basement, that its chambers are all of uniform dimensions, are all alike in embellishment and furniture, and that, in seeing the first of its thousand halls, we have seen all. And what if an unvarying ceremonial, and endless round of dull manœuvres, repeated day after day, through the year, and year after year, comprises the history of the personages of this palace! The very idea is insufferable. Now to apply our illustration to the argument in hand, we consider it inevitable, or nearly so, to conclude that the material universe—this palace of the great king, is as various and vast in the *species* and modes of life it includes, as it is vast in mathematical extent; and also, that it is proportionately vast and various in the destinies and the revolutions of which it shall be the theatre.

The visible extent of the creation *through space*, we take as an indication, by the rule of symmetry, of the incalculable compass of the *varieties of being*, now actually occupying the abodes that constitute the celestial system; and again, this same visible extent of the creation seems to bespeak a corresponding vastness of range in *the changes and revolutions*, the transitions and the fortunes, that shall constitute the history of the entire system.

By freely admitting the hypothesis of this sort of proportion, as involved in the symmetry of the universe, and as placing its extent in space, its extent in species, and its extent in time, on a footing of equality, we seem to have gained an idea of the whole, such as comports with the notion we must entertain of the infinite perfections of Him whose work it is.

Will then the reader go forward with the author upon the ground of this supposition, as not unreasonable—That the vastness of the visible universe, so far as it actually comes within our means of knowledge, may be taken as a sort of guage of the vastness of that range of intellectual and moral existence of which the visible universe is the platform? If this rule of measurement be granted, it will imply a corresponding vastness, or unbounded range of fortunes, as attaching to the intellectual economy, and as yet to be developed in the lapse of time. Presuming upon the reader's willingness to grant the premises now demanded, it will be proper to endeavour to define a little our conceptions of the actual extent of the material system; not, indeed, as if the starry fields were to be measured by the line of human calculation, or as if the mere multiplying of figures would enable the mind to grasp the quantities they represent. Nevertheless there is something which may be done, the doing of which is highly important to the purpose we have immediately in view. In dealing with a theme such as this, wherein the objects spoken of immeasurably transcend as well the powers of the conceptive faculty as the powers of arithmetic and of language, the very plainest style, and the very homeliest terms, are the most appropriate; inasmuch as while employing such a style and terms, the illusion is avoided of supposing, either that our ideas, or our mode of expressing them, bears any sort of proportion to the things spoken of. We will then speak of the probable dimensions of the heavens, as we should of the width and height of a building.

Methods of computation (as every one knows) which are not uncertain, afford us the means of advancing a negative proposition, to this effect, that the nearest of the fixed stars is more remote than the distance, already mentioned, (page 55,) or about twenty billions of miles, a distance which would be traversed by light (passing ninety-five millions of miles in 8 min. 7 sec.) in three years and 216 days. But there are millions of stars so much more remote than those that have been supposed to afford a parallax, that they may actually have ceased to exist three thousand years ago, and yet may appear in their places;—their last ray not having reached our system: these facts every one is familiar with.

But now, in supposing ourselves to pass on beyond the nearer strata of the starry expanse, and towards the most remote which powerful telescopes discover, have we any reason to imagine that we are approaching the confines of creation? or shall we conclude that, beyond the reach of the human eye, and the telescope, nothing remains? This were surely a greater presumption than to admit as probable, the contrary supposition, well as it consists with what we actually know. What is it that encircles the creation, so far as seen? certainly not any limit of the creative power. But the material world is not *infinite:* and yet infinitude allows that the visible heavens should be multiplied or repeated millions of times, and still that it should lie far within the limits of the infinite. The apparent probability is that the universe has no such limits as those which the human eye extends to. The inference we are warranted in drawing is of the same sort as that we should adopt, concerning the expanse of the ocean, in looking at the horizon from successive elevations:—we first measure the watery field from the deck of a ship; and thence we behold a billowy line, not much exceeding a radius of a league or two: but we ascend the shrouds, and at the height of the main yards or cross-trees perceive that a much evener horizon marks a distance at which the waves cease to be discernible, or to present a serrated line: and we accordingly extend our calculations to the distance of eight or ten leagues: thence we climb to the topmast, and again stretch our circle to a double diameter, or more; and if we could borrow the wings of the eagle, and soar to the clouds, we should still gaze upon a widening prospect, and find that the dim distance enlarges at every stage of our ascent, and at a rate surpassing the scale we had assumed at the first.

It is thus that every extension of our means of knowing the starry field, has only served to open to us a vastly wider prospect, without giving any indication of our discerning a limit: on the contrary, new nebulæ, similar to those that have been found to consist of innumerable stars, are revealed, and new vistas of worlds are dimly opened before us. Thus we have every reason to suppose the creation to be immensely more extensive than the space reached by the telescope: and yet this space, in the mode in which it offers itself to our conceptions, suggests a supposition, tending to give consistency, as well as enlargement, to our notions of the universe.

The galaxy, ascertained to consist of innumerable stars, and forming, as seen from our system, a somewhat irregular band, encircling the heavens, obliquely to the ecliptic, gives to the general figure of the starry expanse the form of a flat parallelogram, about the midst of which is placed the sun of our system. Laterally, and looking towards the sides of this parallelogram, the stars are comparatively scanty; but looking in any direction, longitudinally, or towards the extremities, we include, of course, a vast perspective, and see a thickened brightness, constituted of the countless worlds that are ranged within the general figure.

But now, in adhering to the analogy of the celestial mechanism, can we conceive of this parallelogram as being such indeed, and as stretching itself, in obedience to no rule of symmetry, through space, like a raft floating in the ocean? or shall we not rather believe that the portion of the field of space which we see replenished with suns, constitutes really a segment of a sphere so immeasurably vast, that the suns ranged in the *opposite sides* of the hollow globe are far beyond the range of vision, or even beyond the passage of light? In fact, the diameter of this supposed sphere must be such that, if light could traverse it, countless ages must elapse before it could reach us. The supposition we now propound may be readily conceived of by any one who imagines a hollow globe, we will say of three feet diameter, formed of a crust of glass, two inches thick; and this crust containing, pretty plentifully, grains or spangles of gold and silver, evenly distributed in its substance. Now if we think of the eye as stationed at any one of these grains, as its point of view, the speckled glassy crust would present an appearance not very unlike that offered by the starry heavens; that is to say, laterally, to the right and left, the substance would be comparatively clear of grains; but in every direction, longitudinally, and when the eye follows the course of the substance, the grains would seem so thickly ranged as to give a shining opacity to its appearance. At the same time, the opposite side of the globe would be too remote for its grains to attract the eye.

This supposition, consisting as it does with the law which imposes a spherical figure upon all the celestial masses and motions, and so recommending itself as probable, and as agreeable to the analogy of known facts, implies that the portion of the heavens seen by us, bears but a small proportion to the part which is unseen; such a proportion, for example, as is borne by the Australian continent to the entire surface of our globe. To present the appearance which it actually does, this visible portion can hardly exceed the extent of fifty degrees of the circle.

And yet, when we have conceived of a hollow starry sphere, such as has been described, are we to conclude that we have compassed the material universe? If there be *one* such sphere, there may be, in remotest space, another; and if another, many. This world of ours is not the universe; —the solar system is not the universe;—but do our telescopes of twenty feet long sweep the field of the universe? The probability that they do not is nearly as strong as any probability can be: every reason is on the other side; and with the infinity of space as the field, and the infinite creative power and will of the Supreme Being as the means, the belief that this energy reaches its boundary within any circle that created minds will ever be able to measure or to conceive of is not to be entertained. On the contrary, we may far more reasonably suppose, not only that the divine perfections of power and wisdom abstractedly, will always surpass the comprehension of finite beings, but that the *products* of those perfections will stretch out beyond the longest line of created minds: and that not the loftiest seraph shall ever be able to reach a spot whence, with even a seraph's ken, he may be able to descry the lone boundaries of the creation, and to look out beyond the circle of productive power. Rather let us believe that creatures—the highest of them, let them wander where they may, and as far as they may, and let them hold on their course with unwearied curiosity, age after age, and in what direction they may please, shall yet find themselves in the very heart of the populous dominions of the Almighty, and surrounded in all directions by worlds, and by systems of worlds.

Whoever takes the simple facts now ascertained, and which form part of our astronomy, and with laborious and continued effort of the mind follows them out, and brings them within grasp, even faintly, of the conceptive and rational faculties, will find it far more easy to go the length we have now gone, in our hypothesis of the material universe, than to stop short of it, at any point, and to conceive of a limit or a cessation of the creative energy. Such a limit, place it where we may, offends reason; but the unbounded conception gives us the liberty we want in thinking of God and of his works.

Whatever may be the speculations we indulge concerning the vastness or the form of the visible universe, it manifestly transcends all our powers of conception and calculation. The stars of heaven are as the sands upon the seashore—innumerable; and they are planted through space at distances, one from the other, exceeding all means of measurement:—this is enough. But now, in considering the vast structure as THE WORK OF MIND, and as the product, not of power merely, but of wisdom, we are absolutely compelled to assign to the whole some purpose, proportionate to the mechanical preparation for life which it furnishes. The vastness of the platform assuredly implies a corresponding grandeur of intention, and an intention as ample in its compass as the necessary conditions of finite being may admit. That is to say, in looking at the heavens we assume that a theatre so stupendous does, and shall sustain the utmost amount of life, not merely in *numbers*, but in *kinds*, which it might, abstractedly, sustain. The Creator having, as we see, put forth his power unboundedly, in relation to space, shall he not put it forth unboundedly also in relation to the *species*, and modes of existence?

The strength of an inference such as this will be differently estimated by different minds; but there are few, if any, who would not admit it to some extent. For example; none could tolerate the idea, and especially seeing what we do see in our own planet, that the innumerable spheres around us are totally untenanted, and that the stupendous celestial mechanism is a mechanism merely. Not much more admissible is the idea that, our own planet excepted, the lowest forms of life only, as of vegetables and zoophytes are to be found in all the wide fields of creation. Nor, again, can the mind satisfy itself, or get free from a distressing sense of disproportion, in stopping short of the belief that intellectual and moral life on a scale, at least equal to that which has place in this world, has also place in other worlds.

But this is barely enough ; or it is the lowest supposition that can at all be entertained ; and the idea which the author would fain set at work in the reader's mind, involves a principle that carries us much further. It is not merely that we involuntarily expect to find, within so vast a scheme, beings higher in faculty and power than man ; but that a wider range should be taken, as to the modes of existence. In all worlds is there then nothing to be found except animal organization, and nothing more excellent ? Is the creative energy so hemmed in as that the human structure is the highest and the best that can be accomplished ? If nothing restrains it, as we see it is not restrained, in respect of dimensions or numbers, is it restrained in respect of the means and elements of life ? We conclude it is not ; and, on the contrary, must profess to believe that the supposed reach of power, in the one respect, is fully borne out by its reach in the other ; and that the universe is not more amazing in a simply mechanical or mathematical sense, than it is in what we must call its physiology.

The divine attributes, as we have already had occasion to observe, are not to be conceived of like the faculties or the impulses of human nature, as so many distinct and separable qualities or powers, any one or more of which may come into play, while the others remain inert. Nothing less can be admitted, concerning the infinite and absolute Being, than that He is ONE in essence, in a sense exclusive of all partial modes of procedure, or single exertions of particular attributes. We must by no means think that the divine power is put forth in any instance, not accompanied by the divine wisdom; or these again apart from goodness and justice. God is not, in any act, just only, or good only, or wise only, or almighty only; but always, and in every particular act, he exhibits, or if not exhibits, really exercises the complement of his awful perfections; and as we must not think that any one of those attributes which we, from the limitation of our powers, are compelled to speak of distinctively, comes into act alone, so neither must we suppose that any one attribute is ever, or in any case, latent; for the latter supposition, as well as the former, implies what must never be granted—a parting, or a divisibility of the divine nature. This belief of what must be termed the simplicity and integrity of the Infinite Being, which is of the utmost importance in relation to every branch of theology, carries with it the belief that, if God creates at all, he will create in the plenary exercise of his undivided perfections.

Now what we actually see of the celestial system goes little further than to display infinite power. Our scientific deductions indeed give evidence of intelligence in the equipoise of the planetary revolutions; but at this point, we stop. And yet, although deprived of the means of immediately ascertaining, or of witnessing the exertions of the other attributes of Deity, ought we to doubt, or can we, with any consistency doubt, that power and intelligence, thus boundlessly put forth, under our eyes, are moving alone? Rather we conclude, and with a rational confidence, that bare power and intelligence are subsidiary to the exercise of the moral perfections; and that therefore, on the theatre of the material universe, the greatest range possible is taken for putting in movement those loftier attributes.

It is on this ground then, that while we attach little importance to any hypothesis concerning the universe, which is not distinctly sustained by scriptural evidence, or actual facts, we challenge a serious importance for the PRINCIPLE on which all such conjectures proceed, and can by no means admit that the refutation of any one such particular hypothesis involves a rejection of the theory of which it may be an individual expression.

What has now been said concerning that range and variety in the modes of existence which seems implied, by the rule of symmetry, in the mere vastness of the material universe, is plainly applicable also, as we have assumed it to be, to that range and variety of *fortune* which the lapse of time shall devèlop. If we cannot admit the belief that a low uniformity prevails through all worlds, neither can we imagine a dull monotony to be the law of all.

In truth, the very attributes which have given birth to variety at any one moment, must give birth to variety successively, or through the eras of time. That same power and intelligence which expand in the one direction, will expand in the other, by necessity; nor can we assign any value to our argument in its bearing upon space and species, which will not attach to it, in an equal degree, in relation to time.

Moreover, high faculties involve high destinies, whether for the better or the worse: a faculty is a germinating power; and the more profound or expansive it is, the greater will be the difference between its early and its later development. A being endowed with complex faculties will never fail to create to itself A HISTORY. Two such beings associated, will generate a course of events indefinitely various; and a large community of beings, each gifted with active powers, and impelled by various and contrary impulses, must impart a complexity to the course of events such as is not to be unravelled, or brought round to its simple elements, within any brief period. Or perhaps, we should rather say that a course of events, complicated as it must be by springing from the interaction of beings themselves complex in powers and desires, will perpetually involve itself deeper and deeper, with the great principles of moral government; and thus will accumulate its demands upon futurity, wherein laws are to be vindicated, and irregularities are to be reduced to system.

To bring then our present argument to a conclusion, and summarily to state its import, we look upon the visible universe, its immeasurable spaces, and its innumerable spheres, as a fully expressed symbol of Power, and as a partially expressed symbol of Wisdom;—we say partially, because it is hardly at all by the eye, and only in degree by the inferences of science, that the construction of this stupendous work is at present cognizable. But we do not forget that it is by accommodation to our own modes of thinking that we speak of the power and wisdom of God *distinctively*, and that, in truth, these attributes are relations only of the one Undivided and Infinite Nature. This same celestial structure therefore, could we examine it throughout, would be found to exhibit every other attribute, in act, with an equal or proportionate intensity. The power has not gone further than the wisdom has gone; nor these further than the goodness or the rectitude; and the universe is doubtless as great in every sense, as it is great in mere dimension, and in number of parts. It is as if, upon the palace wall of the Supreme, a hand were seen writing—and already it has written, in our view—"Power," and partly

Wisdom; but knowing whose name it is, of which this writing is the initial portion, we well know that the entire inscription must run on much further.

Let every one then—every one capable of holding correspondence with the Creative Mind, let every one read, in the visible heavens, a dim, and yet not fallacious presage of the vastness, and depth, and height, of that unseen economy, with which he shall find his destinies involved; and let him believe that, when this now unseen economy comes to be known, the vastness of the material theatre shall cease to attract regard, in comparison with the stupendous movements and destinies which it sustains.

CHAPTER XX.

ON THE ADVANCEMENT OF PNEUMATOLOGY.

The two pioneers of physical philosophy are Accident and Hypothesis; and so it has been that science, while professing to care for nothing but what is certain, has actually owed the extension of her domain very much to chance, and not less to conjecture. This humiliating fact, if indeed it should be thought of as humiliating, is forcibly felt, and freely acknowledged, during the spring season of any single branch of science; for then the particular instances are fresh in every one's recollection; but afterwards, and when the new truths have acquired firmness and consistency, and when they have settled down into the form of an ascertained system, and when this system begins to exact submission, instead of asking for patronage, then it is apt to shrink disdainfully from its early helps, and to frown upon hypothesis, and to think itself beyond the reach of any further accessions from accident. This feeling and practice, however, ought not to be admitted; and philosophy, in its ripest state, should still favour the means of its early triumphs, and freely yield itself to every new chance of advancement.

All this is especially true in relation to the several branches of intellectual philosophy; and yet the very difficulty of the subject, which should incline those who pursue it to admit and invite every possible aid, seems rather to inspire a prudish jealousy, as if what is felt to be held in an uncertain and precarious manner, were secure only while guarded against every rudeness.

Among the expressions of this sort of latent fear, the following may be named; and first, a stern decision in relation to certain natural subjects of curiosity, concerning the physical constitution of man, that they lie hopelessly beyond the reach of the human faculties; and that it is a proof of ignorance and presumption, and of an incapacity to discern the real limits of mental philosophy, so much as to moot these questions, or to indicate a wish to pursue them; just as it is held to be the sign of a smattering acquaintance with mathematical principles, to go in quest of a perpetual motion. Again, this same unacknowledged feeling would restrict us, not merely in relation to the subjects of inquiry, but as to the mode of conducting those inquiries which, in themselves, are granted to be legitimate.

Mental philosophy must be cultivated, it is said, with clean hands; that is to say, in a rigid avoidance of any process of investigation not strictly analytic and metaphysical; or such as would seem to bring these high themes down from their elevation, and set them upon the common level of physiological researches. All we can know of MIND (as we are taught to believe) is to be found in an analysis of our personal consciousness:—the mental philosopher need never leave his study. Mental philosophy is granted to be inductive; but the materials of the induction are all in the bosom.

Once more; the very same freedom in admitting conjectures which, within the circle of the physical sciences, is allowed and encouraged, on the well understood principle that such conjectures (never confounded with ascertained facts) may lead the way to discovery, and keep the mind alert, and ready to avail itself of happy accidents—this same freedom of conjecture, which has been so fruitful a source of important advancements, is somewhat superciliously discarded from the precincts of Intellectual Philosophy, as worthy only of vulgar and empirical minds. But before conjecture or hypothesis is thus excluded from the range of mental science, it should be proved, that the occult constitution of rational and sentient beings is to be explored by the method of analysis alone; for it is manifest, that if the mental, like the animal structure, may possibly become better known than it is by a collation of various classes of facts—facts assembled under the guidance of a previously assumed theory, then it will follow that it is to the aid of hypothesis we should look for further advancements in this as well as in other lines of physical inquiry. And in truth, by so much as this subject is obscure, and remote from immediate observation, the more need have we of such assistance. Do we not possess mental firmness enough to secure ourselves against the dangers of putting mere conjecture in the place of real science? If we do not, then let us abstain altogether from philosophic pursuits.

But it may be asked, what room is there for hypothesis, or in what direction are conjectures to be hazarded, in relation to the proper objects of mental philosophy? In reply, we grant at once, that there is little room for admitting these pregnant methods of inquiry in relation to that sort of mental philosophy which turns upon the adjustment and exact expression of abstract notions, and which is properly termed METAPHYSICS. But we look wider when we think of intellectual science, and think of it as a branch of physiology. Thus understood, it not merely embraces more objects, but comes under methods of investigation that are more diversified. Metaphysics is analytic simply; but Intellectual Philosophy, while it employs analysis, rests mainly upon induction, (in the physical sense of the term,) and must employ as well hypothesis as observation and experiment.

Metaphysical mental philosophy is the knowledge of MIND; but Physical mental philosophy is the knowledge of MINDS; and this distinction opens before us at once a wide and various field. The knowledge of *minds* we might consent to designate by the term Pneumatology, comprehensively understood; and it will then lead us to make inquiry, not merely concerning the laws of mind, as discoverable by an analysis of our personal consciousness, but concerning those often-recurrent varieties of mental conformation (within the human system) which assume very nearly the distinctness and the regularity that constitute *specific* differences, and which might properly give rise to a classification by orders, genera, and species. If any such classification were effected, it is manifest that a comparison of the differences on the ground of which it was made would immensely extend and advance our knowledge of mind in the abstract; for it is only by setting off the differences, one after another, that any generic body or class of things can be known.

But this is not all; for, on the one hand, with the many indications, some indeed obscure, and some explicit, of the existence of rational orders, other than the human, and, on the other hand, with innumerable sentient and voluntary species around us, partaking with ourselves, in the fullest manner, of all the rudimental faculties of mind, and exhibiting proofs also of the germs, or faint characteristics, of some of the highest faculties, it can never be assented to that mental philosophy should be restricted within the limits of the human system.

Even if it were true that we may know much more of

the human mind than of any other class, and that the knowledge of the human mind is of more practical consequence than the knowledge of any other, it will not follow, if we regard the spirit and rules of our modern physical sciences, that we should so narrow the range of our curiosity. But in truth, it may be made to appear, that the knowledge of the human mind is more likely to be advanced in relation to what still remains obscure, by pursuing these difficulties on other ground than that of the *human* mind, than by arrogantly and pertinaciously continuing to fix our attention upon the facts of our personal consciousness. Let us leave our closets, forsake our dim seclusions, and our lamps, and open our eyes upon the wide world of animated beings.

In relation to the *supernal* branch of pneumatology, alluded to above, it is granted that *science* can go but a little way, with its merely natural means of information; nor is it desirable that an intermixture of philosophical inquiries and Biblical deductions should be encouraged. On this very principle the author, in the preceding pages, has avoided every thing beyond a mere passing reference to facts known to us only through the medium of the inspired writings. The subject is a Biblical one, and might well engage the attention of those qualified to pursue it, in the legitimate methods of interpretation and criticism. And yet, in placing this obscure subject in a clearer light than at present falls upon it, little probably would be done by any who should resolve to entertain none of those mere conjectures which suggest themselves to us in hours of unrestricted meditation. Those numerous passages of Scripture which affirm or imply the existence and agency of superhuman and of extra-human orders, are manifestly imperfect allusions merely to single points of a vast scheme, veiled from our view; and unless we court the aid of hypothesis—and of more than one hypothesis, in expounding these scattered notices, it is not probable that we shall ever advance a step beyond the mere literal interpretation of single texts. On the contrary, it might happen, that a series of suppositions, well devised, might at length lead to some such general notion on the subject as would give consistency to all parts of the evidence, dissipate many difficulties, and even lead to our entertaining more expanded and more affecting notions of that scheme within which our own destinies are involved.

In advancing the conjectures which, in the present work, he has hazarded, the author has briefly stated some of those suppositions he has been accustomed to entertain, in reading the Scriptures, with the very view of catching every faint indication of things unseen, and which often are of a kind so obscure as to escape notice entirely, except when the mind is quickened, in an unusual manner, by the incitement of some general and consistent conception of the unseen economy. No sound mind is seduced from its sobriety longer than a few minutes by any such conception, how plausible soever it may seem. But although not beguiled, the mind may be substantially aided by thus entertaining an hypothesis. Let, for example, some one such theory be distinctly digested, and the mind filled with it; and let it be compared with whatever we know of the system of the universe, whether by analogy or observation; and then let the entire chain of Scripture evidence, critically examined, be gone over, with a view to this particular supposition. The consequence will be, perhaps, its absolute rejection; or perhaps it may so adjust itself with special points of the evidence as to forbid its total rejection, and so as may lead to its being held in reserve, to be compared with the results of inquiries conducted on some other principle.

But are such inquiries altogether futile and vain? Will those venture to say so, who entertain a due reverence for the canon of Scripture, and who believe that every separate portion of it is placed where it is found with a specific intention, and for an important end? Let it rather be believed as probable that, if our Christianity is to recommend itself more extensively than hitherto it has done, to mankind at large, it will be, in part, by our obtaining some more enlarged conceptions of the great spiritual economy—conceptions such as may impart the vividness of reality to our faith in things unseen.

But we turn, at present, from this more obscure and difficult branch of pneumatology, which must always come rather within the range of theology than of science; and advert to that other branch of the same subject, in relation to which all the materials are under our eye, and the methods of proceeding are strictly and simply inductive.

Now whatever may be the prejudices that stand in the way of such a course of inquiry, it appears that, if our object be to analyze the mind, and to learn the conditions and laws that attach, severally, to its faculties, a scrutiny of our personal consciousness is but one of the means to be employed: and indeed it is now acknowledged, by some of the authorities in this department of philosophy, that an attention to the multifarious developments of the intellectual and moral powers, in individual minds, is advantageous or indispensable, for completing intellectual science; and that it is by comparing these various facts with our own consciousness, that either is to be understood. Thus while the method of analysis and abstraction interprets the facts collected by observation, these enlarge and define the results of analysis.

But what principle, admitted as good in any other department of science, will justify our confining our view to *human* nature, while mind is exhibiting itself under ten thousand modifications around us? All the rudiments of the mental constitution, as more fully developed in man, meet our eye and invite our curiosity in the inferior species; and it would seem to be the most natural, and the most auspicious course of inquiry, to begin at the lower part of the scale of intelligence, and to make ourselves familiar, *first*, with the simpler forms of the percipient, voluntary, and reasoning principle. A mere arrogance surely, as if intellectual philosophy were degraded by taking its first steps on so low a path, should not be allowed to have its influence with those who have learned the logic of modern science. Shall the chemist pursue his inquiries, only so far as may be done by examining the nobler elements—heat, light, electricity, the precious metals, and the diamond; but stop when it would be necessary to soil his hands with earths?

There is, however, a branch of intellectual philosophy, or we would rather say of pneumatology, in relation to which an extensive and laborious examination of the corporeal mental structure of the various sentient tribes—our fellows in animal organization, seems to be imperatively demanded, and promises to yield very important results. Once and again, in the course of this essay, the author has had occasion to refer, incidentally, to the subject which he will now endeavour, somewhat more distinctly, to express.

It is well understood that mental philosophy should be pursued irrespectively of any theory we may entertain concerning the structure or functions of the brain; and that the deductions and the distinctions which constitute this science must be precisely such as they are, whatever opinion we may adopt in reference to the purely physical question of the dependence of the mind upon animal organization. This granted, it is yet certain that we must return to the subject of animal organization when the important controversy is entered upon concerning the independent reality and immateriality of the mind, and when we have to deal with the opinion, that mind is nothing but a function of the animal structure; or that thought and perception are products of the medullary mass, just as the bilious secretion is the product of the liver.

In opposition to any such opinions, we may either take the course of metaphysical argument, and show that the soul must be a simple, indiscerptible substance, immaterial, and immortal; or we may take the moral and religious course of argument, and prove, from the instincts, the anticipations, and the grandeur of the human mind, that it must be altogether superior to the body, and must be its survivor. But now, in pursuing the first of these lines of argument (and indeed the second in part) we find ourselves entangled in some consequences not easily avoided or disposed of, in relation to the inferior tribes of the animated world, inasmuch as the reasoning we employ, and the principles we assume, will almost inevitably stretch an inference as far as to include every species of beings that perceives, and acts, and that is wrought upon by emotions allied to those we call moral. It must indeed be confessed that the argument of the immaterialist, as sometimes conducted, if pushed to its consequences, would go near to imply the immortality of birds, beasts, and fishes, of insects and of zoophytes!

Happily however there is another course open to us:

and in the first place, (which we may well afford to do,) let us get completely clear of all the embarrassments alluded to above, by ceasing to seek for any aid in establishing the *immortality* of the human soul, from the doctrine of its *immateriality*, or spirituality, or independence of matter. Man we believe to be immortal, (revelation apart,) not because his mind is separable from animal organization, but because his intellectual and moral constitution is such as to demand a future development of his nature. Why should that which is immaterial be indestructible? None can tell us; and on the contrary, we are free to suppose that there may be immaterial orders, enjoying their hour of existence and then returning to nihility.

But now, taking up the hypothesis that animal life, in all its kinds—every being that has consciousness, perception, and voluntary motion, possesses a principle totally distinct from the animal tissue, and the animal functions—a principle strictly immaterial, (although perhaps always in fact combined with some kind of corporeal congestion of elements,) then it will remain to bring this doctrine to the test of facts; and perhaps we may be able to bring it to the test of experiment. In doing so it is clear that our methods of inquiry will be the most exempt from exception, and our conclusion the most decisive, if we carry on the investigation, chiefly, on the field of inferior animal life. If on *this* field we make good our ground, every thing will be secured, as by anticipation, or *à fortiori.*

And not merely will there be an argumentative advantage in establishing the doctrine of the independence of mind, on the broader and lower basis of merely animal existence, but the almost infinitely varied structures of the animated tribes around us, will be found to offer many instances of so striking and decisive a kind, as will hardly allow of a choice of opinions, but will compel us to adopt a belief such as must utterly exclude the opinion of the materialist. If the *human* animal structure may leave us in doubt, we shall scarcely find it possible to hesitate when we come to examine the structure and physiology of inferior species: we may perhaps be perplexed in considering the question of the immateriality, or rather independence of the *human* mind, but shall be relieved of all difficulty in examining the animal mechanism of insects and worms.

There are those probably, who would not wish even to see the materialist confuted, if it must be on the strange and offensive condition—a condition so derogatory to the dignity of man, of our acknowledging a brotherhood of mind, such as shall include the polypus, the sea-jelly, and the animalcule of a stagnant pool. But science knows of no aversions, and must hold on its way, through evil report and good report. Truth, in the end, will not fail to justify itself, in all its consequences and relations.

The line of investigation necessary for doing justice to our present hypothesis, it would not be difficult to mark out. Let the muscular power be first considered, and a copious comparison of structures be instituted, such as should support a rational conclusion concerning the process, and the mechanism by which it is effected:—as thus—

In all cases of muscular movement, a connection, either with the brain, or with a ganglion sustaining the same office, by the means of the nervous chords, is indispensable:—except when the limb is supplied with galvanic excitement in an artificial manner, in which case motion ensues; but it is motion of one sort only—namely, a convulsive contraction of the stronger muscle or muscles, in each antagonist set. Now this exceptive case, accidentally made known to us, suggests the belief that, what the brain supplies is—galvanic excitement merely; or a stimulus, of whatever kind, equivalent to that which in this instance is furnished by galvanism. What we are to seek for then is—the cause of *discriminative* motion; that is to say, the cause of those movements in which the stronger muscles may remain at rest, while the weaker are called into action. The question is, Does the brain supply, not only the chemical stimulus of contractility, but also the directive or discriminative power, which acts upon certain muscles, and holds others in suspension? Now besides the abstract improbability of any such double function, belonging to the same viscus, we find, upon examining the structure and arrangement of the nervous chords, in all species, that while they are admirably fitted for discharging the office of conveying a stimulus *indiscriminately* to the limbs, they cannot, without the highest difficulty, be considered as the channels of distinct volitions to particular muscles. The one purpose speaks itself in their construction, while the other is as plainly contradicted and excluded. Especially does this seem to be the case in the nervous economy of certain of the inferior classes of the animated world.

In the general scheme then of muscular motion, there are clearly before us the several constituents—*all but one.* There is the bony fulcra or leverage, with its hinges, and the muscular fibre, banded together, secured to its attachments, and supplied with blood; and there is the nervous network, conveying, from the brain or spinal process, the stimulus which produces the vehement contraction of the fleshly tissue. But in all this we yet want the principal agent, namely, that power which determines the kind of motion, and the direction of the movement that in each instance is to ensue. Does then this agency come from the brain? The conclusion we anticipate is that it does not; inasmuch as the line of connection is not at all adapted to any such purpose. But does there remain within the animal apparatus, any system of vessels, or any gland, or any fluid, not otherwise occupied, to which we may probably assign the office of determining motion? There is none; and we therefore attribute the determination immediately to a power distinct from, and independent of, the visible structure—that is to say, the MIND, present throughout the body, and acting and feeling, wherever present, by its inherent faculty in relation to matter.

It need hardly be said that our hypothesis is open to a special mode of attestation, or refutation, by the means of the various accidents that affect the muscular power, in consequence of disease. Thus all the facts connected with convulsive and spasmodic affections, on the one hand, and with paralysis and leipothymic states of the system, on the other, or with delirium, and insanity, and febrile excitement, will, if fairly considered, either confirm or exclude the theory we adopt. Besides these methods, it is easy to imagine experiments, such as should be almost of a decisive kind.

From the examination of the muscular system, we should advance to consider the mechanism of sensation. The organ of sense and the brain, are connected by a chord: there is therefore doubtless a communication going on from the one to the other. But what is it that is conveyed; and in which direction does the current flow? It is said that sensations are transmitted from the organ to the brain;—the stream therefore is in a direction *contrary* to that which takes place in effecting muscular motion; for in that case, the volition flows down from the brain to the extremities.*

* It is not forgotten that the nerves of muscular motion and the nerves of sensation are different.

But according to our hypothesis, the course of the current is the same in both cases; and the influence conveyed is also the same. That is to say, we assume that the brain supplies the organ with galvanic excitement, and nothing else; just as it supplies the muscular fibres with galvanic excitement, and nothing else, and that, as the mind, *in the limb*, determines motion, so the mind, *in the organ*, admits sensation. Sensation, as we suppose, takes place at the tangential point or surface, where the external vibration gives rise to a vibration upon the nervous expansion.

With a view of determining the question, as here stated, we should first examine the sense of touch; and surely it must be granted that the arrangement and reticulation of the nerves of feeling are such as to render the supposition of the conveyance of distinct local sensations, from the surface of the body to the brain, in the highest degree ineligible; while the hypothesis of a mere conveyance of excitement, from the brain to the surface, and of the immediate presence of the percipient faculty, at the point of sensation, is rendered almost certain.

If, on an extensive comparison of facts, permanent and accidental, this were admitted, the same hypothesis would not be denied in relation to the other organs of sensation; and thus, instead of an organ dispatching volitions, and receiving sensations, we should have, in the brain, a secreting viscus merely; and we should then attribute sensation, volition, consciousness, and power, not to an animal organ, but to the MIND, natively fraught with power, active and passive—to the mind, linked indeed to the animal structure, but suffused throughout it, and constituting the LIFE.

The hypothesis we have here stated is surely susceptible of being brought to the test of facts, in the ordinary modes of scientific inquiry. Its consequences perhaps, if established, might be more extensive and various than at first they may appear. At least they would not fail to place Pneumatology on a firmer and a broader basis; and so to open the way for enlarged and definite conceptions of the great Spiritual Economy of the universe.

A CATALOGUE

OF THE

WRITINGS OF ISAAC TAYLOR.

Ancient Christianity,

And the Doctrines of the Oxford Tracts for the Times. Fourth Edition, with Supplement, Index, and Tables. 2 vols. 8vo., pp. 550 and 700. London, 1844.

Ancient Christianity,

And the Doctrines of the Oxford Tracts for the Times. Supplement, including Index, Tables, &c. 8vo., pp. 142. London, 1844

Spiritual Despotism.

Second Edition. 8vo., pp. 504. London, 1835.

Fanaticism. 8vo.

Natural History of Enthusiasm.

Eighth Edition. 8vo. London.

Saturday Evening.

Sixth Edition. 8vo. London. 12mo., pp. 379.

Home Education.

Crown 8vo. London, 1838.

Physical Theory of Another Life. 8vo.

Four Lectures on Spiritual Christianity,

Delivered in the Hanover-Square Rooms, London, March, 1841. 12mo., pp. 203. London, 1841.

Elements of Thought;

Or, Concise Explanations, Alphabetically Arranged, of the Principal Terms Employed in the Different Branches of Intellectual Philosophy. Seventh Edition. 12mo. London.

An Essay,

Introductory to a New Edition of Pascal's Thoughts. 12mo.

Transmission of Ancient Books

To Modern Times. 8vo.

Essay

On the Application of Abstract Reasoning in the Christian Doctrine. Originally published as an Introduction to Edwards on the Will. 12mo., pp. 163. Boston, 1832.

Wesleyan Methodist;

A Review, published in the Edinburgh Review.

Introductory Essay

To a Translation of Pfizer's Life of Luther.

Loyola and Jesuitism

In its Rudiments. 12mo., pp. 416. London, 1850.

Process of Historical Proof. 8vo.

Balance of Criminality,

Or Mental Error. 12mo.

Jane Taylor's Works.

A New Edition. With a Life and Notes. 5 vols. 12mo.

Wesley and Methodism.

Josephus, The Works of.

A New Translation, by the Rev. Robert Traill, with Notes, Explanatory Essays, and Pictorial Illustrations. Edited by *Isaac Taylor.* Royal 8vo. London, 1847.

A

CATALOGUE OF BOOKS

TREATING ON THE

IMMORTALITY OF THE SOUL.

" *For out of th' olde fieldes, as men saith,*
Cometh all this new corne from yere to yere;
And out of olde bookes, in goode faithe,
Cometh all this new science that men lere."

CHAUCER.

" We are all drawn and attracted by the desire of knowledge and science; to excel in which, we think is honourable; while we deem it mean and base to be led astray, and to wander in ignorance and error."

CICERO.

" We have another presumption in favor of this sentiment, growing out of the fact, that in all religions of antiquity the doctrine of a future state is plainly inculcated. It is inculcated, not only in the religious systems of the Chaldeans, Persians, Greeks, and Romans, but in that of the ancient Egyptians, among whom the Israelites dwelt for several centuries. 'We have here,' says Champollion, describing the inscriptions on the tombs of the ancient kings, 'the Egyptian psychological system, in an important and religious point of view, that of rewards and punishments.' We find completely demonstrated all which the ancients have told us respecting the Egyptian doctrine of the immortality of the soul."

GREPPO.

NEW YORK:
WILLIAM GOWANS.

1853.

A CATALOGUE OF BOOKS

TREATING ON THE

IMMORTALITY OF THE SOUL.

A DISCOURSE on the Certainty of a *Future and Immortal State*, in some moral, physiological, and religious considerations. 8vo. $1.00. London, 1741.

A DISCOURSE concerning the Certainty of a *Future and Immortal State*. In some moral, physiological, and religious considerations. By a Doctor of Physic. 12mo. 88 cts. London, 1706.

A FEW THOUGHTS on the Creation, Generation, Growth, and Evolution of the *Human Body and Soul;* on the Spiritual and Immortal Nature of the Soul of Man; and on the Resurrection of his Body at the Last Day. 8vo. Calf, very neat. $2.00. London, 1805.

A FREE INQUIRY into the Nature and Immortality of the Soul, managed by way of a Dialogue between an acute Philosopher and an able Divine. Done out of the French. London, 1704.

A MORAL Essay upon the Soul of Man, in three parts, Done out of the French. 12mo. pp. 447. $1.00. London, 1687.

A NEW METHOD of Demonstrating from Reason and Philosophy the four fundamental points of Religion, viz., Existence and Immortality of the Soul, God, &c., &c. 8vo. $1.50. London, 1756.

A PHYSICO-Theological Discourse upon the Divine Being, or first cause of all things; Providences of God, general and particular; Separate Existence of the Human Soul; Certainty of Revealed Religion; Fallacy of Modern Inspiration and Danger of Enthusiasm. To which is added, an Appendix concerning the Corruption of Human Nature, the Force of Habit, and the Necessity of Supernatural Aid to the acquest of Eternal Happiness. With Epistolary Conferences between the deceased Dr. Anthony Horneck and the author, relating to these subjects. 4to. pp. 222. London, 1698.

A PHILOSOPHICO-Theological Treatise on the Merit which the Christian Religion has on the Doctrine of the Immortality of the Human Soul. 8vo. pp. 111. Leipzig, 1788.

This treatise furnishes the reader with an historical retrospect of the suppositions, opinions, and doctrines relative to the state of man after death, entertained and circulated by the sages of different nations previous to the foundation of the Christian Religion.—German Museum.

A SHORT HISTORICAL View of the Controversy concerning an Intermediate State and the Separate Existence of the Soul between Death and the General Resurrection. 8vo. pp. 183. London, 1763.

A VINDICATION of the Account of the Double Doctrine of the Ancients, in answer to a Critical Inquiry into the Practices of the Ancient Philosophers. 8vo. pp. 38. $1.50. London, 1747.

AN ESSAY. Of Transmigration, in defence of *Pythagoras*. 12mo. $1.00. London, 1692.

AN ESSAY on the immateriality and Immortality of the Soul and its Instinctive sense of Good and Evil; in opposition to the opinions advanced by Dr. Priestly. 8vo. Bds. $1.00. London, 1778.

AN ESSAY on the state of the Soul after Death. 8vo. pp. 45. $1.00. Edinburgh, 1825.

AN ESSAY on Immortality, by the author of the Review of the First Principles of Bishop Berkeley, Dr. Reid, and Professor Stuart. 8vo. pp. 325. London, 1818.

AN EVIDENCE FOR IMMORTALITY, and for Transmigration. To which is added a Treatise concerning those who sleep in the Dust of the Earth. Bound up with Morgan's History of the Spanish Wars in Africa. Small 8vo. Half calf. $1.00. London, 1732.

AN INQUIRY into the knowledge of the Ancient Hebrews concerning a Future State. By Joseph Priestly Johnson. $1.00. 1801.

AN INQUIRY into the Spirit of Truth; being some serious Considerations on the Physical, Physiological, and Moral.

ADDISON, JOSEPH. Evidences of Christianity, with additional Discourses, namely, Immortality of the Soul, Atheism, &c., &c. 12mo. $1.00. Dublin, 1761.

ÆNAS GAZÆUS ET ZACHARIAS MITYLENÆUS Philosophi Christiani de Immortali. Tute Animæ et Mortalite Universi, ex Recensione et cum animadversionibus *Casparis* Barthii. Greek and Latin. 4to. $5.00. *Excessively rare.*

ALLIN, THOMAS. Discourse on the Immateriality and Immortality of the Soul; the Character and folly of Modern Atheism; and the Necessity of a Divine Revelation. 8vo. Half Calf. $1.50. London, 1828.

AMNER, RICHARD. Considerations on the Doctrines of a *Future State* and Resurrection, as revealed, or supposed to be so, in the Scriptures. 8vo. $1.50. London, 1797.

AMYRALDUS, MOSES. A Discourse concerning the Divine Dreams mentioned in Scripture, together with marks and characters by which they might be distinguished from vain delusions, in a Letter to Monsieur Gaches; translated from the French by Fa Lowde, Fellow of Clare-Hall, in Cambridge. 18mo. pp. 132. $1.00. London, 1676.

AMYRALDUS, MOSES. The Evidence of Things not seen; or, Divers Scriptural and Philosophical Discourses concerning the State of Good and Holy Men after Death. Translated into English. 12mo. *Very rare.* $1.28. London, N. D.

ANCIENT PHILOSOPHY. A Critical Inquiry into the Opinions and Practice concerning the Nature of the Soul and a Future State, and their method of Teaching by the Double Doctrine, in which are examined the notion of Mr. Jackson and Dr. Sykes concerning these matters, with a Preface by the Author of the Divine Legation, &c. 8vo. pp. 102. $2.00. London, 1748.

ARISTOTELE'S De Anima de Sensu, de Memoria, de Somno Similique Argumenti: Ex Recensione *Imanuel Bekhere.* 12mo. $2.00. Berloni, 1829.

ARISTOTLE. Treatises, namely, on the *Soul*, Sense and Sensibles, Memory, Sleep and Wakefulness, Dreams, Divination by Sleep, Motion of Animals, Generation of Animals, Length and Shortness of Life, Youth, Old Age, Life and Death, Respiration, &c. With copious elucidations. Translated into English by T. Taylor. 4to. Very scarce. (*Only fifty copies printed.*) $15.00. London, 1808.

ATHENAGORAS. (*The learned Athenian philosopher.*) The Apologetics of. First, for the Christian Religion. Second, for the Truth of the Resurrection, against the Skeptics and Infidels of that age. Together with a curious Fragment of *Justin Martyr*, on the subject of the Resurrection. And two other Fragments, the one attributed to *Josephus*, the other to *Methodius*, concerning the State of the Dead. Translated by D. Humphreys. 8vo. Very rare. $3.00. London, 1814.

ATTERBURY, FRANCIS. (*Bishop of Rochester.*) Legacy to all True Englishmen, in Five Essays. One concerning the *Future State.* 18mo. pp. 71. $1.00. London, 1733.

BAKEWELL, FREDERICK C. Natural Evidences of a Future Life, derived from the properties and actions of animate and inanimate matter. 8vo. pp. 372. $2.00. London, 1835.

BALFOUR, WALTER. Three Essays on the Intermediate State of the Dead. The Resurrection from the Dead, &c. 12mo. 75 cts. Charlestown, 1828.

BALDWIN, O. An Investigation into Principles, among other things, the Immortality of the Soul. 4to. Bds. $1.25. *Title page lost.* 1800.

BARROW, CAPEL. A Lapse of Human Souls in a state of pre-existence, the only Original Sin. 8vo. $1.25. London, 1756.

BARROW, CAPEL. Theological Dissertations, namely, A Lapse of Human Souls, in a state of pre-existence, the only Original Sin. Deism not consistent with the Religion of Reason and Nature, end and design of Christ's Death. Discourses concerning *Origen*, and the chiefest of his opinions, Reprobation and Future Punishment. 4to. $2.00. London, 1772.

BAULLIER, M. Essai Philosophique sur l'Ame des Bêtes. 2 vols. 12mo. Calf. $1.50. Amsterdam, 1837.

BAXTER, A. An Inquiry into the Nature of the *Human Soul;* wherein the Immateriality of the soul is evinced from the principles of reason and philosophy. 2 vols. 8vo. Calf, 2d ed. $3.00. London, 1737.

BEHMEN, JACOB. Forty Questions concerning the Soul, propounded by Dr. Balthasar Walters, and answered by *Jacob Behmen.* (Alias Teutonicus Philosophus. And in his answer to the first question is the turned eye or philosophic globe. (Which in itself containeth all mysteries,) with an exposition. *To which is added a catalogue of books written by Jacob Behmen.* 4to. pp. 185. Rare. $2.00. London, 1647.

BELLAMY, DANIEL. The Truth of the Christian Religion demonstrated both from Reason and Revelation. In twelve discourses. *And the Future State demonstrated from the nature of the soul.* 8vo. $1.00. London, 1744.

BENTLEY, RICHARD. Sermons; chiefly on the confutation of *Atheism.* 8vo. Calf, neat. Very scarce. $2.00. Cambridge, 1724.

BIGLAND, JOHN. Reflections on the Resurrection and Ascension of Christ. 12mo. Bds. 50 cents. London, 1810.

BISHOP WARBURTON'S Divine Legation of Moses examined, in which the Mosaic Theocracy, Hero-Gods, a future, separate state of animal life, and action of the soul after death, with other principles, are occasionally considered. 8vo. $1.00. London, 1742.

BLACKLOCK, THOMAS. A Treatise on the *Immortality of the Soul.* To which is prefixed his Poems, and a Life and Character of the author, by *Spence.* 8vo. Calf. $1.50. London, 1756.

BLACKBURN, B. An Historical View of the Controversy concerning the Intermediate State, and the Separate Existence of the Soul between Death and the General Resurrection; deduced from the beginning of the Protestant Reformation to the present time. 8vo. pp. 432. $2.00. London, 1772.

BLOUNT, CHARLES. *Anima Mundi*, or an Historical Narrative of the opinions of the ancients concerning the *soul of man* after this life, according to unenlightened nature. 12mo. Rare. $1.00. London, 1679.

BOLD, SAMUEL. A Discourse concerning the Resurrection of the same Body; with two letters concerning the necessary immateriality of creating, thinking substances. 12mo. 75 cents. London, 1705.

BROUGHTON, JOHN. Psychologia; or, an Account of the Nature of the Rational Soul. In two Parts. The First—Being an Essay towards establishing the received doctrine of an Immaterial and Immortal Substance, united to the Human Body, upon sufficient grounds of Reason. The Second—A Vindication of that received and established Doctrine, again a late Book, called Second Thoughts, &c., wherein all the author's pretended demonstrations to the contrary, as well philosophical and rational, as scriptural, are fully refuted; together with occasional remarks on his way of reasoning, &c. 8vo. pp. 418. London, 1703.

BROUGHTON, T. Prospects of Futurity on the Nature of the *Life to Come*, and on the general burning of the world. 8vo. $2.00. London, 1767.

BROWN, ISAAC HAWKINS. The Immortality of the Soul; a Poem, translated from the Latin, by John Letece. To which is added the original Poem, with a commentary by the translator. 8vo. Calf. $2.00. London, 1745.

BROWN, ISAAC HAWKINS. Poems on various subjects, namely: on the *Immortality of the Soul*, Latin and English, Pipe of Tobacco, &c., &c. Fine portrait: royal 8vo. Paper. 75 cents. London, 1768.

BROWN, JOHN. Psyche, or the *Soul*, a Poem. 12mo. Bds. 75 cents. London, 1818.

BRUCE, JOHN. Death on the Pale Horse. 12mo. Bds. plate. 75 cts. London, 1827.

BURNET, Dr. THOMAS. A Treatise concerning the departed Souls, before, and at, and after the Resurrection. Translated from the Latin, by Dennis. 8vo. Calf. Portrait. $1.50. London, 1730.

BUSH, GEORGE. The Soul; or, an Inquiry into Scriptural Psychology, as developed by the use of the terms, soul, spirit, life, &c.,

viewed in its bearings on the doctrine of the Resurrection. 12mo. pp. 141. 44 cents. New York, 1845.

BUSH, GEORGE. The Resurrection of Christ; in answer to the question, whether he rose in a spiritual and celestial, or in a material and earthly body. 12mo. Paper. 25 cents. New York, 1845.

CALVINI JOHANNES. Psychopannychia qua refellitur quorundam imperitorum error, quia animas post mortem, usque ad ultimum, judicum dormire putant. 12mo. pp. 104. London, 1839. Published in connection with the first.

CAMPBELL'S (Archibald) Doctrines of a middle state between Death and the Resurrection, of Prayers for the Dead, and the Necessity of Purification; plainly proved from the Scriptures, the Fathers, &c. Folio, *neat, very scarce.*

C. B. D.D. A Discovery of Divine Mystery; or, the Nature and Efficacy of the Soul of Man, considered in all its faculties, operations, and divine perfections, and how it governs in divine and secular affairs of life. In three Parts, &c., with many other curious matters. Being a complete body of divine and moral philosophy. C. B. D.D. 8vo. pp. 447. London, 1700.

CHAPPELOW, LEONARD. Two Sermons concerning the State of the Soul on its immediate separation from the body; written by Bishop Balle. Together with some extracts from writers of distinguished note and character. 8vo. pp. 120. Cambridge, 1765.

CICERO, The Tusculan Disputations of. (*Embracing his views of the Immortality of the Soul.*) 8vo. $1.00. London, 1840.

CLARKE, SAMUEL. A Letter to Mr. Dodwell; wherein all the arguments in his epistolary discourse against the Immortality of the Soul are particularly answered, and the judgment of the Fathers concerning the matter truly represented. A defence of an argument made use of in a letter to Mr. Dodwell, to prove the natural immortality of the soul. A second defence of the above; also a third and a fourth defence of the above. Bound in one vol. 8vo. Scarce. $1.50. London, 1711.

COLLIBER. Thoughts concerning Souls. 8vo. $2.00. London, 1734.

COLLIBER, S. Free Thoughts concerning the Soul, in four Essays; namely, Nature, Pre-existence, Souls of Brutes, and *Future State.* 8vo. pp. 168. $1.00. London, 1735.

COLLIER, JOHN. Essays on the Progress of the Vital Principle, from the vegetable to the animal kingdoms, and the *Soul of Man.* 8vo. Bds. $1.50. London, 1800.

COLLIER, JEREMY. Human Souls Naturally Immortal. Translated from a Latin manuscript. Bound up with *Melmoth* on the Sublime and Beautiful of Scripture. Thick 12mo. $1.00. London, 1707 and 1777.

COOKE, NATHANIEL. Creed Philosophic; or, Immortality of the Soul. 4to. $1.25. London, 1813.

COPLAND, ALEX. The Existence of other Worlds, peopled with living and intelligent beings, deduced from the nature of the Universe. 12mo. $1.25. London, 1834.

COWARD, Dr. W. The Grand Essay; or, a Vindication of Reason

and Religion against Imposture and Philosophy. That the existence of immortal substances is a philosophic imposture, and impossible to be conceived. 2 vols. 12mo. $1.50. London, 1704.

COWARD, Dr. W. Second Thoughts concerning Human Souls. 8vo. Calf. $1.50. London, 1702.

COWARD, W. Just Scrutiny; or, a Serious Inquiry into the Modern Notions of the Soul, with Second Thoughts Concerning the Human Soul. 2 vols. 8vo. Neat, but not uniform. Rare. $4.00. London, 1702.

This work excited so much attention and dislike, that it was burnt by order of Parliament; it is an elaborate defence of the doctrine of Materialism.—Orme.

CRAVEN, W. Discourses on the Jewish and Christian Dispensation, compared with other institutions; and the Future State of Rewards and Punishments, in answer to Hume. 8vo. pp. 480. $1.50. Cambridge, 1802.

CRAWFORD, CHARLES. A Dissertation on the Phædon of Plato; or, Dialogues on the Immortality of the Soul. With some observations upon the writings of that philosopher. To which is annexed, a Psychology; or, an Abstract Investigation of the *Nature of the Soul;* in which the opinions of all the celebrated metaphysicians on that subject are discussed. 8vo. pp. 291. $2.00. London, 1773.

D'ARGENES, Marquis. Philosophical Dissertations on the uncertainty of knowledge, namely: of history, logic, general principles, philosophy, metaphysics, judicial astrology, with remarks on the theology of the Grecian philosophers. To which is added, Maupertuis's Dissertation on Gravity, *including a treatise on the Immortality of the Soul.* Portrait. 2 vols. 12mo. $2.00. London, 1753.

DAVIS, WILLIAM. The true dignity of Human Nature; or, Man viewed in relation to *Immortality.* 12mo. 75 cents. London, 1830.

DAVIS, W. True Dignity of Human Nature; or, Man viewed in relation to Immortality, 12mo. 88 cents. London, 1830.

DEAN, PAUL. A Course of Lectures in defence of the Final Restoration. 8vo. Cloth. pp. 190. 75 cents. Boston, 1832.

DEMONT, G. D. On the Materiality of Mind, the Immateriality of the Soul, the Vital Principle, and Nervous System. 8vo. Pamphlet. 50 cents. London, 1830.

DEMONSTRATING, A New Method of, from reason and philosophy, the four fundamental points of Religion, viz: The existence and the immateriality of the spirit or *Soul* of man; the existence of the Supreme Spirit or God; the Immortality of the *Soul;* the certainty of a future state. 8vo. $1.00. London, 1756.

DICK, THOMAS. The Philosophy of a Future State. 12mo. 50 cts. New York, 1829.

DIGBY, KENELM. Two treatises. The Nature of Bodies and the Nature of Man's *Soul,* in the way of discovering the Immortality. 4to. $1.75. London, 1645.

DODWELL, HENRY. The Natural Immortality of the Soul, clearly demonstrated from the Holy Scriptures, and the concurrent testimonies of the primitive writers. Being an explication of the famous passage in the dialogue of St. Justin Martyr, with Typhon, concerning the soul's immortality. In a letter to a friend; with an appendix, consisting of a letter to Mr. John Norris, of Bermerton and an expostulation relating to the late insults of Mr. Clark and Mr. Chishull. 8vo. pp. 157. London, 1708.

DODWELL, Henry. An Epistolary Discourse, proceeding from the Scriptures and the first Fathers, that the Soul is a principle naturally mortal; but immortalized actually by the pleasure of God to punishment or to reward, by its union with the divine baptismal spirit. Wherein is proved that none have the power of giving this divine immortalizing spirit since the Apostles. London, 1706.

DREW, S. An Original Essay on the Immateriality and Immortality of the Human Soul, founded solely on physical and natural principles. 12mo. pp. 210. 50 cents. Baltimore, 1811.

ENGEL, C. C. "We shall meet again in another World." A philosophical dialogue. 8vo. pp. 216. Germany, 1800.

"*The author has, in this elegant dialogue, adduced the most satisfactory arguments possible for the confirmation of an expectation which is intimately connected with the repose of every feeling, and ably refuted in the most important objections that may be raised against it.*"—German Museum, 1800.

ESSAYS ON SUICIDE and the Immortality of the Soul, by the late *David Hume*, with remarks by the editor. To which is added, two letters on Suicide, by Rousseau. 12mo. *Very rare.* $1.25. London, 1789.

ETERNAL PUNISHMENT, proved to be not suffering but privation; and Immortality dependent on Scripture Regeneration. 8vo. $1.50. London, 1817.

EXISTENCE OF THE SOUL after Death. A Dissertation opposed to the principles of Priestley, Law, and their respective followers. By R. C. 8vo. pp. 114. Paper cover, $1.25. London, 1834.

FAWCETT, J. Dialogues on the other World, namely: Angelical Heaven, Nature and Fall of Angels, State of the Dead, Resurrection, Millennium, Future Renovation of all things. 12mo. 75 cents. London, 1759.

FELLOWS, ROBERT. The Religion of the Universe, with consolatory views of a *Future State.* 12mo. $1.00. London, 1836.

FLAVEL, JOHN. Pneumatologia. A Treatise on the Soul of Man. 8vo. pp. 466. $1.50. London, 1824.

FLEMING, CALEB. A Survey of the Search after *Souls*, by Coward, Clarke, Baxter, Sykes, Law, Packard, and others. Wherein the principles for and against the materiality, are collected. 8vo. $1.00. London, 1758.

FREE THOUGHTS, in defence of a Future State, as discovered by natural reason, and stripped of superstitious appendages; demonstrating against the nominal deist, that the consideration of future advantages is a just motive to virtue; of future loss and misery a powerful and becoming restraint of vice. With occasional remarks on a book, entitled An Inquiry concerning Virtue. And a refutation of the revived *Hylozoicism* of *Democritus* and *Leucippus.* 8vo. pp. 111. London, 1700.

FREE THOUGHTS concerning Souls; in four essays, namely: An Inquiry into the Scripture meaning of the word Satan, and its synonymous terms. Kinnicott, two dissertations; one, the Tree of Life in

Paradise, and the Creation and Fall of Man. Bound in one vol. 8vo. $2.00. London, 1735.

GASTRELL, BISHOP. A Moral Proof of the certainty of a Future State. 8vo. 75 cents. London, 1737.

GENTLEMEN INSTRUCTED in the conduct of a virtuous and happy Life. To which is added a Dialogue, *If the Soul* be Mortal, it is better to be a Beast than a Man. 8vo. $1.00. London, 1716.

GROVE, HENRY, Some Thoughts concerning proofs of a *Future State*, from reason, occasioned by the discourse of J. Hollett, on the same subject. 8vo. $1.25. London, 1730.

HADDOCK, J. Psychology; or, the Science of the *Soul*, considered Physiologically and Philosophically. 12mo. pp. 112. New York, 1850.

HALLENBERG, J. An Historical and Philosophical Inquiry into the origin of the Doctrine of the Resurrection of the Body, and whether it be asserted in the Book of Job. 12mo. pp. 45. London, 1799.

HARMER. T. Miscellaneous Works, among other things contains an account of the *Jewish Doctrine of the Resurrection of the Dead.* 8vo. $1.50. London, 1823.

HARWOOD, EDWARD. Discourses on St. Paul's description of death, and its consequences. 8vo. pp. 294. $1.25. London, 1790.

HAUGHTON, G. D. On Sex in the World to Come, An essay on. 12mo. pp. 333. $1.50. London, 1841.

HILLS, H. A Short Treatise concerning the Propagation of the Soul.—Justice done to human Souls, in a short view of Mr. Dodwell's late book, entitled An Epistolary Discourse, proving from the Scriptures and the first Fathers, that the Soul is a principle naturally mortal. By John Turner.—Human Souls naturally immortal. Translated from a Latin manuscript by S. E., with a recommendatory preface by Jeremy Collier.—The above three bound up in one vol. 18mo. $2.00. London, 1667.

HINTS to Medical Students upon the subject of a *Future State.* 12mo. pp. 48. 50 cents. York, 1823.

HOBART, JOHN HENRY. (*Late Bishop of New York.*) The State of the Departed, set forth in a funeral address, delivered at the interment of Bishop Moore, and a Dissertation on the same subject. 8vo. Half bd. pp. 98. 63 cents. New York, 1825.

HOBBES, THOMAS. Human Nature; or, the Fundamental Elements of Policy; being a Discovery of the Faculties, Acts, and Passions of the *Soul of Man;* from the original cause. 12mo. pp. 317. $2.50. London, 1684.

HODGES, WALTER. (*Sheol.*) Being a brief Dissertation concerning the place of *Departed Souls*, between the time of their Dissolution and the general Resurrection. 8vo. $1.00. London, 1745.

This treatise is bound up with the author's Christian Plan, and Reflections on the Life of King David.

HOLMS, EDWARD. An Attempt to prove the Immortality of the Soul, by Reason and Scripture. With an appendix, showing the influence of this opinion upon the faith and practice of Christians. 8vo. pp. 96. 2*s.* London, 1789.

HOMES, NATHANIEL. The Resurrection revealed; or, the Dawning of the Day-star about to rise. Folio. $2.00. London, 1659. *Recommended by Peter Sterry and Joseph Caryll.*

HOPE, ELIZABETH. The Immaterial System of Man, contemplated in accordance with the Beautiful and Sublime, and in reference to a Plan for General Education. 2 vols. London, 1835.

HORBERY, MATTHEW. An Inquiry into the Scripture Doctrine concerning the duration of Future Punishment. In answer to Bishop Warburton on Hell Torments. 8vo. pp. 313. $2.00. London, 1744.

HOUGHTON, P. Five Essays on the Proof of Man's Future Existence; to which are added seventeen sermons on important subjects. 8vo. London, 1809.

HUMPHREY, DITTON. A Discourse concerning the Resurrection of Jesus Christ. Wherein the consequences of the doctrine are stated. The nature and obligation of moral evidence. The proofs of the fact of our Saviour's resurrection. Together with a Treatise concerning the impossible production of thought from matter and motion; the nature of human souls, and brutes, &c. 8vo. pp. 510. $1.25. London, 1714.

HUNTINGFORD, THOMAS. Testimonies in proof of the separate existence of the Soul in a state of self-consciousness between death and the resurrection. To which is added, John Calvin's *Psychopannychia*, (*in Latin.*) 12mo. pp. 500. $2.25. London, 1829.

IMMORTALICUS. Original and serious reflections concerning our ideas of the *Supreme Being*; the importance of matter or substance, and its *Immortality*; of Death, and of a future ameliorated existence of mankind. 8vo. pp. 26. New York, 1811.

IMMORTALITY, An Essay on. By the author of a review of First Principles of Bishop Berkeley, Dr. Reid, and Professor Stewart. 8vo. Bds. pp. 328. $1.00. London, 1814.

IMMORTALITY, or Annihilation? The question of a Future State discussed and decided by the arguments of reason. 12mo. pp. 270. $1.25. London, 1827.

IMMORTALITY OF THE SOUL. Arguments natural, moral, and religious for. 12mo. 50 cents. Worcester, 1805.

IMMORTALITY OF THE SOUL. A Discourse concerning the certainty of a *Future and Immortal State*. In some moral, physiological, and religious considerations. 12mo. pp. 194. $1.50. London, 1741.

IMMORTALITY OF THE SOUL. A Philosophical Dissertation on the Essence of the Soul, &c. 8vo. pp. 56. Upsal, 1707.

IMMORTALITY OF THE SOUL. Chiefly demonstrated by the Apparitions of departed spirits to many persons well known and now living. With a serious Address to the people of this nation, upon the pernicious and prevalent doctrine of Atheism. With some observations on the queries propounded to Thomas Paine by the Bishop of Llandaff, in his Apology for the Bible. From the manuscript of an eminent divine. 8vo. London, 1799.

IMMORTALITY OF THE SOUL. A Poem (on the Immortality of the

Soul) delivered before a Society at Andover, Sept. 22d, 1829. 8vo. pp. 15. By Richard H. Dana.

IMPARTIAL THOUGHTS upon the nature of the Human Soul, and some passages concerning it in the writings of Mr. Hobbes and Mr. Collier, occasioned by a book entitled Second Thoughts. By a Divine of the Church of England. London, 1704.

INTERMEDIATE STATE, Historical View of the controversy concerning an, and the separate Existence of the Soul between Death and the Resurrection. 8vo. Scarce. $1.50. 1772.

JACKSON, JOHN. The Belief of a Future State proved to be a fundamental article of the Religion of the Hebrews.—A Defence of the Ancient Philosophers, concerning their doctrine and belief of a Future State.—Dr. Priestley's Inquiry into the knowledge of the Ancient Hebrews concerning a Future State.—Jackson's Remarks on Dr. Middleton's Free Inquiry.—The four bound in one volume. 8vo. $1.75. London, 1749.

JENNINGS, J. C. History of the Soul of Man and Brutes, *in German.* 8vo. Portrait. $1.25. Hull, 1774.

KEMICK, T. On the State of the Dead. (A Sermon.) 8vo. pp. 42. London, 1805.

KERATRY, M. De l'Existence de Dieu, l'Immortalité de l'Ame. 12mo. Paper cover. 75 cents. Paris, 1815.

LADENFROST, J. G. Account of what experience has taught him concerning the Human Soul. 8vo. pp. 300. London, 1794.

LANCASTER, T. W. The Harmony of the Law and the Gospel with regard to a *Future State.* 8vo. pp. 470. $5.00. Oxford, 1825.

L'ANIMA. Di Ferrante Pallavicino. Divisa in sei vigilie Vigilia Prima Ultima Impressionne. 32mo. Vellum. 50 cents. Licon, 1664.

LAW, EDMUND. (*Late Lord Bishop of Carlisle.*) Considerations on the Theory of Religion. To which is prefixed a Life of the author, the late William Paley, and an appendix concerning the use of the words *Soul* or *Spirit,* in the Holy Scriptures, and the state of the dead there described, with a copious index. A new edition, by *George Henry Law,* Lord Bishop of Chester. 8vo. pp. 555. Bds. $2.00. London, 1820.

LAYTON, HENRY. Arguments and replies in a dispute concerning the nature of the Human Soul: viz., Whether the same be immortal, separately subsisting, and intelligent; or be material, unintelligent, and extinguishable at the death of the person. Observations upon Dr. Nigholl's book, entitled, A Conference with a Theist; being proof of the Soul's Immortality, and an answer to the objections made against that doctrine, in a book entitled "*Second Thoughts concerning Human Souls.*" Observations upon a treatise entitled, Psychologia; or, an account of the Nature of the Human Soul. Observations upon Mr. Broughton's Psychologia. Observations upon a treatise entitled, A Vindication of the Separate Existence of the Soul, by John Turner. Observations upon the Happiness of Good Men in the next World; also, Proofs of the Immortality of the Soul, by Dr. Sherlock. The above all bound in one thick volume. 4to. $3.00. London, 1703.

LAYTON, H. Search after Souls; or, the Immortality of a Human Soul, theologically, philosophically, and rationally considered. 2 thick vols. 4to. Calf. Very neat. $5.00. London, 1706.

MALLOCK, DAVID. The Immortality of the Soul, with other Poems. 12mo. 75 cents. New York, 1833.

MANLOW, TIMOTHY. The Immortality of the Soul asserted, and practically improved; showing by Scripture, reason, and the testimony of the ancient philosophers, that the soul of man is capable of subsisting and acting in a state of separation from the body; and how much it concerns us all to prepare for that state. With some reflections on a pretended refutation of Mr. Bentley's Sermon. 18mo. pp. 164. Very rare. $1.00. London, 1683.

MARAT, M. (*The Celebrated French Revolutionist.*) A Philosophical Essay on Man, being an attempt to investigate the principles and laws of the reciprocal influence of the *Soul on the Body.* 2 vols. 8vo. Calf. $4.00. London, 1773.

MARMORIERES, BARTHES. Elnathan; ou, Les Ages de l'Homme, traduit du Chaldéen—Elnathan; or, the Age of Man, translated from the Chaldean. 3 vols. 8vo. $5.00. Paris, 1802.

MATERIALISM Philosophically examined; or, the Immortality of the Soul asserted and proved on philosophical principles, in answer to Dr. Priestley's Disquisition on *Matter and Spirit*, by John Whitehead. 8vo. Boards. $3.00. London, 1778.

MATHER, COTTON. Awakening Thoughts on the Sleep of Death; with a Debt paid unto the memory of some that sleep in Jesus. Boston, 1712.

M'CANN, GEORGE. An Inquiry into the Moral Regeneration of Human Nature. 8vo. pp. 192. $1.00. Edinburgh, 1828.

Twenty-eight pages of the above book are taken up with a Discussion on the Immortality of the Soul.

MILLES, THOMAS. The Natural Immortality of the Soul asserted and proved from the Scriptures, and First Fathers; in answer to Dodwell's Discourse, in which he endeavours to prove the soul to be a principle naturally mortal. 8vo. pp. 504. $1.25. Oxford, 1707.

MILLS, W. The Belief of the Jewish people and the most eminent Gentile philosophers, more especially *Plato* and *Aristotle*, on the *Future State*, briefly considered. 8vo. pp. 130. $2.00. Oxford, 1828.

MORE, HENRY. The Immortality of the Soul, so far set forth as it is demonstrable from the knowledge of nature and the light of reason. 12mo. pp. 580. $1.00. London, 1659.

MORE, H. Psychozoia—the Life of the Soul—the Immortality of the Soul, &c. 8vo. Hf. bd. 3*s.* Cambridge, 1647.

MUSTON on Recognition in the World to Come, or Christian Friendship on Earth perpetuated in Heaven. 8vo. Bds. 2*s.* 1830.

MYSTICAL DIVINITY, the French Academie; or, History of the Body and Soul of Man, the Creation, Matter, Composition, Form, Nature, Virtues, Vices, &c., &c., and on the Immateriality of the Soul, by Peter de la Primaudaye, Esq. 4to. Vellum, *scarce.* 12*s.* 6*d.* London, 1605.

NEWMAN, FRANCIS WILLIAM. The Soul, her Sorrows and Aspirations: an Essay towards the Natural History of the Soul, as the true basis of Theology. 12mo. pp. 222. London, 1849.

NICHOLS, WILLIAM. A Conference with a Theist, being a proof of the Immortality of the Soul, wherein is contained an answer to the objections made against the Christian doctrine. In a book entitled Second Thoughts concerning the Human Soul, &c. 8vo. pp. 248. London, 1703.

NORRIS, JOHN. A Philosophical Discourse concerning the Natural Immortality of the Soul. Wherein the great question of the Soul's Immortality is endeavoured to be rightly stated and fully cleared. Occasioned by Mr. Dodwell's late epistolary discourse. In two parts. 8vo. pp. 127. London, 1708.

OBSERVATIONS on the Chronology of Scripture—Strictures on the Age of Reason. The evidence which reason, unassisted by revelation, affords us with respect to the nature and properties of the Soul of Man. Argument in support of the opinion that the Soul is inactive and unconscious from death to the resurrection, derived from Scripture. 8vo. pp. 141. $1.00. New York, 1795.

O'LEARY, ARTHUR. A Defence of the Divinity of Christ, and the Immortality of the Soul, and other Tracts. 8vo. Calf. $1.00. Dublin, 1781.

O[VERTON's], (R.) Man's Mortalitie; or, a Treatise wherein is prooved, both Theologically and Philosophically, that whole Man (as a rationall Creature) is a Compound wholly Mortall, contrary to that common distinction of *soule* and *body*, &c.; also, divers other mysteries, as of Heaven, Hell, Christ's humane residence, &c. 4to. *scarce*, *uncut*, 8*s*. 6*d*. Amsterdam, 1644.

PAINE, THOMAS. Private Thoughts on a Future State. Essay on Dreams, New Testament examined, and the Origin of Free Masonry. 8vo. $1.00. New York, 1810.

PARKER, HENRY M. The Draught of Immortality and other Poems. 8vo. pp. 204. $1.00. London, 1827.

PARKER, SAMUEL, Letters and Essays by; among others, The Soul. The doctrine of the identity of the body at the resurrection, vindicated. 8vo. Binding loose. 75 cents. London, 1701.

PATUZZI, FATHER. A Dissertation on the Seat of Infernal Spirits or Demons. 4to. Venice, 1764.

PETERS, C. Critical Dissertation on Job, wherein a Future State is shown to have been a popular belief of the Jews. 4to. $2.50. London, 1751.

PHILOSOPHICAL LETTERS, upon Physiognomies. To which is added, Dissertations on the inequality of *Souls*, Philanthropy and Misfortunes. 12mo. 75 cents. *From the Duke of Sussex's Library.* London, 1751.

PLATO. Phædon; or, a Dialogue on the Immortality of the Soul. To which is added, *Crito;* or, what we ought to do, with an introduction to each. Translated into English. 12mo. Portrait. $1.00. London, 1783.

PLATO. Phædon; or, a Dialogue on the Immortality of the Soul. Translated from the original Greek, by Madame Dacier, with notes and emendations; to which is prefixed a Life of Plato, by Archbishop Fenelon. A new edition, with the opinions of ancient, intermediate, and modern philosophers and divines on the *Soul's Immortality*. To which is appended a catalogue of books written by various authors on the Immortality of the Soul, (*in all*, 211.) 12mo. pp. 252. $1.25. New York, 1849.

PLATO. Phædon; or, the Immortality of the Soul. Translated from the Greek by Charles Stuart Stanford. 8vo. pp. 130. $2.00. Dublin, 1835.

PLATTE, N. On the Sleep of the Soul, Intermediate State, &c., &c., 1813.

PLATTS, JOHN. Reflections on Materialism, Immaterialism, on the Sleep of the *Soul*, an Intermediate State, and the Resurrection of the Body; being an attempt to prove that Resurrection commences at Death. 4to. pp. 20. London, 1814.

POLIOHELE, H. An Essay on the Evidence from Scripture that the Soul, immediately after the Death of the Body, is not in a State of Sleep or Immortality, but of Happiness or Misery, and on the Moral Use of that Doctrine. 8vo. London, 1820.

PRIESTLEY, JOSEPH. An Inquiry into the Knowledge of the Ancient Hebrews concerning a *Future State*. 8vo. pp. 67. $1.00. London, 1801.

PRIMAUDAYE, PETER. Mystical Divinity. The French Academie; or, History of the Body and Soul of Man, Form, Nature, Virtues, Vices, &c., on the Immateriality of the Soul, &c. 4to. Vellum. 1605.

RALEIGH, SIR WALTER. Ghost; or, his Apparition to an intimate friend, willing him to translate into English this learned *Book of L. Lessius*, entitled De Providentia Numinis, and Animi Immortalitali. 18mo. pp. 384. $2.00. Very rare. London, 1651.

R. C. Existence of the Soul after Death. A Dissertation opposed to the principles of Priestley, Law, and their respective followers. 8vo. Paper. 75 cents. London, 1834.

REDFORD, G. Body and Soul; or, Life, Mind, and Matter. 8vo. Plates. $2.00. London, 1847.

REYNOLDS, F. A View of Death; or, the Soul's Departure from the World. A Philosophical and Sacred Poem. To which is added, the Life of the author. 12mo. Very scarce. $2.00. London, 1735.

ROWE, HENRY NATHANIEL. The Rainbow of the Mind, explained in a Dialogue between the Materialist and the Author, with the Five Senses in council assembled; proving the Immortality of the *Soul* by evidence of sight. 8vo. pp. 48. London, 1846.

RUST, BISHOP. Lux Orientalis; an Inquiry into the opinion of the *Eastern Sages* concerning the Pre-existence of Souls. Being a Key to unlock the grand mysteries of Providence. Two parts. 8vo. Calf. $1.50. London, 1682.

SERMONS, Five: namely, against Atheism, God's Government, Human Nature, natural and moral proofs of a *Future State*. 8vo. 50 cents. London, 1738.

SHERLOCK, WILLIAM. A Discourse on a Future State. 8vo. Gilt. $2.00. London, 1760.

SLADE, JOHN. The Transmigrating Soul; or, an Epitome of Human Nature. A Moral Satire. 12mo. 63 cents. London, 1760.

SMITH, JOHN. (Of Cambridge.) Select Discourses, viz.: *Immortality of the Soul*, Superstition, Atheism, Existence of God, Divine Knowledge, &c. 4to. pp. 512. $5.00. Cambridge, 1673.

SMITH, LAWRENCE. The Evidence of Things not Seen; or, the Immortality of the Soul proved from Scripture and Reason. Together with an examination of the opinion of a Middle Place of residence. 8vo. $1.00. London, 1708.

SMITH, W. A Dissertation upon the Nerves, namely, the Nature of Man. The Connection of the *Soul with the Body*, &c., &c. 8vo. $2.00. London, 1768.

SOUL OF MAN. A Moral Essay upon the Soul of Man. 12mo. pp. 447. 75 cents. London, 1687.

STURMEY, DANIEL. Discourses on several Subjects; but principally on the *Separate State of Souls.* 8vo. $1.00. Cambridge, 1716.

STURT, JOHN. The Resurrection: a Poem. 12mo. pp. 253. London, 1808.

SUMMARY VIEW of the Platonic Doctrine, with respect to a Future State. (*Bound up at the end of Dante Inferno.*) 12mo. $1.00. London, 1785.

TAYLOR, HENRY. Considerations on Ancient and Modern Creeds. To which is added by another Author, *A Treatise on the Existence, Immateriality, and Immortality of the Soul, proving the same from self-evident principles.* 8vo. pp. 242. London, 1782.

TAYLOR, ISAAC. Physical Theory of Another Life. 12mo. pp. 336. 2d edition. London, 1847.

TAYLOR, JEREMY. The Doctrine of Scripture concerning the Middle State of the Soul, and the Traditions of the Church for Prayers for the Dead. 4to. pp. 8. London, 1696.

THE HOPES OF IMMORTALITY. A Poem, in four parts. $2.00. Edinburgh, 1839.

THE GREAT SOUL of Man. 12mo. 75 cents. London, N. D.

THE UNIVERSALIST. A Periodical, containing, among other things, Psychology; or, the Doctrine of the Soul. Resurrection, Anthropology; or, an Essay on Man. 8vo. Bds. 87 cents. Utica, 1825.

THE PRE-EXISTENCE OF SOULS and Universal Restoration. From the minutes and correspondence of the *Burnham Society.* 8vo. $1.50. Taunton, 1798.

THE FUTURE STATE; or, a Discourse attempting some display of the Soul's Happiness in regard to that eternally progressive knowledge, and the consequence of it, which is amongst the Blessed in Heaven. 18mo. pp. 159. $1.00. London, 1683.

THOMAS, FREDERICK SAMSON. Poetical Fragments, containing the Psychologist; or, Whence is a knowledge of the Soul desirable? And the Deluge, a midnight reverie. 8vo. pp. 237. $1.25. London, 1836.

THOMSON, THOMAS. The Immortality of the Soul, and other Poems. 12mo. Glasgow, 1819.

THOUGHTS on the Probability of our being known to each other in another Life. 8vo. London, 1815.

THOUGHTS on the Grounds of Man's Future Hopes, drawn from the Principles of Reason, for the use of a gentleman who doubted whether we had any thing to hope or fear beyond the Present Life. 8vo. *Very curious and scarce.* 1739.

TOLAND, JOHN. Letters to Serena: namely, Origin and Force of Prejudice; the History of the *Soul's Immortality* among the Heathen; Origin of Idolatry; Spinoza's System of Philosophy without foundation. 8vo. $1.50. Rare. London, 1704.

TRANSNATURAL PHILOSOPHY; or, Metaphysics: demonstrating the Essences and Operations of all Beings. By J. S. 60 pages are taken up with *demonstrating* the Immortality of the soul. 8vo. pp. 480. *Very rare.* $5.00. London, 1700.

TURNER, JOHN. A Brief Vindication of the Separate Existence and Immortality of the Soul, from a late Author's Second Thoughts: wherein he pretends to demonstrate the notion of the Human Soul, as believed to be a Spiritual Immortal Substance, united to a Human Body, to be a plain Heathenish Invention, and not consonant to the principles of philosophy, reason, or religion. Printed for J. Wyatt, 1702. Quarto. pp. 64.

TURNER, JOHN. Justice done to Human Souls in a short view of Mr. Dodwell's late book, entitled an Epistolary Discourse, proving from the Scriptures and the First Fathers that the Soul is a Principle naturally Mortal. 12mo. pp. 124. London, 1706.

VINDICIÆ MENTIS. An Essay on the Being and Nature of *Mind.* To which is added, an Inquiry into the Life and Immortality of the Soul. 12mo. $1.00. London, 1702.

WADSWORTH, THOMAS. The Immortality of the Soul explained and proved by Scripture and Reason. A confutation of that irrational irreligious opinion of the Soul's dying with the Body, and interruption of its communion with God from death until the day of judgment. The several theological, moral, and philosophical absurdities thereof are discovered, and the most considerable objections answered.—To which is added, Faith's Triumph over the fear of Death. 18mo. pp. 118, 115. $1.50. London, 1670.

WAIT, DANIEL G. An Inquiry into the religious knowledge which the Heathen Philosophers derived from the Jewish Scriptures. 8vo. pp. 80. $1.50. London, 1813.

WARREN HASTINGS. (*Governor-general of India.*) Reflections on the Immortality of the Soul. N. D.

WATSON, T. Intimations and Evidences of a *Future State.* 8vo. Bds. $1.00. London, 1792.

WATTS, ISAAC. Philosophical Essays on various Subjects, viz.: Space, Substance, Body, Spirit, the Operations of the Soul in Union with the Body, Innate Ideas, Perpetual Consciousness, Place and Motion of Spirit, the Departure of the Soul, the Resurrection of the Body, &c., &c. 8vo. pp. 410. $2.00. London, 1793.

WATTS, ISAAC. The World to Come; or, Discourses on the joys or sorrows of departed Souls at death, and the glory and terror of the Resurrection. To which is prefixed, an Essay towards the proof of a separate state of Souls after death. 8vo. $1.25. Haverhill, 1816.

WEDDRED, JOHN. A Future State discovered by Reason. A Sermon preached in the cathedral of Peterborough. 4to. 1*s*. Rivingtons.

WEEKS, JOHN. A Discourse on the State of the Soul between Death and Judgment. 12mo. Bound with other pamphlets. 63 cents. London, 1749.

WENSTOVIUS, LEWES. The Place of the Soul; or, a Dissertation upon the seat of the Rational Soul in the Body; where the vulgar opinion, asserting that the whole Soul exists at one and the same time in every part of the Body, is refuted, and proved to be uncertain and false. To which is added an appendix, containing some moral admonitions concerning the care of the Soul. 12mo. pp. 109. Copenhagen, 1704.

WEST, GEORGE MONTGOMERY. Miscellaneous Writings of, including a Philosophical Essay on the Immortality of the Soul. 2 vols. 8vo. $1.50. London, 1829.

WHATELEY, R. (*Archbishop of Dublin.*) A View of the Scripture Revelation concerning *A Future State*. 12mo. $1.38. Scarce. London, 1829.

WHELPLY, SAMUEL. A Sermon on the Immortality of the Soul. Delivered at Newark, April 11th, 1804. 8vo. pp. 21. Newark, 1804.

WHISTON, WM., Sermons and Essays by. One against the *Sleep of the Soul*. 8vo. $1.25. London, 1711.

WHITBY, DANIEL. An endeavour to connect the certainty of Christian faith in general and of the Resurrection of Christ in particular. 12mo. pp. 411. Oxford, 1671.

WIGRAM, G. Essay on Man; or, the Mortal Body and Immortal Soul, explained. 8vo. pp. 180. London, 1828.

N. B.—The names having prices affixed are for sale by the publisher.

www.ingramcontent.com/pod-product-compliance
Lightning Source LLC
LaVergne TN
LVHW010219110826
845151LV00004B/1148

9781425526269